TREASURES OF THE
SMITHSONIAN

TREASURES OF THE
SMITHS

ONIAN

National Museum of American History · National
Museum of Natural History · National Air and Space
Museum · Hirshhorn Museum and Sculpture Garden ·
Arts & Industries Building · Freer Gallery of Art ·
National Museum of American Art · National Portrait
Gallery · National Museum of African Art · National
Zoological Park · Renwick Gallery · Anacostia
Neighborhood Museum · Cooper-Hewitt Museum

Edwards Park

Edwards Park

Smithsonian Books
Washington, D.C.

Trade distribution by
Harry N. Abrams, Inc.
New York, New York

Page vi: Steel, brass, and bronze gates designed and built by Albert Paley for the entrance to the gift shop at the Renwick Gallery.
Pages x-xi: An unusual and stunning example of two corals from the Indo-Pacific: king coral (Melithaea ochracea Linnaeus) has grown on a deerhorn coral (Pocillopora damicornis Linnaeus). National Museum of Natural History.
Pages xii-xiii: This "crazy" quilt, worked between 1897 and 1929, was made out of irregular pieces of fabric as a parlor throw. National Museum of American History.
Pages xiv-xv: A forerunner of today's data processing equipment, this 1853 "difference machine," designed by Georg Scheutz, was the first patented mechanism to print its results. National Museum of American History.
Pages xvi-xvii: Sotatsu. Waves at Matsushima (detail). Japan, 17th century. Ink, color, and gold on paper, 4'11⅞" x 11'8" (1.52 x 3.56 m). Freer Gallery of Art.

Copyright © 1983 Smithsonian Institution. All rights reserved. No part of this book may be reproduced or utilized in any form or by any means, electronic or mechanical, including photocopying, recording, or by any information storage and retrieval system, without permission in writing from the publisher.

Manufactured in the United States of America

Library of Congress Cataloging in Publication Data

Park, Edwards.
  Treasures of the Smithsonian.

  Includes index.
  1. Smithsonian Institution. I. Title.
Q11.S8P37 1983 069'.09753 83-40203
ISBN 0-89599-012-1
ISBN 0-8109-1680-0 (Abrams)

First Edition
5 4 3 2 1

TO JEAN

with whom 40 years of marriage
has been an institution even more
delightful than the Smithsonian

Contents

Foreword

What is there about the Smithsonian which promotes curiosity, wonder and a sense of mystery? Why is it that the Institution remains enigmatic and in many ways, unknown? The word *Smithsonian* itself is a household expression, connoting uprightness and verity. Like Webster or Oxford, dictionaries par excellence, the definitions contained in the world of Smithsonian are always taken as the "last word," the labels on the exhibits beyond question, the epitome of veracity. Letters from our curators in answer to questions coming in from around the world are quoted, their statements taken at face value.

This is a weighty responsibility. Are we really as correct and as profoundly so as we sound? Are we really keepers of the mysteries, arbiters of the truth? I do not know, suspecting only, as a scientific sceptic, that the ultimate truth on almost any subject will always remain elusive, slipping between the sentences, intriguing us by the very *exceptions* which can never be explained by footnotes alone, or by formulae yet to be devised. Let the final truth always remain a particle in doubt, so that future generations can still go on to discover yet more.

Time and tradition are on the side of the Smithsonian. The truth which lies in objects, so much better than in words, will out, but not necessarily today, or even tomorrow. Let it come to us in measured form. I hope that those who work at the Smithsonian will always cherish this ideal of the Institution, infallible of course, but flexible enough to view the future as confirming the true efforts of the past to reach the infallible even at the risk of temporarily being proved wrong. My own philosophy has always been that it is better to make

a statement of belief, even if it only elicits debate, for in the debate itself the truth is advanced. It is refreshing, as a teacher will find, to be able to say to a student, "I don't know. I cannot answer that question just now because I do not have an answer. Let us seek it together." Let us then never be keepers of the mysteries to which we cannot testify, any more than we would tamper with the perceived truth of the time, at our peril.

So this book of history, the tale of our "Treasures," embodies the perceived truth as seen at the time by those who have shaped the Smithsonian. It explains our chronology, in a series of flashbacks of the author, a man skilled in the subject and possessed by a love of the Institution which surely does not veil his eyes from the truth. For affection does not conceal all the warts and kinks of the persons written of or gloried in the telling. The Smithsonian bears telling and retelling, for its story is part of an unending saga of renewal and of cultural as well as scientific aspiration. Americans yearn for increased knowledge. Idealistically we yearn to spread the results.

What could be better than to follow our mandate, "for the increase and diffusion of knowledge among men," by telling and retelling this fascinating and evanescent story of how we grew, step by step, into the pyramid of achievements represented by 135 years of trial-and-error learning about America and Americans, and the persistence of truth and tradition through it all.

S. Dillon Ripley

There is so much good in the
worst of us,
And so much bad in the best
of us,
That it scarcely behooves
any of us
To talk about the
rest of us.

1897

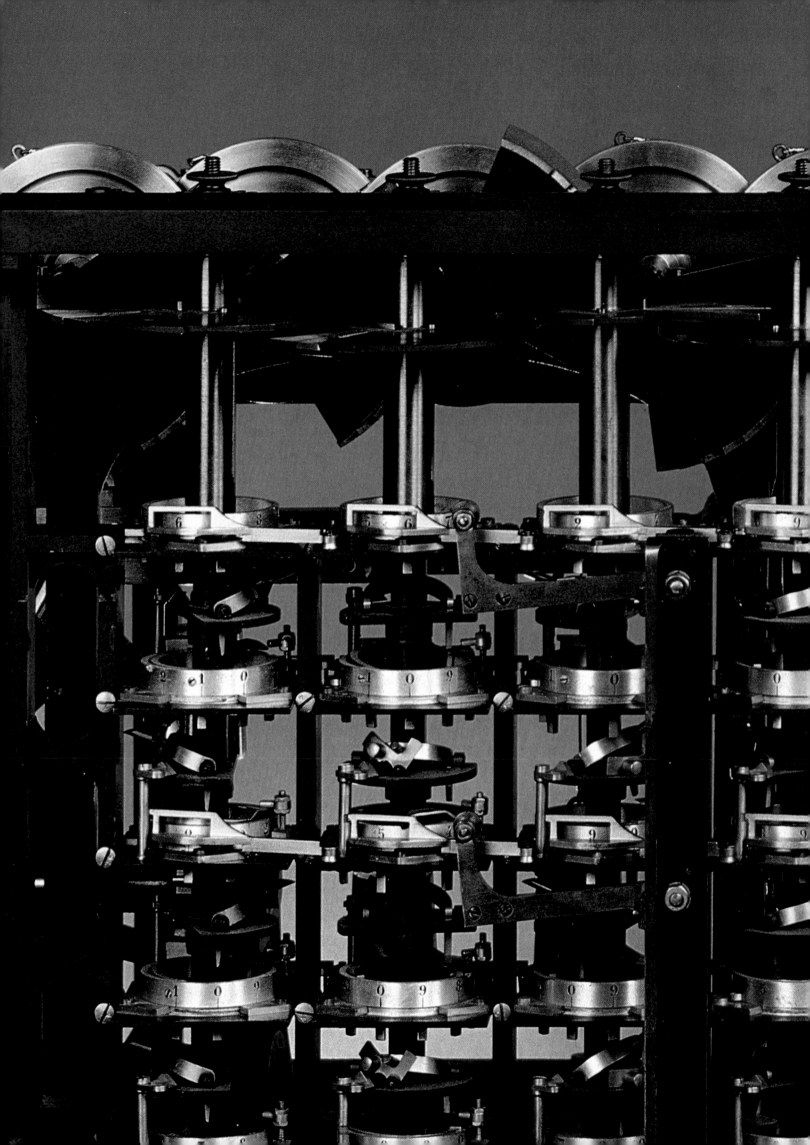

Preface

They work in the monumental museums that flank Washington's Mall and appear elsewhere in the nation's capital. They do their jobs in establishments in New York and Cambridge and Tucson, on broad acreages in Virginia and Maryland, on an island in Panama and beside a canal in Florida, as well as other small field stations all over the world.

These people comprise a broad, amorphous presence called the Smithsonian Institution. They carry on research in its name, they add to its collections and display and maintain its prize objects, explaining their meaning to more than 20 million visitors a year. They safeguard the Institution and do its enormous housekeeping. There are some 3,600 of these people, and most of them don't know each other. But if you must come up with a unifying thought about them, you might best say that they share in a search for excellence.

Over the decades, this search has resulted in a significant expansion of human knowledge. And tangibly it has produced enormous collections—some seventy-eight million items—of which a few, a mere two-and-a-half million, have been chosen with great discrimination to be displayed in the Smithsonian museums. These objects, products of the search for excellence, can all rightly be called treasures. Trying to do a book with that word in the title seems almost impossible.

But this task is a team effort by a great many Smithsonian people. Museum directors, curators, researchers have thrown their expertise behind these selections as choice samples from an overflowing trove.

For the most part, you won't find them simply listed, museum by museum. Instead they are linked by ideas, by trends and anecdotes, with unfettered digression from one museum to another.

Each chapter starts with a place or two, for the Smithsonian buildings must surely be counted among its treasures. The buildings, either because of their history or because of what they contain, suggest an era, a window of time, such as the Civil War or the turn of the century. The objects that fall within an era then pick up meanings that go beyond their beauty or intrinsic value. On some occasions these rules are broken—as rules are often meant to be.

The great, well-known treasures, of course, are here—the Hope Diamond, the Wright *Flyer,* the first ladies, George and Martha portraits, pandas—all are found in these pages. But with these popular items are many others, lesser known and sometimes more significant, that we have rated as treasures. Surprise is an element of delight at the Smithsonian, and we hope you will find it here.

Up to now that word "we" has been a pleasant backstop in discussing this book. Now, however, it must give way to "I." One person's treasure may be another's dross, and if the choice here doesn't suit you, I must take the responsibility. My experience as a columnist on *Smithsonian* magazine gave me a rudimentary knowledge of the Smithsonian, but I now realize how very sketchy that knowledge was. Again and again I battled with subjects and lost. I went into the ring with the worlds of art, history, and science and was left sagging on the ropes until rescued by experts. The fact is, writing a book like this quickly bangs all the conceits out of you.

How then, do I go about thanking the veritable army of people who saved my neck time and again? I've tried not to name names in the chapters that follow unless individuals demanded identification by their efforts. But now I must try to express gratitude to just about the entire Smithsonian staff.

Mr. Ripley, ever supportive and encouraging, added some of his own store of knowledge about the Institution he heads. His knowledge, in fact, is so vast and varied that it really doesn't seem fair. After all, here is an administrator of Cabinet status who makes a trained journalist look pathetic. I can understand his scholarly knowledge of the Castle, because he works there, and about birds, because he's an ornithologist. But why does he know so much about American Impressionists? What's he doing with information about General Sheridan's horse? His wealth of information makes me uneasy—and very glad he's in my corner.

James M. Goode, Keeper (I love that title) of the Castle, has long been my friend and guide in exploring that grand old building.

Museum and bureau directors at my time of writing proved enthusiastic and devoted to the cause and made things as easy as possible. All need a mention: Alan Fern of the National Portrait Gallery and Charles C. Eldredge of the Museum of American Art, Roger G. Kennedy of the Museum of American History, Walter J. Boyne of Air and Space and Abram Lerner of the Hirshhorn, Richard S. Fiske of Natural History and Theodore H. Reed of the Zoo, Thomas Lawton of the Freer, Sylvia Williams of African Art, Lisa Taylor of the Cooper-Hewitt, Lloyd E. Herman of the Renwick, John Kinard of the Anacostia Neighborhood Museum.

Often the directors turned my education over to trusted aides, handpicked for unbelievable patience: Susan Hamilton and Garnett McCoy of the Archives of American Art; Marc Pachter at the Portrait Gallery, and Marge Byers at the Museum of American Art; a host of experts at American History, but specifically, for knowledge that fattened this book, Margaret Klapthor, Bob Post, Herb Collins, Bob Vogel, John H. White, Cynthia Hoover, and John Stine. And of course Sylvio Bedini and Ellen Wells of The Dibner Library.

At the Hirshhorn I was brilliantly tutored by Ted Lawson, and at Air and Space I basked in the culmination of material gleaned from, especially, Claudia Oakes, Tom Crouch, Paul Garber, Don Lopez, Lou Purnell, and Bob Mikesh. A similar horde at Natural History guided my steps, particularly Porter Kier, Walter Adey, John S. White, and Fred Collier. Martin Amt of the Freer crammed me with Orientalism, barely leaving room for Roz Walker to tamp in some African Art and David McFadden at the Cooper-Hewitt to enlighten me about design.

Special thanks are due to Peggy Thompson, an old friend and associate, whose research is so broad and meticulous that it is impossible for me to touch on any aspect of the Institution without feeling a sense of appreciation.

Finally, throat-lumping gratitude to the exceptional staff at Smithsonian Books, who collectively took my adequate efforts and transformed them into what I feel is truly a splendid book.

Edwards Park
Annapolis, Maryland
October 1983

Front Royal

Renwick

National Zoo

Air and Space

Hirshhorn

Arts + Industries

Whipple Observatory

Tropical Research Institute

Carrie Bow Cay

American Art / Portrait Gallery

Cooper-Hewitt Museum

Barney House

Freer

Castle

American History

Natural History

Anacostia Neighborhood Museum

African Art

The Garber Facility

Chesapeake Bay Center

Introduction

In 1976, the year of our nation's bicentennial, the noted Smithsonian anthropologist Lawrence Angel opened the great urnlike crypt in the Smithsonian Castle where the bones of James Smithson had reposed since they were brought to the United States at the turn of the century. Dr. Angel, whose interpretive analyses have earned him the nickname Sherlock Bones, put his skill to work on the dusty remains of the founder of the Smithsonian Institution and came up with the sort of deductions that have long made police forensic experts regard him with awe.

Smithson, said Angel, stood about five feet six inches, was right-handed, had a well-muscled, athletic build with longish arms, had possibly suffered an injury to his right shoulder when he was a boy, had strong features, and had smoked a pipe, holding it on the left side of his mouth. A picture of the man emerged from the description and was drawn for the edification of his admirers.

The remarkable thing about all this isn't just that Dr. Angel was able to flesh out old bones—his Smithsonian colleagues knew he could do that. What was more surprising was that this was the first indication of what James Smithson, endower of perhaps the world's best-known and most beloved institution, looked like in his maturity.

The story of Smithson and his bequest is well known today, thanks to the fame of his Institution. But when he died in 1829 in Italy at age 64, he was a half-forgotten expatriate Englishman, known only for his family bloodlines and, among his colleagues, for his work in chemistry. Despite his illegitimacy (he was, in John Quincy Adams' tactful euphemism, "antenuptial"), indications are that Smithson's father, who became the first Duke of Northumberland, loved the boy, wished him happiness, gave him a fine education and encouraged him in his chosen field—a rather arcane one at that time.

As a young man, Smithson used his mother's maiden name, Macie. When later he adopted the name of Smithson, he determined that it would "live in the memory of man when the titles of the Northumberlands . . . are extinct and forgotten." It lives, all right.

Smithson spent most of his later life in Europe and died in Genoa. His will provided that his estate—pretty sizeable for those days—should go to his nephew. But if the nephew died childless, the money was to be used for the establishment of an institution in the United States "for the increase and diffusion of knowledge among men." Curious, old-fashioned words as we read them today. "Diffusion" is ambiguous, "among men" is sexist. But there were no misunderstandings about some of the wording of the will when, upon the death of that childless nephew in 1835, the United States was notified that it stood to inherit more than half a million dollars—a great deal of money in those days.

And here occurs yet another curiosity in the Smithson story. For the United States responded to its remarkable good fortune not with gratitude and excitement, but with suspicion and possibly a touch of greed. Remember, this was the age of Andrew Jackson. Americans were reacting against the aristocratic leadership of Virginians and New Englanders. Intellectualism was out. Gallus-snapping, tobacco-chewing, good-ol'-boy frontier Americanism was in. As Lyman Butterfield, editor of The Adams Papers, points out, "most

Congressmen of the 1820's and 1830's would as soon have been caught in adultery as in writing a book."

It was to such Congressmen that the task fell of deciding what to do about all that money and that strange will. Some thought Smithson had been insane. One wanted to return the money to England on the assumption that surely that nephew of Smithson's had left a "bastard slip" somewhere. And the inevitable element of greed displayed itself when Congress invested the money in state bonds that proved to be generally worthless.

One relic of the old intellectual leadership of the country remained. Former President John Quincy Adams, now an aging, embittered, acerbic Representative from Massachusetts, saw the Smithson bequest for what it undoubtedly was—simply an idealistic gesture from a fellow intellectual who wanted to make the world a better place and who looked upon the youthful United States as the most hopeful environment for his dream. Adams roused himself to battle and took on the enemies of the bequest: the "cormorants," the "total indifference" of then President Martin Van Buren, "the utter prostration of all public spirit in the Senate."

Fighting for the notion that the money should be used to increase knowledge, Adams settled upon a national observatory as the best investment. He stated his case most thoroughly in two lectures which he gave in Quincy and in Boston, where the old gentleman, despite his dour crankiness, remained popular. It is through these lectures that we can glean more about the bequest than in any other records, including Smithson's enigmatic will.

Adams points out the circumstances of Smithson's birth; mentions with admiration his family, including the half brother, Lord Percy, who fought bravely for the British at the opening of the American Revolution; reveals the exact amount of the endowment, $508,318.46; and decries the use of it to buy Arkansas and Michigan bonds ("one of the worst abuses of Legislative power").

"I declared explicitly," he reported, "that no part of the money should be applied . . . for the education of youth." He explained his belief by saying that education doesn't increase and diffuse knowledge. Its purpose is "the instruction of children in that which is already known." He wanted the terms of the bequest meticulously met.

This final struggle of John Quincy Adams is what finally, after eight years, produced the Smithsonian Institution. Adams didn't get his observatory, but he would see immediately that the truest value of the Harvard-Smithsonian Center for Astrophysics—today's version of the observatory he sought—is in the minds of the people who use it to increase knowledge. The hardware, the giant Multiple Mirror Telescope, which is high atop a mountain peak in Arizona, is indeed wonderful. Six 72-inch reflectors combine and are mounted on a square building that rotates like a gun turret. This is an extraordinary treasure, but not a patch on the intellects that use it and learn from it where we belong in the cosmos.

Similarly, the Smithsonian Environmental Research Center with its two locations in Maryland—one in Edgewater on the Chesapeake Bay, where scientists have long studied one of the world's greatest estuaries, and the other in Rockville, formerly the Radiation Biology Laboratory, which has carried out observations of the effect of sunlight on cellular biology since 1929—displays the same treasure—the human intellect—in full panoply.

The Smithsonian Tropical Research Institute (STRI), headquartered in Panama City, tells us of the ecology of coral reefs, of the differing biology of Atlantic and Pacific waters, and what we might expect if ever we dig a waterlevel canal linking the two oceans. One of its research centers perches on an impossibly steep hill on Barro Colorado, an island where the present canal widens into Lake Gatun. Here is a fascinating physical treasure—rain forest, swampy glades, a varied shoreline. Scientific studies here have touched everything from the howler monkeys that wake you at dawn to the insects that prowl through the forest litter.

John Quincy Adams didn't foresee the Smithsonian museums—although he would have appreciated their necessity in the "diffusion" process. As he admitted, he didn't want the Smithson money spent on education. But surely he would have approved of the Anacostia Neighborhood Museum. Anacostia is a predominantly black section of Washington with a long, proud history. In 1967 the Smithsonian acquired a former movie theater on a busy street and converted it into a community museum. In the years since, this museum has become a powerful local enticement for exploring and celebrating black American history.

Like any intellectual, Mr. Adams would insist on authentic, contemporary records of our history, and I know he would enjoy sampling the rich resources of manuscript and memorabilia of yet another Smithsonian collection—the Archives of American Art.

The Archives, with centers in Detroit, New York, Boston, Washington, D.C., San Francisco, Houston, and Los Angeles, has grown into the largest body of documentary materials on American art history. Fascinating letters, drawings, photographs, diaries, art gallery records, and more abound—it's all here for scholars and anyone else who's interested.

To attempt to describe the Smithsonian in terms of statistics would lead to madness, I should think. The number of items constantly changes, the number of scientific projects fluctuates, the number of museums is equally variable. But the values of the Institution—the old dream, we think, of that curious, perhaps embittered Englishman—are constant. Excellence in scholarship and in the collection and display of its tangibles remains firm.

It is an odd fact that the cornerstone of the Castle—the original Smithsonian—has somehow vanished. I like to think that it isn't stone at all. It's human excellence. I'm sure John Quincy Adams would approve.

An Age
of Heroes

When I first joined the staff of the Smithsonian—an event that had seemed to me about as unlikely as being presented at court—I found myself hurrying along the Mall late one afternoon, engrossed in new duties and concerned about fulfilling them. Head down, I strode toward my office. Then I glanced up, and suddenly there was the Castle looming beside me.

Atop its tallest tower the flags were being hauled down, crackling in the winter wind. Lights glowed from the arched Romanesque windows. Pigeons murmured as they found roosting room on stone lintels and in the crenellations of the sandstone walls. Wrapped in its ivy, the old edifice seemed to be settling down for the night.

I stopped, and we stared at one another, the Castle and I—it with splendid indifference, I with sudden wonder that I should belong to such a place and, in a way, to such a building. As more lights came on in the growing darkness, it seemed to become a great ship on a sea of grass, intent on a distant harbor, fired with some particular purpose. And I felt stirrings of what has since become affection for the old place.

The Castle is the Smithsonian's first building, erected in the 1840s and '50s to house an institution that seemed pretty harebrained at that time. It still serves as the Smithsonian's administrative heart and is one of the best-known landmarks in Washington, a ready reference point for the capital's taxi drivers.

James Renwick designed the Castle in a style variously called Romanesque Revival or Norman, but perhaps best described as Victorian Folly. Its center section stands tall; its asymmetrical wings spread wide. Towers of

Overleaf: *The setting sun slips behind darkened towers of the Castle, softly silhouetted against an autumn sky. Once housing all of the Smithsonian's activities, the Castle is occupied mostly by administrative offices today.*

Above: *Photographed by Mathew Brady in the 1860s, the Castle dominates this view of Independence Avenue and lends an incongruous touch of elegance to what was then a remote part of Washington.*

various shapes and sizes soar above it with abandon, sprouting from random corners and gables. Many end in those curved, pyramidal caps that come straight from the illustrations of *Grimm's Fairy Tales*.

Yet gables and towers and battlements and arches and rose windows come together as a reflection of the people who have worked here to keep James Smithson's enigmatic idea alive. On my first real look at the building I thought myself back in a university, feeling about me the aura of scholarship, the mystique of bright minds. At night the Castle seems secretive, turned in on itself. Yet I have seen it on sunny mornings when it positively beamed, opening its broad wings in welcome to the thousands who would visit the Smithsonian as soon as the doors opened.

When the Castle was sufficiently completed in 1855, Joseph Henry, first Secretary of the Smithsonian, moved in with his family. He had come to the job without much enthusiasm, for he had achieved some fame at Princeton as a physicist (the unit of electrical inductance, the henry, is named after him), and when the first Board of Regents appointed him in 1846, he hesitated to take on nebulous duties at an ill-defined establishment. He was urged to accept the job as a patriotic gesture.

Dr. and Mrs. Henry, a son, and three daughters lived in the east wing. His study is still the office of the Secretary, and the Henry family parlor may or may not be the Secretary's present "inner sanctum." The Henrys were joined in the Castle by other scientists (unmarried) who were given rooms there. Sometimes, on damp days, I think the building still carries the lingering scent of their old books and their frayed academic gowns.

A photograph dated 1865 shows the Henrys in front of their stately home, the Secretary seated on a folding chair, his wife and daughters surrounding him, all armed with croquet mallets. I suppose the grass upon which they pose so naturally is the edge of Washington's Mall, for it would have been the Castle's front lawn as well as a city park.

Not much of a park in the 1860s. A canal sliced through it that reeked with sewage. Drunks and vagrants wandered across the grass, and army cattle grazed on it. Yet the Mall witnessed a good deal of drama in these Civil War days, and certainly the Henry family must have shared exciting moments: the flight of Professor Thaddeus Lowe's balloon, *Enterprise*, in 1861; the drilling of Union troops; the appearance of Abraham Lincoln to test or inspect new military gadgets like the breech-loading carbines slated for his cavalry.

President Lincoln knew Dr. Henry and occasionally visited the Castle. Mr. Lincoln apparently attended an abolitionist meeting there in 1862 when Horace Greeley, the famous editor, turned upon him and charged that the war was being fought over slavery and that slavery must end. They say Lincoln remained impassive. Yet emancipation followed within the space of a few months.

Lincoln invited Secretary Henry to the White House. Once it was to meet a visiting delegation of Indian leaders from the West. Lincoln wanted Dr. Henry to explain to them, by using a globe, how their tribes fitted into the vast world of which they were a part.

Joseph Henry was interested in weather forecasting, among many other things, and in pursuing this interest used the tallest Castle

This c. 1865 photograph shows Joseph Henry, founding Secretary of the Smithsonian, enjoying a relaxed moment on the grassy Mall with his wife and three daughters.

tower, the Flag Tower. It is said that Lincoln went up with him at least once to watch the army experiment with semaphor signals. And there's a wonderful story, unfortunately undocumented in the Smithsonian's massive Joseph Henry Papers, that after that expedition a zealous Union officer nabbed Dr. Henry and hauled him before the President. "It's just as I suspected, Mr. President," he panted. "This man is in communication with the secesh across the Potomac!"

Lincoln, of course, was delighted. He asked Dr. Henry if there was any good reason why he shouldn't be shot as a spy. Then he admitted to the officer that he, too, had been up in the Flag Tower.

So have I. A small elevator took me to the attic of the Flag Tower where an iron ladder rises through a hatch in the roof. If Lincoln and Henry aimed for that height, they wouldn't have had that elevator, but would have had to climb the ladder all the way up the tower. Perhaps so. Human legs were stronger in those days. Anyway, it was remarkable to me to shinny up the last lap, perhaps in their distant wake. A vertical ladder is hard for a tall man, and I could picture President Lincoln swinging his knees aside so he wouldn't bark them on the rungs. I didn't have that trouble. He would have towered over me by at least six inches.

The little roof of the Flag Tower is cool on a hot day and bitter on a cold one. Under it, on one side, the Mall sweeps past from the Capitol to the Washington Monument. In the early 1860s neither was completed. The Capitol dome was still abuilding, and money had temporarily run out for the monument. Facing around, I found the Potomac. I was looking toward the site of the Long Bridge (close to today's 14th Street Bridge) and I thought of the beaten northern troops streaming across it after the First Battle of Bull Run, a mob without organization, filled with panic and shame, their bright militia uniforms caked with what the poet Walt Whitman called a "coating of murk and sweat."

The Victorian furnishings in the Smithsonian Secretary's office, opposite, *and the adjacent parlor,* above, *reflect an ongoing program to restore the Castle to its original appearance. The iron beams in these rooms, once occupied by Joseph Henry and his family, are original; they enabled this part of the Castle to survive the fire of January 1865.*

Whitman described the soldiers reaching Washington:

> queer-looking objects, strange eyes and faces, drench'd (the steady rain drizzles on all day) and fearfully worn, hungry, haggard, blister'd in the feet. . . . They drop down anywhere, on the steps of houses, up close by the basements or fences, on the sidewalk, aside on some vacant lot, and deeply sleep. A poor seventeen or eighteen year old boy lies there, on the stoop of a grand house; he sleeps so calmly, so profoundly. Some clutch their muskets firmly even in sleep. Some in squads; comrades, brothers, close together— and on them, as they lay, sulkily drips the rain. . . .

Had Dr. Henry or any of the other Smithsonian scientists seen this drama from the tower? Did anyone, from this lofty place, hear the distant thunder of the great guns?

Just before the Civil War ended in 1865 the Castle burned. Workmen setting up a stove led the stovepipe into the attic instead of a flue, and so the roof over the center section went up in flames and collapsed. More of the building would have gone had it not been for iron floor beams—the first used in a major

Washington structure. As it was, the losses were great: collections which had barely been started suffered badly. So did the Smithson papers. So did paintings of Indians.

The Henry quarters weren't damaged. The tall mahogany bookcases in the Secretary's Office are thought to be the originals, and the Victorian curtains with their scalloped valances in the "parlor" are in the style of the originals. And on the ground floor, the Great Hall with its lofty ceiling and the rose-windowed old Library which has become the "Commons," where staff members eat lunch, survived and now gleam with refurbishment. But upstairs in the central section, new floors were inserted during the restoration in 1968. Only in the library of the Wilson Scholars can you see the way the upper floor used to look—the ceiling so high that it seems to be lost in a misty, cloudless sky.

Abraham Lincoln expressed his sympathy to Dr. Henry for the tragedy of the fire and offered the use of troops to help put up a temporary roof. This was all in the winter of 1865. Lincoln's last winter. . . .

We have Lincoln in a number of ways at the Smithsonian. We have paintings of him

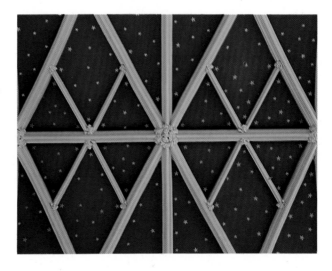

and lithographs, engravings, photographs, etchings, busts, and casts. Some pictures show him unbearded and gaunt, some have him bearded and weary. He appears pensive sometimes, and often worried, and now and then confident. Most of the Lincoln art is in the National Portrait Gallery. There is a cast of his hands—big hands, strong and capable, yet gentle. He had life masks done, as was the custom, and the National Museum of American History has the last one, done about the time of the Castle fire. But the portrayal of Lincoln that hits me between the eyes and leaves me shaken is the cracked-plate photograph in the Meserve Collection at the National Portrait Gallery.

On April 10, 1865, just four days before he was assassinated, Abraham Lincoln visited the Washington studio of photographer Alexander Gardner to sit for a portrait. The glass plate broke during the albumen-silver printing process, and Gardner threw it away after making one print. The crack shows up, all right—it runs through the top of Lincoln's head, not far from where Booth's bullet was going to strike him. But the blemish doesn't affect the rest of the face or its impact.

I found myself studying the face, wanting to return to it after seeing the rest of the Meserve Collection. The feeling that I got was that I verged on *knowing* the man. I had seen reproductions of that print many times before, but they are necessarily clouded, the dark areas too muddy for detail, the light places too washed out. The original print— the only print—reveals a strong, resourceful character at a dramatic moment, for the news of Lee's surrender to Grant at Appomattox Courthouse had barely reached the President.

He has lines of fatigue, but the lines, like the eyebrows, have an indomitable lift, the mouth is quirked in the faint beginnings of a smile.

There are wonderfully human touches. Lincoln's left eye is watering just a little. After all, he had to hold his pose, dead still, for about 45 seconds so that the image would not be blurred. He undoubtedly needed to blink.

His photograph gives other evidences of warm-blooded imperfection. The presidential necktie is askew. And the beard, neatly trimmed though it is, has apparently sprouted a distressingly undisciplined hair. A white hair, at that. Every man knows that a wild hair—usually white—always seems to crop up at the wrong time. Nothing could remind us more that President Lincoln was, after all, a mere mortal.

Frederick Hill Meserve considered the cracked-plate Lincoln his treasure of treasures. He began gathering photographs of faces and scenes, mostly dating from Civil War days, in 1897, and maintained them until his death in 1962. There are far too many for the room that the Portrait Gallery devotes to them, so those on display are rotated. Unfortunately, the Lincoln portrait is so fragile that it, too, is rotated. Lincoln never saw it for he was dead by the time it was developed and printed. Had he seen it he probably would have described it, as he did other portraits, as a good likeness, "but not pretty."

On the day I visited the Meserve Collection, other photographs from original negatives in the collection from the Lincoln days stared down at me from the walls. There was Oliver Wendell Holmes, "Autocrat of the Breakfast-Table," whose son was wounded three times during the war. When Jubal Early's Confed-

Alexander Gardner.
Abraham Lincoln (1809–65). 1865. Photograph, albumen-silver print, 17¹¹/₁₆ x 15³/₈" (45 x 39 cm). Frederick Hill Meserve Collection, National Portrait Gallery (NPG).

Christian Schussele. Washington Irving and His Literary Friends at Sunnyside. *1864. Oil on canvas, 52 x 78" (132 x 198 cm).* NPG. *As a tribute to writer Washington Irving— shown seated, facing forward—the artist has him surrounded by mid-19th-century literary giants, such as Ralph Waldo Emerson, sitting at Irving's left, and Henry Wadsworth Longfellow, leaning on the chair in the left foreground.*

erate force raided to the outskirts of Washington, and rebel snipers sent bullets whistling close to Abraham Lincoln's tall top hat—he was at Fort Stevens to see the action—young Captain Holmes is said to have grabbed him and shouted "Get down, you damned fool!"

And there was Henry Wadsworth Longfellow, who reached his height before the Civil War with such narrative poems as *Evangeline* and *The Song of Hiawatha*. His wife died in 1861, and for a while he was silenced, barren of words. In 1862 he began to stir again, and translated Dante.

In contrast to this Yankee feeling about the collection is the superb photograph of Robert E. Lee. Mathew Brady found the great Confederate general in Richmond a few days after the surrender at Appomattox. He persuaded Lee to don, once more, the old rebel uniform and then photographed him on the porch of his house.

Another photograph at the National Portrait Gallery to remind us of the Civil War is a cabinet card (a commercially produced picture) of Sojourner Truth, the black abolitionist, suffragist, and evangelist who spent the war gathering supplies for Negro volunteer regiments. In 1864 she came to Washington to help integrate the streetcars (almost a century before Rosa Parks's Alabama bus ride!) and was received by Lincoln at the White House. Along the bottom of this cabinet card is printed "I sell the shadow to support the substance." Sojourner Truth never learned to read or write but as a lecturer she drew heavy crowds for more than 50 years. To support herself she sold her likeness to her admirers for about fifty cents.

Musing about the Smithsonian's Civil War connections, I dropped in at a logical place, the Museum of American History. I eventually battled my way past enticing diversions to the military history section on the third floor where the weapons and uniforms of all our wars are displayed. As always, I was struck by the contrast between the mannequins wearing enlisted men's uniforms (lean

I SELL THE SHADOW TO SUPPORT THE SUBSTANCE.
SOJOURNER TRUTH.

Randall

East Grand Circus Park,
DETROIT.

Mathew Brady. Oliver Wendell Holmes
*(1809–94). 1860s. Photograph, albumen-
silver print, 3⁷/₁₆ x 2³/₈" (9 x 6 cm). Frederick
Hill Meserve Collection,* NPG.
*Oliver Wendell Holmes, physician and author,
was among the famous faces photographed by
Mathew Brady during the Civil War. Holmes
was in his 50s and had already published some
of his witty and urbane writings when Brady
took this picture.*

*Two other notable photographs owned by the
National Portrait Gallery are these of
Sojourner Truth,* above, *and Robert E. Lee,*
opposite. *Sojourner Truth, an early activist
for both black and women's rights, had her
picture taken about 1870 by an unknown
photographer at a Detroit studio. Robert E. Lee
was photographed by Mathew Brady a few days
after his surrender at Appomattox.*
Randall Studio? Sojourner Truth *(c. 1797–
1883). c. 1870. Photograph, albumen-silver
print, 5¹¹/₁₆ x 4¹/₁₆" (14 x 10 cm).* NPG.
Mathew Brady. Robert Edward Lee *(1807–
70). 1865. Photograph, albumen-silver print,
8 x 6" (20 x 15 cm).* NPG.

Thomas Buchanan Read.
General Philip Henry
Sheridan *(1831–88). 1871.*
Oil on canvas. 54 x 38⅞"
(137 x 99 cm). NPG; *transfer
from the National Museum of
American History (*NMAH*);
gift of Ulysses S. Grant III.*

as whips—we all should have such waistlines!)
and those wearing officers' uniforms (amply
reflecting the good life).

But the figure I sought proved to be just
about perfect: Rienzi, General Philip Sheridan's horse. Toward the end of the Civil War
Rienzi carried the general on a tremendous,
emotional ride from Winchester, Virginia,
down the Shenandoah Valley to rally fleeing
Federals and turn a defeat into a smashing
victory. The North, which needed heroes, was
fed an idealized description of the swarthy little commander on his big, black horse, galloping full tilt past straggling soldiers, waving his
hat and gesturing toward the sound of the
guns while they all cheered and followed.

Thomas Buchanan Read, poet and painter
of, I think it is safe to say, minor stature, became so carried away by the drama of Sheridan's ride that he wrote a real rouser called,
of course, *Sheridan's Ride,* which gave a few
generations of school children something
lively to recite on speech days. The stanzas
lead off by telling how the roar of the distant
guns drifted "Up from the South at break of
day, / Bringing to Winchester fresh dismay,"
so that everyone realized the rebels were coming, "And Sheridan twenty miles away."

But the general sets off to save the day (a
natural rhyme, and don't for a moment think
Mr. Read doesn't use it):

*General Philip H. Sheridan's
horse, called* Rienzi *and later*
Winchester, *has been preserved and is on display in the
Hall of Military History at the
National Museum of
American History.*

> *A steed as black as the steeds of night*
> *Was seen to pass, as with eagle flight,*
> *As if he knew the terrible need;*
> *He stretched away with his utmost speed;*
> *Hills rose and fell; but his heart was gay,*
> *With Sheridan fifteen miles away.*

So the stanzas chip away at the distance:
"Every nerve of the charger was strained to
full play, / With Sheridan only ten miles
away." And then (I still almost know it by
heart), "He is snuffing the smoke of the roaring fray, / With Sheridan only five miles
away."

16

General Sheridan's brass-hilted, steel-bladed service saber is in the Hall of Military History at the National Museum of American History.

17

And finally:

With foam and with dust, the black charger
*   was gray;*
By the flash of his eye, and the red nostril's
*   play,*
He seemed to the whole great army to say
"I have brought you Sheridan all the way
From Winchester, down to save the day!"

This second battle of Winchester and the poem about it gave Rienzi a new name, Winchester. It also inspired Read to do an oil painting of the ride in 1871, shortly before his death. It's in the National Portrait Gallery. There's Rienzi/Winchester flying out of the battle fog, eyes blazing and nostrils aquiver, while Philip Sheridan brandishes his sword.

Rienzi stands today in apparent modesty in his glass case, wearing a plain blue army blanket. He's strong and well-built. Horse lovers will be pleased to know that he didn't *really* gallop the whole 20 miles on his great day. Records show that General Sheridan paused along the way to cheer up the wounded and threaten the skulkers with damnation, so Rienzi got chances to rest a bit. Considering that the horse has been dead since 1878, he looks in great shape, quite capable of carrying Fighting Phil on another yelling, saber-swinging dash any old time.

Elaborately framed painting of Ulysses S. Grant shows the General in the trenches at Vicksburg in 1863. Grant's wife Julia had this to say of the likeness: "The General looks careworn and weary and the picture, I think, really portrays him as he looked at this time." Ole Peter Hansen Balling. Ulysses Simpson Grant *(1822–85). 1865. Oil on canvas, 40 x 30" (102 x 76 cm).* NPG.

Close to Rienzi is another, grimmer Civil War memento. This is the stump of a tree, 22 inches in diameter, from the battlefield of Spotsylvania. The tree was felled by the hundreds of bullets that just happened to plow into it during that savage, close-range fight in 1864. You can see some of the heavy lead gobs still embedded in the stump; you can see how they grooved and furrowed and slashed away the wood until at last the tree toppled. The soldiers who fought there didn't aim at that tree. But they were fighting desperately in a pall of smoke and fog, and the sheets of lead that ripped back and forth as the volleys were exchanged shattered everything in their way, pruning the undergrowth, gnawing into the breastworks, and felling trees like this one. No display could more graphically show what a Civil War battle was like.

General Ulysses S. Grant, who supervised the Union attacks at Spotsylvania Courthouse—and many other places—in 1864, appears in a portrait at the National Portrait Gallery. He is depicted in military uniform, though he takes his place among the nation's presidents. The most remarkable thing about the painting is the frame. It surrounds a rather vague and seedy-looking Grant, messily attired in an unbuttoned uniform and a pink shirt, and it overwhelms him with heavy, convoluted wood bearing the names of his battles

and crowned by an eagle which is craning down at the portrait as if to see if that really is the General down there.

Mrs. Grant, however, shows up in the first ladies exhibit at the Museum of American History. I find this a good place to visit when I'm on a history kick. It's not that I'm enraptured by all those first ladies' gowns, nor by the faces of the mannequins which are, of course, all the same face—that of Cordelia, King Lear's feisty youngest daughter, sculpted by Pierce F. Connelly of Louisiana in 1865. The original bust is in the Museum of American Art, outside the gallery devoted to American sculptor Hiram Powers. Pierce's Cordelia looks just like Hiram's Proserpine (or vice versa). Actually *all* the faces of classical female busts and statues look pretty much alike, a fact I have come to realize while wandering among them in our museums.

But it's the settings of our first ladies that I like best. They introduce themselves to us in groups, each group in a reconstructed room of the presidential quarters. Thus Martha Washington sits in the simple colonial drawing room of the Philadelphia house that served her husband. To keep her from being lonely two other first ladies join her: Abigail Adams and Thomas Jefferson's daughter Martha Randolph, even though both actually lived in the nearly completed White House.

Julia Grant is in the Blue Room as it was from 1869 to 1891. With her are Lucy Hayes

Mannequins of first ladies and White House hostesses during the years 1845 to 1869 include, from left: Martha Johnson Patterson, Mary Lincoln, Jane Pierce, Abigail Fillmore, and Harriet Lane.

(called Lemonade Lucy because she refused to serve liquor), Lucretia Garfield, President Arthur's sister, President Cleveland's sister, President Harrison's wife Caroline Scott, and the Harrison daughter who served as First Lady after Caroline died.

Mrs. Lincoln is in another group, separated from Julia Dent Grant with great curatorial tact because in real life the two were so often thrown together with disastrous results. Never a stable person, poor Mary Lincoln teetered on the edge of mental illness during her husband's administration, throwing tantrums of jealousy at the slightest suggestion that any other woman was uppity enough to chat with the President. When the Lincolns made visits to Grant's headquarters, Mary would become outraged at the mere presence of other generals' wives, and when one rode too close to Lincoln during a review Mary became quite manic. She embarrassed everyone around, but her episodes were particularly shattering to her husband—and to warm, friendly Julia Grant who was always placed in the position of being the one to calm her down.

Just as well they are in different rooms now. Mary Lincoln stands in the reproduction of the Victorian Parlor along with Sarah Polk, Betty Bliss, who was President Taylor's daughter, Abigail Fillmore, sorrowful Jane Pierce in mourning for the son who died in a train wreck shortly before Franklin Pierce's inauguration, Harriet Lane, who was President Buchanan's niece, and President Andrew Johnson's daughter Martha Patterson.

Mary Lincoln dominates them all, standing regally, bristling with good breeding. Her pose is similar to that in the photograph Brady made of her, now in the Meserve Collection. I can't look at her without thinking of the line attributed to Lincoln after his first meeting, back in Illinois, with this imperious Mary Todd. Asked how he liked her, he is supposed to have replied, "One *d* is good enough for God."

To me, the great marvel of the first ladies exhibit, where carpeting is worn out faster than anywhere else at the Smithsonian, is the feeling it gives of glimpsing real people in their niches of time. I sense that they were gossipy, loving, backbiting, joyous, and, too often in the case of the Lincolns, tragic. "Why is the lighting so dim?" I hear as visitors stare into those settings. To keep the gowns from fading is the official answer. Also, for me, the dimness enhances the strange feeling that here one can touch the life of yesterday.

Just outside these misty, haunted galleries of White House life there are sometimes displayed mementos of another presidency. They don't occupy more than a small case, for they serve no national purpose; they teach little. These are trivial items connected with Jefferson Davis, President of the Confederacy, and I find it a good thing that this figure, castigated in his defeat as the villainous leader of rebellion or, if you were a Southerner, as the architect of catastrophe, should be remembered here at the Smithsonian simply as a person who had ideals, worked hard, loved his wife, enjoyed his friends.

It has often been said that in the Civil War, God was firmly entrenched on both sides. So, for the first time in our history, were railroads. North and South, trains ran troops to the front and supplied the encampments—and were, naturally, the targets of the enemy. A small six-wheeler locomotive, *Pioneer*, stands in the Railroad Hall at the Museum of American History to remind us. It was partially destroyed in Chambersburg, Pennsylvania, when Jeb Stuart's Rebel Cavalry tore through on a whooping, shooting raid and burned down the Union train sheds. Little *Pioneer* was rescued and refurbished—and here it is, safe and sound at last.

Lincoln appreciated his railroads. Shortly before he took office, his predecessor, James Buchanan, got a letter from the King of Siam offering "several pairs of young male and female elephants." The idea was that the Americans would let nature take its course and then could use the resulting population of pachyderms for heavy work and transportation.

I recently saw the letter while a nice exhibit of Thai artifacts was being opened by a very old, saffron-robed holy man, the Supreme Patriarch of Thailand, at the National Museum of Natural History. The items were gifts that had been sent to various United States presidents by Thai rulers. They were beautiful—model chariots and royal barges. But we never got those live elephants. Lincoln's answer, written in 1862 (the mails were terrible then, too), expressed thanks for various gifts, then explained, "Our political jurisdiction . . . does not reach a latitude so low as to favor the multiplication of the elephant, and steam on land, as well as on water, has been our best and most efficient agent of transportation in internal commerce."

It must have been hard for Lincoln to say no to those elephants. They were rare beasts in those days, exotic enough so country lads would trudge miles to see one. In fact, the phrase "seeing the elephant" came to symbolize the experiencing of any big, strange, maybe frightening event. Young people headed for the western wilderness would say they were going to see the elephant. And veteran Civil War regiments, coming out of action to refit after one of those fierce, tree-felling battles, would tell the wide-eyed recruits that they had seen the elephant.

A curator at the Museum of Natural History once told me that ivory is relatively easy to carve. You get through the outer enamel and into the somewhat softer innards of a tusk—the dentin, I suppose—and away you go. He produced a beautiful oriental carving, a long, narrow display of tiny figures and designs. "It's simply a small tusk," he said. "See how it curves."

Wonderful carved ivory was brought home by American sailors who had reached exotic places on the clipper ships—those superb vessels, deep and slender of hull and heartbreakingly beautiful when all sail was set—which for a decade that ended with the Civil War absolutely ruled the waves. Clippers, British as well as American, set record after record in reaching the California gold fields from the East Coast, in crossing the wild Atlantic with immigrants, in sailing to China for tea.

Mementos of this China trade can be seen in the Hall of American Maritime Enterprise in the National Museum of American History. There are beautiful objects like vases that Yankee skippers brought home to their white waterfront mansions with the widow's walks on the roofs. But more meaningful are the tea chests. I am stirred by the authenticity of

Overleaf: *The* Pioneer, *built in 1851, chugged and steamed its way up and down the Cumberland Valley for some 30 years before taking up permanent residence at the Smithsonian.*

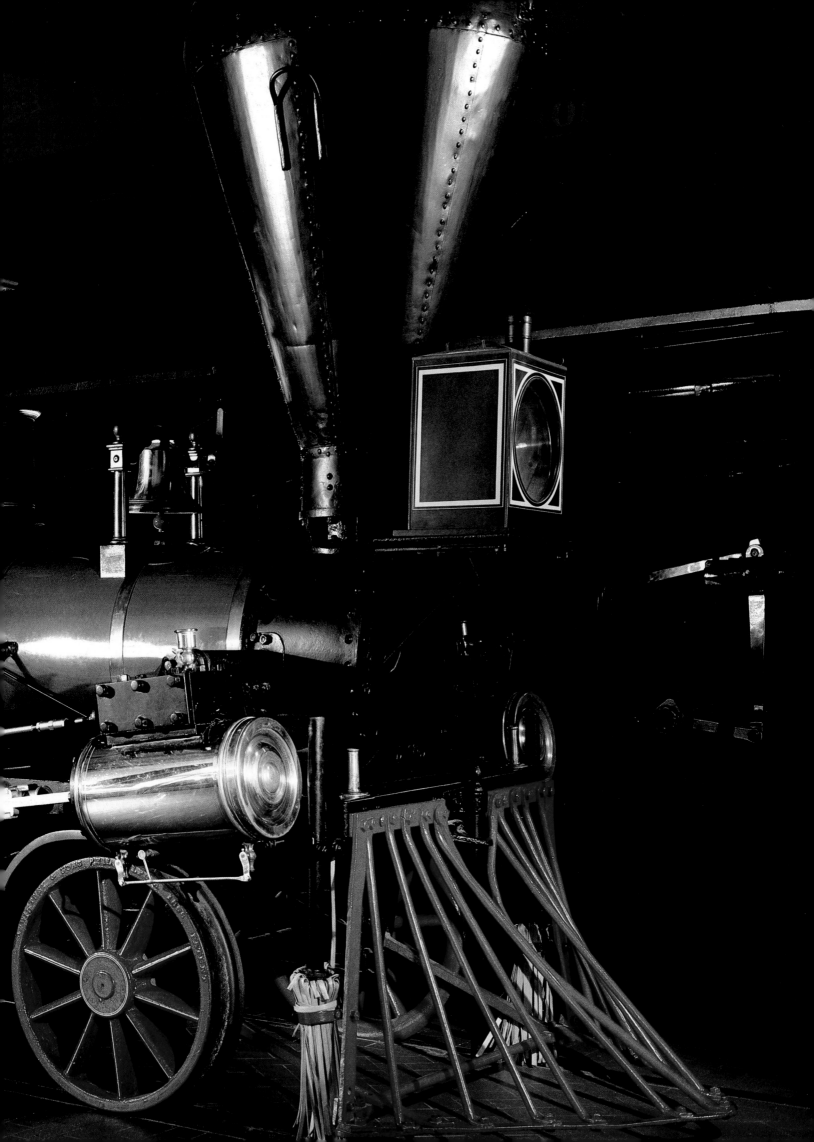

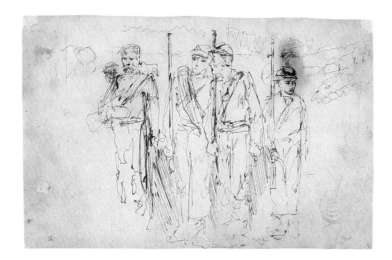

Winslow Homer. The Walking Wounded. *1861–62. Pen and brown ink, 4¹³/₁₆ x 7⁹/₁₆" (12 x 19 cm). Cooper-Hewitt Museum (CHM).*

these somewhat battered wooden boxes that once held the produce those great ships raced home to sell.

Young men in the mid-1800s saw the sea as the pathway to exotic places, new experiences, beauty, danger, zest. In short: adventure. Many people still feel that way about the sea, even though the waters are murkier today—and far more crowded with pleasure boats. Yet anyone who has ever taken a sloop out of harbor will look at William T. Richards' water-

color, *Rocky Cove*, at the Museum of American Art, and recall moments almost like this, an instant of shimmering light, of serenity, of that suddenly broadening horizon that seems to expand the soul and entice the sailor away from the embracing land and off to the unknown. Not far away you can see the other face of the ocean, *Coast of Maine*, by that Civil War sketcher-turned-painter, Winslow Homer. Here are furious waves smashing against tortured rocks. The sailor hears the

Opposite: *Winslow Homer.*
High Cliff, Coast of Maine.
*1894. Oil on canvas, 30⅛ x
38¼" (77 x 97 cm). National
Museum of American Art
(NMAA), gift of William T.
Evans.*

Above: *William Trost
Richards.* Rocky Cove. *1876.
Watercolor, 9 x 14⅜" (23 x
37 cm). NMAA, gift of Oliver
I., David, George C. Lay, and
Alice Lay Lane.*

scream of the wind and feels the sting of the spray and is damned glad he's safely ashore.

Homer lived on the Maine coast after the Civil War, perhaps as an antidote to the furious, often senseless time of conflict. His letters in the Archives of American Art reveal that he was almost reclusive, shunning compliments, fame, and even company. Years later, between 1912 and 1918, almost 300 of his drawings and watercolors and 22 of his oil paintings were given by his family to the

Cooper Union museum-library in New York, which later became the Cooper-Hewitt, the Smithsonian's National Museum of Design. Homer's war sketches are here, also many of his paintings of the sea which so occupied Americans in that time of the beautiful ships.

Whaling was the greatest nautical adventure. Young men from inland towns, dressed in their Sunday clothes, would shyly venture onto the New Bedford or Nantucket waterfronts, seeking a berth on a whaler and a

chance to wash the mud and manure off their country boots. Father might have been the minister of a white-steepled church on the green, and grandfather before him, but no matter. Many a husky Yankee lad, well reared on Shakespeare and the Bible, had dreams in his head of learning this salty trade, making port in some voluptuous South Seas island, of daring his life to slay the boat-crunching mammoths of the deep, and of becoming so all-fired rich that he could drive down his old Main Street in a shiny carriage behind a matched pair of bays—the greatest swell in the whole county.

So they came and signed on for three-year cruises in wretched discomfort, with back-breaking work, miserable food, and horren-

dous danger thrown in. Go look at the full-size whaleboat in the maritime exhibit. Picture the sailors rowing it through mid-ocean swells from ship to lolling whale. The harpooner, his knee in the notch of the small foredeck, or cuddy, poises with his iron. The boat's officer, a mate, exhorts the sweating oarsmen. Pick it up from your copy of *Moby Dick*:

"The harpoon was hurled. 'Stern all!' The oarsmen backed water; the same moment something went hot and hissing along every one of their wrists. It was the magical line. An instant before, Stubb had swiftly caught two additional turns with it round the logger-head, whence, by reason of its increased rapid circlings, a hempen blue smoke now jetted up. . . ."

You can see how the harpoon line went aft to the loggerhead, a short post in the stern, furrowed by the singing line. The nearest oarsman would splash water on it to keep the rope from burning through.

"The boat now flew through the boiling water like a shark all fins," writes Melville, describing what came to be known as a Nantucket sleighride—when the whaleboat was towed at terrific speed by the plunging, outraged, harpooned whale. And at this point the strange hierarchy of the sea took over with as foolhardy a custom as sailors could ever conceive on their wettest night ashore. As official an act as actually killing the whale could not devolve on the harpooner, who was simply a specialized crew member: that final lance,

thrust deep into the great animal's vitals, had to be delivered by an officer, not a crewman. The only officer in the whaleboat was in the stern, steering. So while the boat was slashing through the waves, often rolling wildly in its career, the mate in the stern and the harpooner in the bow changed places, skipping over the crowded thwarts, passing each other, leaping into their new positions. Then, tradition upheld, social caste maintained, vanity appeased, the mate, now in the bow, could rightfully deliver the fatal iron.

"The red tide now poured from all sides of the monster, like brooks down a hill. His tormented body rolled not in brine but in blood, which bubbled and seethed for furlongs behind. . . ." And so, finally, horribly, and yet with the same strange elegance as Hemingway described in bullfights, the splendid prey died. Go look at the whaleboat with a copy of *Moby Dick* in your hand.

American ships reached distant places. Long after the Civil War had ended, a Confederate raider, unaware of Lee's surrender, caught a Yankee whaling fleet in Arctic waters and destroyed it. Other whalers plied the Pacific, even down to the Antipodes. I knew an editor in Melbourne whose name was pure New England, and I asked him about it. "My great-grandfather jumped ship from a New Bedford whaler to join the Australian gold rush," he said.

Merchant vessels made port in the Dark Continent, as we then called Africa. They had once, sadly, dealt in slaves. Now they dealt in ivory. Tons of it. And yet African culture barely touched us and is still, after so many decades, relatively little known.

Once more we make the magic transition from museum to museum. We have been in the maritime hall of the Museum of American History. But now we are in the National Museum of African Art and we are astonished to see so many things we didn't know existed. For example, symbols of authority, of hopes and fears, have always been a basic theme of

The Deji (King) of the Yoruba town of Akure in Nigeria, dressed in full ceremonial regalia, sits holding a horsehair fly whisk with which he occasionally gestures. The renowned Life *photographer, Eliot Elisofon, took this photograph, along with 68,000 others that make up the Eliot Elisofon Archives at the Museum of African Art.*

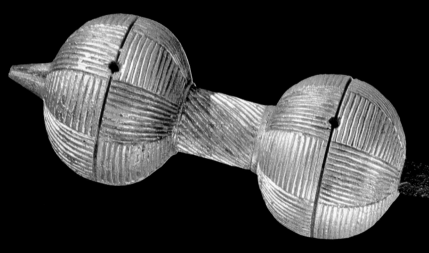

This 45-inch long 20th-century ceremonial sword signifies the presence of an Ashanti king in Ghana. Carried by sword bearers during state occasions, swords like this are held by the seated bearer with the rounded, gold handle pointing toward the king. Such traditions are still alive among the Ashanti. Gift of Emil Arnold.

A pair of men's handmade leather-and-velvet slippers are a recent example of a traditional style still worn by wealthy men of the Hausa people in northern Nigeria. Gift of Ambassador and Mrs. W. Beverly Carter, Jr.

Official messenger staff or "recade" represents kingly authority among the Fon people of the Republic of Benin. The king's messenger carries it when on missions for the ruler. Gift of Ernst Anspach.

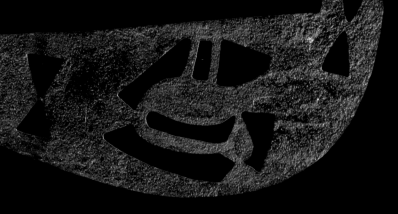

African art. Some are strange to us: the fly whisk that is carried by the village official, the masks that recall ancestors. Ivory, along with gold and other metals, survives the African climate, whereas wood does not. Even the hardest woods, treated with palm oil and stored under the roof of a hut to be thoroughly smoked by cooking fires, seldom date back beyond the 19th century.

Visiting this museum, I was drawn to a very impressive looking chair. The carving around the bottom was intricate and symbolic, and its substantialness indicated that it belonged to someone of elevated status—as indeed it had. The chair was the symbol of the authority of the paramount chief and accompanied him wherever he went to signify his presence.

The sight of this object delighted me. My mind went straight back to where this chapter began—to the Castle. There, in that splendid

Regents' Room, high above the garden, are nine chairs that survived the fire of 1865: the Regents' chairs. When Queen Elizabeth II visited Washington during her tour to honor our Bicentennial, she sat on one. It's still called the Queen's chair.

But on it was placed a pillow. The Queen likes to have one, so somebody among her attendants tries to remember to bring one along for her—just like the portable chair of an African tribal chief.

And as if that were not enough to link Africa with the Castle, note that one of the symbols of an African king is a staff. And if you pause at the front lobby of the Castle and look to your left, toward Smithson's tomb, you will see the Smithsonian Mace. It's gorgeous. It's ornate, adorned with precious metals and stones, meaningfully designed and etched. And what it is, really, is a staff of authority. ✺

Seats of power, past and present, the 19th-century chairs and table, left, *are in the Regents' Room of the Castle, while* at right *is a 20th-century African Chokwe chief's chair from northeast Angola (gift of Mr. and Mrs. Paul Tishman), now at the National Museum of African Art. The Regents, the governing body of the Smithsonian, meet in this room, with the Chief Justice usually seated at one end of the table and the Smithsonian Secretary at the other end. The Chokwe chair is only two feet high, a functional miniature of the chief's larger throne. It was made for occasional use when the chief passed through a village or visited a market.*

Inventions and
Discoveries

No.12208
W. Wright
Steam Engine
Value Gear
Patented Jan. 24th
1856.

No.23.737
D.A. Woodbury
Cut Off Gear for
Steam Engines

No. 635
Baker & Baldwin
Rotary
Steam Engines
Patented Aug. 21st
1839.

No.23352
Miller Rotary
Steam Engine
Patented May 3rd
1859.

A few blocks north of the Mall stands one of Washington's most cherished buildings. It is monumental in size, classical in design, rich in history. And it belongs to the Smithsonian, housing two important museums and the Archives of American Art. We call this building the Old Patent Office, for among its many occupants has been the whole tangled bureaucracy of patents and in its spacious halls were once displayed the fascinating models of American inventions.

Whatever goes on inside the Old Patent Office, whether invention, art, military service, medical care, or presidential festivities (all of which *have* gone on here), its exterior dominates the Washington streets around it. It is square, with Doric porticoes on all four sides and long granite stairways urging you upward to the promised land. In the center of the edifice is an open courtyard where two splendid old elms—surely Smithsonian treasures in their own right—cast shade over fountains, benches, sculptures, and the art lovers who gather here on warm-weather days to sip a cold beer and munch a sandwich.

Art lovers? Yes indeed. For this is the home of the National Portrait Gallery and the National Museum of American Art. It was on my first visit that I stumbled innocently into the Lincoln Gallery of American Art and became an instant admirer of the Old Patent Office and its wonderful collections.

The Lincoln Gallery has been called the greatest room in Washington. It extends the entire length of one of the building's four sides: 88 yards—most of a football field—by 21 yards in width. Its vaulted ceiling is supported by 32 pillars. The walls are bright with paintings; sculptures stand at intervals.

Here, and in the adjoining north hall, on March 6, 1865, Abraham Lincoln's second inaugural ball was held, filling the whole structure with the sounds of waltzes and gallops, the chatter of the rich and powerful, and the aroma of equally rich and powerful food and drink. Walt Whitman, gadfly of Civil War Washington, poked his head in before the

Overleaf: *These diminutive steam engines from the Arts and Industries Building were once kept at the Patent Office Building, which now houses the National Museum of American Art, the National Portrait Gallery, and the Archives of American Art.*

Above: *When this lithograph appeared around 1855 the Patent Office Building was filled with objects of natural history and works of art as well as with patent models.* Top: *Today, its halls are lined with the works of American artists and the portraits of famous Americans.*

event started and couldn't believe how different the place looked from when it had been "fill'd with a crowded mass of the worst wounded of the war."

For in the early years of the Civil War, this huge building, not quite finished, was first a barracks for Rhode Island troops and then a hospital jammed with 2,000 beds. Whitman came to visit the "sick, badly wounded and dying soldiers." So did Lincoln. Clara Barton, later founder and first president of the American Red Cross, rented rooms nearby and worked as a clerk in the Patent Office.

Not long ago, Union Army boots were found in the basement. Also rhymed graffiti. By Walt Whitman? The notion is fascinating, but not very likely. He was only a visitor, after all. And somehow the thought of Whitman creeping down into the cellar to knock off a little doggerel doesn't fit our notions of the "good gray poet." Whitman wasn't much for doggerel. He wasn't even much for rhymes.

The Old Patent Office was a very long time abuilding and even longer in its gestation. Major Pierre Charles L'Enfant, the capital's original city planner, set aside the site as the right place for a national church. It would be nondenominational, in keeping with all these new democratic ideas, and it would rise in a politically neutral position, half way between the Capitol and the White House.

No building arose, however, until 1836. By then L'Enfant's idea for a church had been scrapped by Congress in favor of a "temple of the useful arts." That started its career in patents, and opened the door to other uses. Although the original design for the building was William Parker Elliott's, work began with Robert Mills, who might be called the father of the American Greek Revival, supervising a number of other architects. The design emerged with a feeling of the Parthenon about it, and it's still considered one of the finest examples of the style in the nation.

The south wing was finished by 1840, and here went the collection of the National In-

An illustration in the April 8, 1865, Illustrated London News, right, *shows gaily dressed guests at Lincoln's second inaugural ball held in the Patent Office. Opposite: Lincoln's Cabinet chair, beaver hat, and shawl, now at the Museum of American History, were some of his favorite possessions. He wore the beaver the night he was assassinated at Ford's Theater.*

stitute, a sort of catchall for great documents (including the original Declaration of Independence on loan from the State Department), historic gadgets, stuffed birds, and works of art. These last were later transferred to the newly built Smithsonian.

Fire swept through the building in 1877 and destroyed more than 75,000 patent models. Fortunately many had been placed in the Castle and so survived. You can see them in various crannies and offices in many of the museums of the Institution.

The Department of the Interior shared space in the building with the Patent Office until World War I. The Civil Service Commission moved in during the Depression and stayed until 1963. By then the still-splendid old edifice had been turned over to the Smithsonian—just in time to keep it from being torn down in favor of a parking lot.

The Smithsonian restored the interior to its original spaciousness, hacking away the walls and dividers that had provided offices and cubicles, clearing out decades of mess and scraping off layer after layer of that green paint so dear to the Federal Government. When our workers finally cleaned off the pillars in the Lincoln Gallery they found gleaming marble at the bottom of it all.

Those works of art that had originally been displayed in the Old Patent Office back in the 1840s and had been eventually tucked into corners of the Natural History Building were finally returned, greatly augmented by new acquisitions, to their former home in 1968. That collection became known as the National Collection of Fine Arts, and in 1980 it was renamed the National Museum of American Art. Some of its paintings then helped form a second museum in the building—the National Portrait Gallery. Within a couple of years the Archives of American Art, a research collection of the letters and other writings of American artists, found a home here.

The Old Patent Office has, of course, strong Civil War memories. But because of its beginnings, the art that came here when it

first opened, the patent models that lined the walls, the very style of the architecture, it shouts to me of the 1830s and '40s. When I look up at it as I approach along the F Street Mall I feel a sense of that earlier America, of Yankee inventiveness, of Indians in the West and the Greek Revival in the East, of a national capital consisting of a handful of fine buildings surrounded by an ocean of mud, dust, and hope. . . .

We were introduced, the old building and I, on a spring morning when the Doric columns gleamed at the end of that pedestrian mall. Peddlers' pushcarts and display tables lined the broad, slightly climbing walkway that leads to the southern facade. The hucksters were more interested in soaking up the sun than in calling attention to their bright bits of clothing and silvery costume jewelry. I passed them untempted and mounted the impressive steps toward the shade of the portico. By the time I reached it, I felt a sense of peace, of thoughtfulness.

The Old Patent Office stands today like an island of elegance and serenity above a sea of blaring portable radios, whirling traffic, and forgettable shopfronts proclaiming every product from brass fittings to printed T-shirts. And inside, that contrast is enhanced: instead of racket, conversational murmur; instead of exhaust fumes, that faint, evocative scent that oil paintings, no matter how old they may be, seem to retain.

I was in the National Portrait Gallery. A double stairway opened before me; long corridors stretched away on either side, hung with American faces and figures. It was quickly clear to me that here was a museum devoted as much to history as to art. Here are not just the great works of Copley and Peale and Stuart and Sargent and Trumbull, but busts, lithographs, pencil sketches, everything. And the subjects range from George and

Martha Washington to a sexy life-size figure of Raquel Welch, done for a cover of *Time*. The National Portrait Gallery presents, in every possible way, the people who have made our history thus far, and those who are still working at it.

Ahead of me, doors opened onto the central court. Across that was the Museum of American Art, the MAA as we call it, a twin to the National Portrait Gallery in all but content. I decided to have a look upstairs first, then cross to the Museum of American Art through the upper chambers.

On the second floor of the National Portrait Gallery, I checked up on the Gallery of Presidents. Then on to the third floor where I emerged in a splendid open hall, unadorned by paintings, its pilasters and ceiling gleaming after their restoration from the dingy effects of a 19th-century fire. This great room is called, in fact, the Grand Hall and is frequently used for the Portrait Gallery's famous literary lectures and symposia.

Literary? In an art gallery? I guess it's because literature often (maybe not often enough) contains thought, and thought is supposedly the exclusive product of people—"I think, therefore I am," or if you will, "Je pense, donc je suis," or if you insist on showing off, "Cogito, ergo sum." Anyway, portraiture deals mostly with people, so there is a connection. Explain it however you may, hundreds of people have enjoyed these literary meetings in a true architectural salon. Me too.

Follow this lofty hallway in one direction and you reach the domain of the Archives of American Art: library, files, offices. Head off in the other direction between those elegant walls, and you are following the path of equally elegant guests to the receiving line of the 1865 inaugural ball. Thus you enter, as I did that day, the spectacular Lincoln Gallery, and it becomes your first stop in the Museum of American Art.

It's a marvelous room. It seems to stretch endlessly before you (88 yards is a long way) so that the items at the opposite end are

At the National Portrait Gallery, three Presidents from modern memory—Dwight D. Eisenhower, John F. Kennedy, and Lyndon B. Johnson—sit in a corner of the Gallery of Presidents, a grand marble hall lined with portraits of our leaders.

THE NATIONAL PORTRAIT GALLERY

In this museum, established by an Act of Congress, are portraits of "men and women who have made significant contributions to the history, development, and culture of the people of the United States."

Opposite: *Edward Harrison May.* Isaac Merrit Singer *(1811–75). 1869. Oil on canvas, 51¼ x 38½" (130 x 98 cm). NPG, gift of the Singer Company.*
Right: *Augustus John.* Tallulah Brockman Bankhead *(1902–68). 1930. Oil on canvas, 48 x 24½" (122 x 62 cm). NPG, gift of the Hon. and Mrs. John Hay Whitney.*

Opposite: *Thomas Eakins.* Walt Whitman *(1819–92). 1979 print from 1891 negative. Photograph, platinum print, 4³/₄ x 3⁷/₈" (12 x 10 cm).* NPG.
Right: *Unidentified photographer.* Frederick Douglass *(1817?-95). 1856. Ambrotype, 4³/₁₆ x 3³/₈" (11 x 9 cm).* NPG, *gift of an anonymous donor.*
Below: *John Singleton Copley.* Self-portrait *(1738–1815). 1780–84. Oil on canvas, 18" (46 cm).* NPG, *gift of The Morris and Gwendolyn Cafritz Foundation and matching funds from the Smithsonian Institution.*

THE NATIONAL MUSEUM OF AMERICAN ART

Colonial portraitists, landscape painters, impressionists, Ashcan school members, WPA artists, realists, abstractionists, expressionists—all are represented at this museum, which spans more than 200 years of American painting and sculpture.

John Hesselius. Mrs. Richard Brown. *c. 1760. Oil on canvas, 30 ⅛ x 25⅛" (77 x 64 cm). NMAA, museum purchase in memory of Ralph Cross Johnson.*

John Hesselius. The Reverend Richard Brown. *c. 1760. Oil on canvas, 30⅛ x 25⅛" (77 x 64 cm). NMAA, museum purchase in memory of Ralph Cross Johnson.*

Charles Willson Peale.
Mrs. James Smith and
Grandson. *1775. Oil on*
canvas, 36³/₈ x 29¹/₄" (92 x
74 cm). NMAA, gift of Mr.
and Mrs. Wilson L. Smith, Jr.

Thomas Wilmer Dewing. The
Spinet. *c. 1902. Oil on wood,
15½ x 20" (39 x 51 cm).*
NMAA, *gift of John Gellatly.*

Childe Hassam. The Island Garden. *1892. Watercolor on paper, 17½ x 14" (44 x 36 cm).* NMAA, *gift of John Gellatly.*

51

Edward Hopper. Ryder's
House. *1954. Oil on canvas,*
36⅛ x 50" (92 x 127 cm).
NMAA, *bequest of Henry*
Ward Ranger through The
National Academy of Design.

Helen Frankenthaler. Small's
Paradise. *1964. Acrylic on
canvas, 8'4" x 7'9⅝" (2.54 x
2.38 m). NMAA, gift of
George L. Erion.*

blurred by distance. The placement of objects in any museum is subject to change, but when I went through the Lincoln Gallery, its collection ranged from historical to contemporary paintings and sculptures.

Around me were colonial paintings, those strange, primitive portraits done by itinerant artists who recorded families just as photographers do today. Perhaps it was the style in those days, but all the women and children appear to have eyes like cats'. The men look overfed and uncomfortable. I don't know—it may be that this is an utterly faithful representation of the way we were in the 1700s: gouty men and cat-eyed women. Perhaps these features were prerequisites to beauty.

Anyway, I hurried past these early works of art and abruptly discovered George Catlin. A special niche has been set aside for Catlin's work, and when I poked into it I was surrounded, as surely as any mountain man of the 1830s, by haughty Indian faces with deep-seeing eyes and strong mouths and noses.

George Catlin's obsession with Indians went back to his boyhood friendship with an Indian he met hunting in the woods near his home in New York state. This would have been soon after the turn of the 19th century, so, though the great Iroquois tribes of this region had been pretty thoroughly broken up at the end of the American Revolution, finding individ-

uals ranging the still-wild forests was unusual but not unheard of. Catlin's friend was killed—apparently by a white hunter—and the lad always remembered his sad, dignified eyes.

To please his father, Catlin studied law and set up office in Lucerne County, Pennsylvania. Within two years, his love of art overcame his sense of filial duty and he sold out and launched himself as a miniaturist in Philadelphia. The self-confident, self-taught young artist was quickly successful, but still restless. A chance encounter with a group of western Indians brought east to visit the great cities and to meet the President decided him. He would paint Indians, "rescuing from oblivion the looks and customs of the vanishing races of native man in America."

In 1830 he headed for St. Louis, made friends with the governor of the Territory of Missouri (William Clark, of Lewis and Clark) and got his help in meeting Indians on their own lands. He spent eight years traveling through the wilderness on horseback or by canoe, facing up to the great chiefs and warriors of some of America's "fiercest" tribes and somehow persuading them to pose for him.

You have to hand it to Catlin. He was no mountain man, just a rather undersized Philadelphian (there's a painting of him in the National Portrait Gallery by William Fisk), but he had the guts to look the chiefs in the eye

Sunlight filters through the stained glass dome of the Grand Hall (detail, right) on the third floor of the National Portrait Gallery. Once filled with patent models, then badly damaged by the fire of 1877, the Grand Hall now gleams with all the splendor of the Victorian Renaissance.

and tell them what he wanted, and they must have found him bright and interesting. A good thing, too, for Indians like the Pawnee Horse Chief, whose portrait is, I think, Catlin's best, would not have suffered fools gladly. When George and his friend John Dougherty, an Indian agent called (no kidding) "Honest John," came to call on the Pawnees, the warriors put on a special show for them, charging toward them on horseback, weapons flashing, horses and men painted for battle, the feathers of cardinals and orioles stuck in scalp locks. And Catlin went wild, getting all that ceremonial color on canvas while women and children crowded around his ea-

sel, giggling. People criticize George Catlin's portraits for lacking depth, for being two-dimensional. Perhaps Rembrandt's, too, might have suffered had he been jostled while he worked by a hundred ardent kibitzers.

During his journeys in Indian country, Catlin gathered a collection of Indian objects—clothes and furs as well as paintings—and kept this "Indian Gallery" with him, displaying it wherever he traveled in Europe as well as America. He lectured for funds and tried to sell the gallery, but he failed to do so, and died broke and unhappy. He had turned the Indian Gallery over to a Philadelphia boiler-maker who paid his debts, and the new owner

Catlin's Indian Gallery, *opposite,*
crammed into the Arts and Industries
Building at the turn of the century.
Indian peace medal, lower right, *issued*
in the name of President Jefferson, now at
the Museum of American History.
Above: *William Fisk.* George Catlin
(1796–1872). *1849. Oil on canvas,*
4'2" x 3'4" (1.27 x 1.02 m). NPG,
transfer from the NMAA, *gift of Miss May*
C. Kinney, Ernest C. Kinney, and
Bradford Wickes, 1945.
Right: *George Catlin.* Osceola
(c. 1800–38). 1838. Oil on canvas,
30¾ x 25¾" (78 x 65 cm). NPG, *on loan*
from NMAA, *gift of Mrs. Joseph*
Harrison, Jr.

Overleaf: *Catlin may well have used these*
items which he collected from the Indians to
whom he had devoted his career. Now safely
preserved at the Museum of Natural History,
they once traveled around the United States
and to Europe as part of his Indian Gallery.

had stashed the collection in the basement of his factory. Spencer Baird, the second Secretary of the Smithsonian, heard about it and rescued it. The paintings badly needed restoration and the clothing was mildewed and mouse-gnawed.

Wanting to see more of what Catlin had seen, I knifed resolutely through Washington traffic to the Museum of Natural History. (In this book we can make this transition in the space of a sentence, but actually it took me quite a while.) At last, among the displays in the anthropology section, I found items of the life that Catlin had lived: the skins, tents, knives, hatchets, tools, ornaments, pottery, travois, and other tangibles of the Plains Indians that he knew and that filled out the meaning of his art.

Over in the Arts and Industries Building, across the Mall from Natural History, there are more western Indian items. These are part of the 1876 exhibit, a reminder that even as late as that, many Plains Indians were relatively untouched by white settlement—except for an ominous scarcity of the buffalo on which their lives were based. That year, 1876, was the year of Custer and the Battle of the Little Bighorn; 1877 was the year of Chief Joseph of the Nez Perce and the Battle of the

Captain William Clark carried this pocket compass when he ventured west for the first time with Captain Meriwether Lewis in 1803. Patrick Gass, a member of the exploring party, published an illustrated journal of the famous expedition, here opened to show Lewis and Clark holding council with Indians. Both compass and journal are in the Museum of American History.

In 1839, the American Society for the Diffusion of Useful Knowledge in New York City published The American School Library, *a traveling library to be sent to the frontier territories. The only complete set known to exist is this one from the Museum of American History. Its most worn book is* The Swiss Family Robinson.

Asher B. Durand. Dover Plain, Dutchess County, New York. *1848. Oil on canvas, 3'6½" x 5'½" (1.08 x 1.54 m). NMAA, museum purchase and partial purchase by Mr. Thomas M. Evans.*

Big Hole. So the buckskins and beads in these Centennial cases recall a time when some Indians had changed little from Catlin's day, except that they were getting desperate enough to take on the U.S. Army.

It was the loss of land that pushed the tribes to the wall. And what land! To get the impact of what Catlin and others saw when they went west in the early decades of the 19th century, we have to return to art—landscape painting, this time, back at the Museum of American Art. On the second floor is a gallery of landscapes that beautifully and effectively illustrates the difference between eastern and western scenes in the eyes of 19th century artists—in fact, in the eyes of anyone, even today, who keeps them open to nature's displays while traveling in this country.

This museum has a number of paintings of the Hudson River School, the name given to those early American landscapes, mostly along the Hudson with its mountains and misty val-

Albert Bierstadt. The Sierra Nevada in
California. *1868. Oil on canvas, 6' x 10'¹/₂"
(1.83 x 3.06 m).* NMAA, *bequest of*
Helen Huntington Hull.

leys, that expressed the then new interest in the land. Until the early 19th century, Americans had thought of wilderness as a thing to be defeated and tamed. It was hostile, savage, threatening. Then, appreciation of nature began to seep into this country, partly from England where John Ruskin and his followers were promoting this theme.

American writers picked up the concept of glorious nature. Writing in the 1840s, James Fenimore Cooper described with relish the eastern wilderness of a century earlier, "affording forest covers to the noiseless moc-

casin of the native warrior, as he trod the secret and bloody war-path." Cooper's delight in the wild scene, blended with his dispassionate view of its early threat, appealed vastly to his readers in both England and the United States. In the same decade, Henry David Thoreau went to live at Walden Pond, finding in his patch of forest not a vestige of the old colonial fear, but only a soothing environment for measured thought.

American artists reacted the same way to nature. In this above-mentioned gallery is a painting by Asher B. Durand called *Dover*

Left: *Thomas Moran.* Cliffs of the Upper Colorado River, Wyoming Territory. *1882. Oil on canvas, 16 x 24" (41 x 61 cm). NMAA, bequest of Henry Ward Ranger through The National Academy of Design.* Above: *George Catlin.* Horse Chief, Grand Pawnee head chief. *1832. Oil on canvas, 29 x 24" (74 x 61 cm). NMAA, gift of Mrs. Joseph Harrison, Jr.*

Plain, Dutchess County, New York. This is of a Hudson River site, done in 1848, a serenely pastoral view with small, friendly hills, soft meadows, placid cattle grazing beside calm pools and gentle trees. It is filled with the new American love for the landscape.

The *eastern* landscape, that is. On the same floor look for Albert Bierstadt's *The Sierra Nevada in California.* Here are towering peaks that seem to lose themselves in boiling clouds; vertical cliffs streaming with waterfalls; great trees, bent and twisted by violent storms; wild elk and waterfowl. It's a scene of incredible

power and size and impact—a reflection of how the West looked to this German-born, New England-reared artist, and to other easterners. Bierstadt did this 20 years later than Durand's work, but the effect of the western landscape on eastern eyes is timeless. I, too, am a New Englander, filled with affectionate memories of rocky meadows slanting upward to a fringe of maples, of the ever-changing light across the face of my own regional mountain. And when I first drove west, and the car seemed to flag as it crossed the prairies of west Kansas, seemed even to be constantly climbing—which indeed it was—and then in the far distance before me stood a bank of clouds, their tops etched against the western sky, and I realized they were *not* clouds . . . wow! I felt the impact, all right.

It demanded little of my own imagination to feel that first view of the front range of the Rockies beckoning me, had I been a mountain man, or chilling my heart, had I been an early settler crossing the frontier. Here was the whole mystique of the American West. *Anything* was possible beyond those soaring peaks: Utopia; the land of Oz. And even today, with smog, overcrowding, greed, phoniness, enough of the western grandeur remains in its original purity to stir the juices as it did to Bierstadt and all the others.

Seek out Thomas Moran's *Cliffs of the Upper Colorado River, Wyoming Territory*. The painting shows a sweep of open prairie beneath up-right formations carved by millennia of erosion; four mounted warriors ambling homeward toward a distant cluster of tipis, highlighted by a shaft of sunlight; a backdrop of tumbling clouds, streaked with rain. Another scene to wrench the boundaries of the

Built in 1881 by the Abbott, Downing company, this Vermont hack passenger wagon at the Museum of American History is of the type built and used in remote western regions not reached by rivers or railroads.

William Stanley Haseltine.
Rocks and Trees, Mt.
Desert Island, Maine.
*1860–65. Pen and black ink,
watercolor, 22 x 15" (56 x 38
cm). CHM, gift of Helen
Haseltine Plowden.
A landscape painter in the
Hudson River School
tradition, Haseltine created
almost topographical paintings
of eastern views.*

orderly eastern mind. This was painted in 1882, but that wasn't too late for the visual wallop of the old West. It would be 20 years before Owen Wister published *The Virginian,* the prototype western novel, set right in this Wyoming country. It would be a year before Wister's friend, a bright, energetic young New York assemblyman named Theodore Roosevelt went west for the first time and became so overwhelmed with the wild splendor that filled his eastern eyes that he bought a ranch in the Badlands.

Thomas Moran was another easterner. He first saw the West as artist with a geological survey and was intensely affected. His daughter described his feeling as "a great spiritual revelation and upheaval . . . as he journeyed on horseback through an almost unbelievable wilderness. To him all was grandeur, beauty, color and light—nothing of man at all, but nature, virgin, unspoiled and lovely."

Moran did a great deal, through his huge canvases, to get across the idea that beautiful landscape should be preserved as national parks, a permanent heritage that feeds the soul considerably more than does openpit mining. As a result, he is remembered in geography books with Mount Moran, Moran Canyon, and a few Moran Points. He, in turn, was called by his western trailmates T. Yellowstone Moran. Nearly a hundred of his drawings and watercolors are in the collection of the Cooper-Hewitt Museum in New York.

Vertical cliffs, soaring peaks, and writhing cloud formations are not, of course, the sole property of the western United States. With a snap of the fingers we transport ourselves to the Freer Gallery of Art and gaze at *Clearing Autumn Skies Over Mountains and Valleys,* a wonderful Oriental title for an 11th-century Chinese hand scroll. Such a scroll has a wooden rod at each end so that as you unroll it from one, you roll it up around the other. The painting then passes before you, generally taking you along on a journey, perhaps down a river or through mountains or villages. In this case, you go through the whole experience of autumn in a particular part of China that is rich indeed with the cliffs, peaks, and clouds that both Bierstadt and Moran enjoyed so much.

This Freer treasure dates from the Northern Sung Dynasty, which means it's about 900 years old. It was attributed to Kuo Hsi, who was revered in China as a great landscape artist of that time. But a Smithsonian expert more recently decided that it probably was done by some very good follower. The painting, on silk backed by paper, is in black ink and has taken on a light green hue with age.

I couldn't look at this ancient Chinese scroll without another ridiculous mental leap occurring. Cliffs? Clouds? A journey? Why my feeling of déjà vu? Where had I seen all that before? And then I remembered: as an old friend of the National Air and Space Museum, I encounter those very same elements every time I enter that great new building from Independence Avenue. Huge murals flank the broad lobby of this entrance. To your right, as you enter, is Robert McCall's spectacular concept of space exploration; to your left is Eric Sloane's *Earthflight Environment*—cliffs, mesas, monoliths, roiling clouds pierced by shafts of sunlight. And a journey: an airliner streaks past the clouds, spinning its contrail behind it. All of which shows, I suppose, that artists can think alike even though separated by 900 years.

Admittedly, Sloane's jetliner strikes a false note in our theme of western exploration. George Catlin traveled by horseback and canoe. The familiar Conestoga wagon carried the settlers as soon as trails were established. And trains were soon on the way, rattling along stretches of track in the East, soon threatening the future of the booming canals. It's a strange fact that the Chesapeake and Ohio Canal, laboriously constructed to link the eastern seaboard with the farms and coal-fields beyond the Alleghenies, was begun on the very same day that work began on the Baltimore and Ohio Railroad—which in due course would put the canal out of business.

Thomas Moran. West Wall of the Canyon, Yellowstone. *1892. Pencil on paper, 9⅞ x 7⅞" (25 x 20 cm). CHM.*
Moran drew this view, and many others, while on an expedition to Yellowstone and the Grand Tetons with a government survey team.

Unidentified artist. Clearing
Autumn Skies Over
Mountains and Valleys.
Northern Sung, 11th century.
Handscroll, ink and light color
on silk, 10¼ x 81⅛" (26 x
206 cm). Freer Gallery of Art
(FGA).

The Smithsonian has a number of tangible reminders of the early days of railroads, but one little engine stands paramount among the displays and that is *John Bull*, built in Britain in 1831 and put to work on a few miles of track in New Jersey. It now rests on the first floor of the Museum of American History, rating special billing—a place apart from other railroading memories in the Railroad Hall. It is oiled and clean, its boiler sheathed in polished wooden slats. It looks perfectly ready to rumble back to work.

It *is* ready. *John Bull* celebrated its 150th birthday, in 1981, by taking possession of a mile or so of track beside the Potomac River and showing the world it could still carry a load of passengers at a breathtaking 13 miles an hour. (It can do more, if pressed). It chugged back and forth while onlookers cheered and the Marine Band played Sousa. It worked just fine. I know, because I drove it.

My experience as *John Bull's* engineer didn't occur on that same festive day, but a year earlier when the curator of this little treasure decided to see if he could get the diminutive locomotive going again.

This curator, John H. White, had long carried on a surreptitious romance with *John Bull*. Back when he was a newcomer at the Smithsonian, White eyed the little engine covetously. Finally, on an evening when the sightseers had gone home and the guards weren't looking, he crept onto the engineer's platform and twiddled the controls. White told me that just before a guard was due to appear on his rounds, he was suddenly seized by an irresistible spasm of mad daring, and bonged the bell. It was still echoing in the dark hall as the Smithsonian gendarme panted into sight, and White scuttled away into the shadows.

Later, as curator, White and his remarkable assistant, John Stine, mechanic extraordinaire, spent another quiet evening (this time with the cooperation of the guards), jacking the engine's drive wheels off their little bed of track to see if they would turn. They fed compressed air to the engine, opened the throttle, and watched the wheels turn with a creak and groan. By the time White and Stine had finished cleaning and oiling and greasing that night, the locomotive was ticking over like a smooth-running sewing machine.

Thus it was that on a bright autumn day, the two devotees and their crew of fellow aficionados—all as secretive as commandos starting on a raid—trucked *John Bull* into the Virginia countryside and lowered it onto a piece of track that had been reserved for the coming performance. As evening fell, the crew fed wood to the firebox and tried raising steam. The pressure gauge needle twitched

John Bull *blows its whistle and rings its bell as it returns to the tracks to celebrate its 150th birthday. Built in England in 1831 by Robert Stephenson & Co., this little train is the world's oldest working steam locomotive. Its steam pressure is measured by the gauge,* left.

John Bull *stops for a rest along the C & O Canal, which was put out of business by the expanding railroads.*

and rose—and then a gasket blew with a mighty hiss. It was too late for repairs, so the troops turned in for the night in their trailer.

Early next morning a new gasket was put in place and a fresh fire built. By the time other chosen guests had arrived, steam was up. We all scavenged for scraps of wood, and finally the pressure was enough to open the ancient safety valve. With that, the piping whistle blew, and off went the little engine that could, while we all shouted and waved, just like the frock-coated and bonneted onlookers of an earlier time who watched its original run.

The first "chuff" sent a small eruption of dust and debris (probably a few carefully thrown pennies) and hot, black water shooting into the air from the smokestack, to rain down upon us, but we laughed with joy and ran beside the engine like children. And in the course of the day, nearly all of us got to drive. You turn a long iron rod, the throttle, and you expect the wheels to move with a jerk, but they start gently and easily and only the first lurch of the engine shows that you are moving. And then, triumphantly, you pull a cord and hear the shrill peep of the whistle.

So *John Bull* can rightly be called the world's oldest working locomotive. What's more, it's one of my special treasures. But it's not the oldest American locomotive. One of the first to run in this country was *Tom Thumb*; the

product of an inspired mechanic, inventor, tinkerer, and financier, Peter Cooper. As he grew wealthy (a machine for cutting cloth in mills was one very profitable invention), he set up a foundation in New York to give free technical training to adults. He had always felt that individual success should be shared among one's fellows. Cooper was, remember, born in the 18th century, a time of tumultuous upheaval in minds as well as nations, and he was raised in the glow of the Age of Enlightenment and infected by its ideals. And so he expressed them with the Cooper Union.

As the training classes at the Cooper Union got underway, and lecturers were lured to its podium, Peter Cooper found himself yearning for a museum. And in his old age his enterprising granddaughters, Sarah and Eleanor—Miss Sally and Miss Nelly—and Amy Hewitt, got it started for him.

With their social and family connections, the Hewitt sisters inveigled enough gifts to build an impressive collection of the decorative arts. Today, these and newer acquisitions form the Smithsonian's Cooper-Hewitt Museum on upper Fifth Avenue in New York City. Among the prints, wallpapers, furniture, lacework, tapestries, art, and sculpture are many treasures from the Orient. It's almost as though what the Freer didn't get the Cooper-Hewitt did.

Opposite: *Sparks flying,* John Bull *chuffs down a stretch of track beside the Potomac River, reliving its journeys on the Camden and Amboy Railroad in New Jersey a century and a half earlier.* **Right**: *A drawing by curator John White shows the locomotive as it appeared in 1831.*

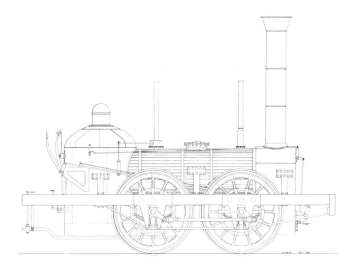

Japan during the Edo period (1615–1868).
Ukiyo-e prints and paintings—or "Pictures of
the Floating World"—depict scenes from
everyday life, affording us a delightful glimpse
of old Japan. Mount Fuji, the highest
mountain in Japan, was a favorite subject of
both Hokusai and Hiroshige, who painted this
symmetrical, snowcapped volcano from every
angle and in every season.

Opposite: *Ando Hiroshige.* One Hundred
Famous Views of Edo. *1858. Woodblock
print, 13¼ x 8⅞" (34 x 23 cm). FGA, gift of
Alan, Donald, and David Winslow, heirs of
the estate of the Hon. William Castle.*

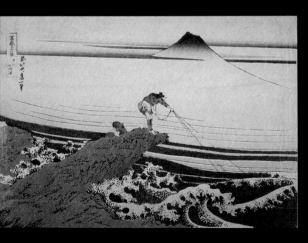

Above: *Ando Hiroshige.* The Suido Bridge
and Suruga Plain *from* One Hundred
Famous Views of Edo. *1857. Woodblock
print, 13⁵⁄₁₆ x 8¾" (34 x 22 cm). CHM.*
Left, top to bottom: *Katsushika Hokusai.*
Yoshida on the Tokaido *from* Thirty-Six
Views of Mount Fuji. *Woodblock print, 10 x
14⅞" (25 x 38 cm). FGA, gift of Eugene and
Agnes E. Meyer.*
Katsushika Hokusai. Kajikazawa in Kai
Province *from* Thirty-Six Views of Mt.
Fuji. *1823–31. Woodblock print, 10¼ x
14⅞" (26 x 38 cm). CHM.*
Attributed to Katsushika Hokusai. Clam-
gatherers on the Shore. *Color and ink on
silk, 22¼ x 31" (57 x 79 cm). FGA.*

So it was that I discovered Oriental art and items that had come to the United States at just the time of our westward expansion. The Chinese put their talent and industriousness to work in the 19th century to meet growing demands from the west. They produced porcelains on order from Europe, designing them as Europeans wanted. Many of these are in the museum. And since my own tastes in these matters hew sternly to the obvious and well-known, I rather like these.

As for Japanese art, I am attracted to the Freer's paintings from the Edo period, and at the Cooper-Hewitt I instantly gravitated toward one of Hokusai's *Thirty-six Views of Mt. Fuji*—prints of fishermen or farmers working against a background of staggering mountains or delicious pools or wistful trees and dazzling flowers—those I love.

Contemplating that these, too, were exported to the world's markets, I began to think about Matthew Calbraith Perry who took his United States vessels to Japan in 1853 with the purpose of working out a treaty that would open the island nation to trade. Japan had managed to stave off attempts by Euro-

82

Below: *Eliphalet M. Brown, Jr., after Bernard William Heine.* Exercise of Troops in Temple Grounds Simoda Japan. *1856. Lithograph, 20%/16 x 32½" (52 x 83 cm). NPG, gift of August Belmont IV.*
Left: *Unidentified photographer.* Matthew Calbraith Perry. *c. 1855. Daguerrotype, 5½ x 4⁵/16" (14 x 11 cm). NPG.*

pean powers to open her ports and commence trade; Commodore Perry, an experienced and highly capable officer, wasn't about to be staved off in turn, so he arrived with the decks of his gunboats cleared for action. He talked gently to the Japanese dignitaries, but they had little doubt that the "black ships" would blast them and their villages if they tried to wriggle out of commitments—which they had generally succeeded in doing before. The result was the first real crack in Japan's door. Perry's treaty didn't accomplish all that the merchants had hoped for, but it made further commercial agreements possible. It certainly introduced Japanese art and culture to many Americans.

Commodore Perry was a military hero of the best kind—he kept the peace. And in the National Portrait Gallery, back in the Old Patent Office Building where we started this long and digressive peregrination, is a rather omi-

nous portrait of him done by an unnamed Japanese artist; also a somewhat self-conscious daguerrotype of him done by an unnamed photographer after his return to the States; finally a picture of the Commodore in Japan with his troops. This last is a fine scene, a lithograph showing soldiers lined up, Japanese citizens milling in the foreground, Perry and the Imperial Commissioners watching from the temple veranda. It tells you more about Perry's expedition than *I* could.

Thus it was that in those pre-Civil War years, we Americans met each other, race to race, discovered nature both in the familiar East and the incredible West, began our railroading career and stretched our minds even as far west as China, and finally, secluded, reclusive Japan. And all along this path, the tangibles of our expansion have been fashioned and have been dropped off at the Smithsonian and are our treasures. ✻

Experience

At 10 a.m.
this spot
was at the
pendulum.

At 10 a.m.
this spot
was at the
pendulum.

Some museums are as high, wide, and open as Grand Central Station. You walk in and there it all is. You see everything in one synapse-searing instant, one gasp of wonder. Ohhh, *wow!* Others are labyrinthine, intricate, clearly designed by someone who wants to slow your pace, lure you into bewildering cul-de-sacs, startle you with unexpected revelations, maybe even lead you astray. Well, if you wander into one of these and don't lose your nerve at the prospect of being locked in at closing time, then you may find yourself savoring the delights and wonder of serendipity, discovering things you never even thought about coming to see.

Such a place is our National Museum of American History, a massive rectangle of pink Tennessee marble that, with grounds and parking lots, takes up two full blocks along the Constitution Avenue side of the Mall. Unless you have time to spare, don't venture into it. Its displays will ensnare you with their siren song, and you will amble from one delightful digression to another, eyes wide, mouth agape, schedules forgotten.

More than 35 galleries of various sizes tempt you with offerings that vary from a 280-ton locomotive to Muhammad Ali's boxing gloves. An average of four-and-a-half-million people explore these and uncountable other marvels each year. Of course a few may be those who got happily lost the year before.

The building is new (as compared to most of the Mall, that is—it opened in 1964); many of the collections are not. Some originated in the "National Cabinet of Curiosities," among the "useful arts" displayed in the Old Patent Office. Other items—hundreds of thousands of them—have been added. For years they crammed the complicated bays of the Arts and Industries Building, the old U.S. National Museum. Now they find a home here.

Large displays rate a proper margin of space around them so visitors can really take them in. But some exhibits are deliberately crowded. A Nation of Nations, designed to

Left: *Judy Garland danced her way through the film* The Wizard of Oz *(1939) wearing these sequined ruby slippers, now owned by the Smithsonian. They are one of several pairs used in the film's production.* Opposite: *Neon-lit restaurant signs in the Nation of Nations exhibit highlight our country's diverse ethnic heritage.* Overleaf: *A multiple exposure photograph captures the dramatic image of the 240-pound Foucault pendulum bob. The arrow is set daily at 10:00 a.m., and the pendulum then appears to travel in an arc, knocking over the pegs as it moves. In fact, its circular movement is caused by the rotation of the Earth, not by its own motion.*

illustrate the diversity of American origins, presents our polyglot culture with a collage of items, pictures, and films as crammed as a Brooklyn tenement. Here are the things that have made us: school desks, hobbies, movies, games, sports, junk food, bills to pay, great moments of the American past. Here are Sandy Koufax's baseball glove and Archie Bunker's chair. Here are a Cheyenne saddle frame of hide-covered wood and antler, and a motorized railroad handcar. Here are a colonial kitchen with a huge apple pie and a red Yankee Stadium ticket booth with graffiti. Your eye has trouble taking it all in: an army barracks latrine; a cross that tells us to "Get Right With God"; the emblem of De Matha High School, 1966 champions of the Metropolitan Catholic League; the badge of the East Ohio Gas Company; a motorman's uniform from street car days; a police uniform right out of the Keystone Cops.

And the sounds! Here is a cacophony of audible memories: children chanting the Pledge of Allegiance, Eddie Cantor singing "Margie," the roar of a crowd as a bat cracks against a ball, the wheeze of a switching engine, the violin of Jascha Heifetz, the sounds of "You Wore a Tulip," of Irish tenor John Mc-Cormack, of Frank Sinatra, of the golden coloratura of Amelita Galli-Curci.

The RCA Victor logo, left, *evokes the early days of sound reproduction. Three generations of American puppets cavort on this poster,* opposite, *from a recent Smithsonian puppet exhibit.* From left to right: *Ventriloquist's figure, Charlie McCarthy, created in 1923 by Edgar Bergen; Kermit the Frog, one of Jim Henson's still popular Muppets; Howdy Doody, marionette and star of the TV show bearing his name from 1947 to 1960.*

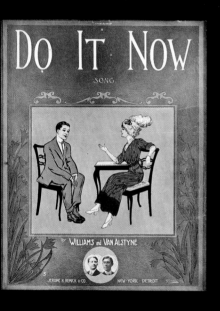

TERRY BRADSHAW | QUARTERBACK
STEELERS

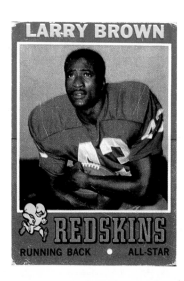

LARRY BROWN

REDSKINS
RUNNING BACK ● ALL-STAR

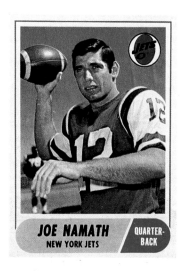

JOE NAMATH
NEW YORK JETS | QUARTER-BACK

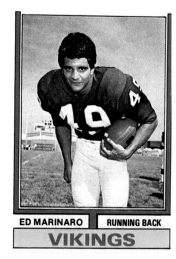

ED MARINARO | RUNNING BACK
VIKINGS

Historically we Americans have been a nation of sports lovers, both as active participants and as devoted followers of our favorite teams. The Museum of American History has thousands of objects related to the history of sports, some of which are illustrated here. Above: An array of football cards highlights some of that sport's "greats" from recent decades. Left: Sandy Koufax's glove, Willie Stargell's cap, and Hank Aaron's Milwaukee Brewers shirt are some of the prized possessions in the baseball display at the Nation of Nations exhibit. And in the same exhibit is the ticket booth from Yankee Stadium, opposite—graffiti, chipped paint, and all. It dates from 1923 when the Stadium first opened its gates to the public.

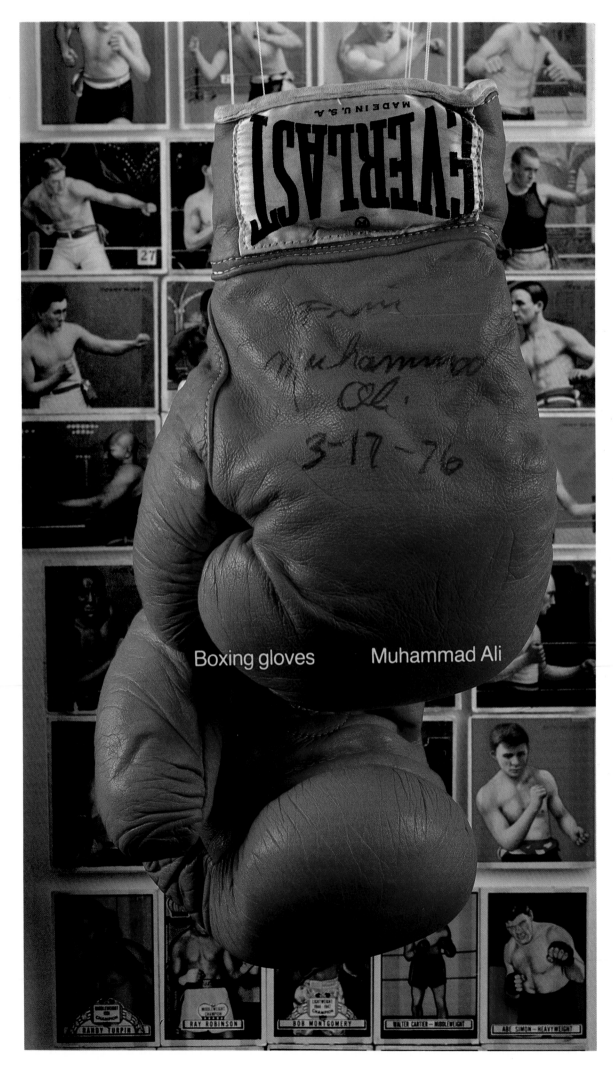

Boxing gloves   Muhammad Ali

Opposite: *Muhammad Ali's boxing gloves which he wore in his successful 1974 world heavyweight title match are on exhibit— autographed by "the Champ."* Above: *Sports artifacts at the Museum of American History include a 1980 U.S. Winter Olympics jacket, Bobby Orr's hockey glove, track star Bobby Morrow's 1956 gold medal.* Right: *Painting shows Jack Dempsey in his famous crouch during the 1919 bout with Jess Willard in which he won the world heavyweight title.*

James Montgomery Flagg. Dempsey-Willard Fight. *1944. Oil on canvas, 6 x 18' (1.83 x 5.49 m).* NPG, *gift of Mr. and Mrs. Jack Dempsey.*

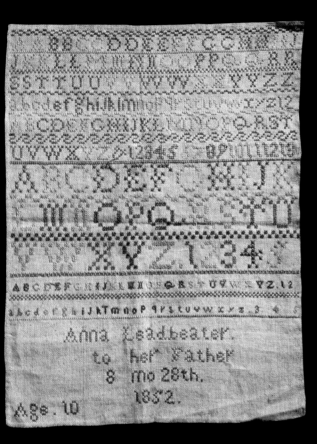

Above: *This sampler was stitched by ten-year-old Anna Leadbeater of Alexandria, Virginia, in 1852. By making samplers, young girls learned sewing and fancywork and practiced the three R's.* Right: *This 1863 Connecticut schoolroom is typical of one-room American schoolhouses a century ago. The portrait of George Washington above the door and the "God is Love" homily epitomize the mix of patriotic and religious themes that were taught to the schoolchildren of that day.*

Overleaf: *Part of the Nation of Nations exhibit, this section of the U.S. Army barracks from Fort Belvoir, Virginia, reflects the Spartan existence of the common soldier. Built in 1940, the barracks were in use during the Korean War and for part of the Vietnam conflict. The uniforms and equipment on display are of World War II vintage.*

GOD
IS
LOVE.
Stay after
George Washington
is the father of his
Country
bark
pick
cord
cart
lost
farm

In a decade of wandering through this museum (thoroughly dazzled and lost, too, I might add) I've come to realize that the sounds really do it for me. Down on the first floor is the great locomotive, old 1401 of the Southern Railway (known to the staff as the Jolly Green Giant). Seven miles of tape were used to catch the sounds of a steam locomotive so that when you stand beside this one you hear it as well as see it, and, if you happen to date from the age of steam, your nostalgia is just that much heightened.

You hear it approaching from the distance, losing speed, safety valve blowing off excess steam. The brakes take hold with a screech and the cars lurch to a stop at the depot. Beside you, mysterious burbles and hisses and long sighs emanate from the engine so that you can almost feel the heat radiating from the great boiler. Then the conductor shouts in the distance, a bell rings somewhere, and with

a great *chuff* you can feel the throb as the drive wheels begin to turn, gritting and crushing a measure of sand spilled from a box above the wheels to give them traction. And finally, from half a mile away, there is the note of the whistle down at the crossing. And in the silence you sense the return to normal life—the newly arrived passengers driving off in open Buicks and air-cooled Franklins, the station master trundling a cart to the baggage room, the barn swallows darting back under the broad eaves.

In the silence, you can test for boiler heat with your hand and feel none. But I once watched a three-year-old boy stand directly in front of the engine, arms akimbo, looking up at that baleful headlight towering above him. The noises were starting—the rumblings of the engine's innards—and then came that first mighty chuff, and the boy's father reached out and snatched him off the track.

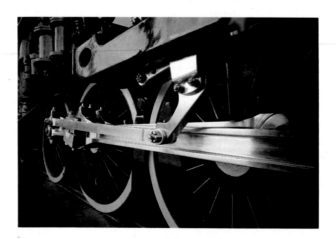

Left: *The six-foot driving wheels of the steam engine, 1401, express the awesome power of the age of steam.* Opposite: *The towering 1401 is one of nearly 7,000 locomotives of this type built largely for passenger service from about 1905 to 1930. It served the Southern Railway's Carolina line for almost 30 years before it was retired in 1951.*

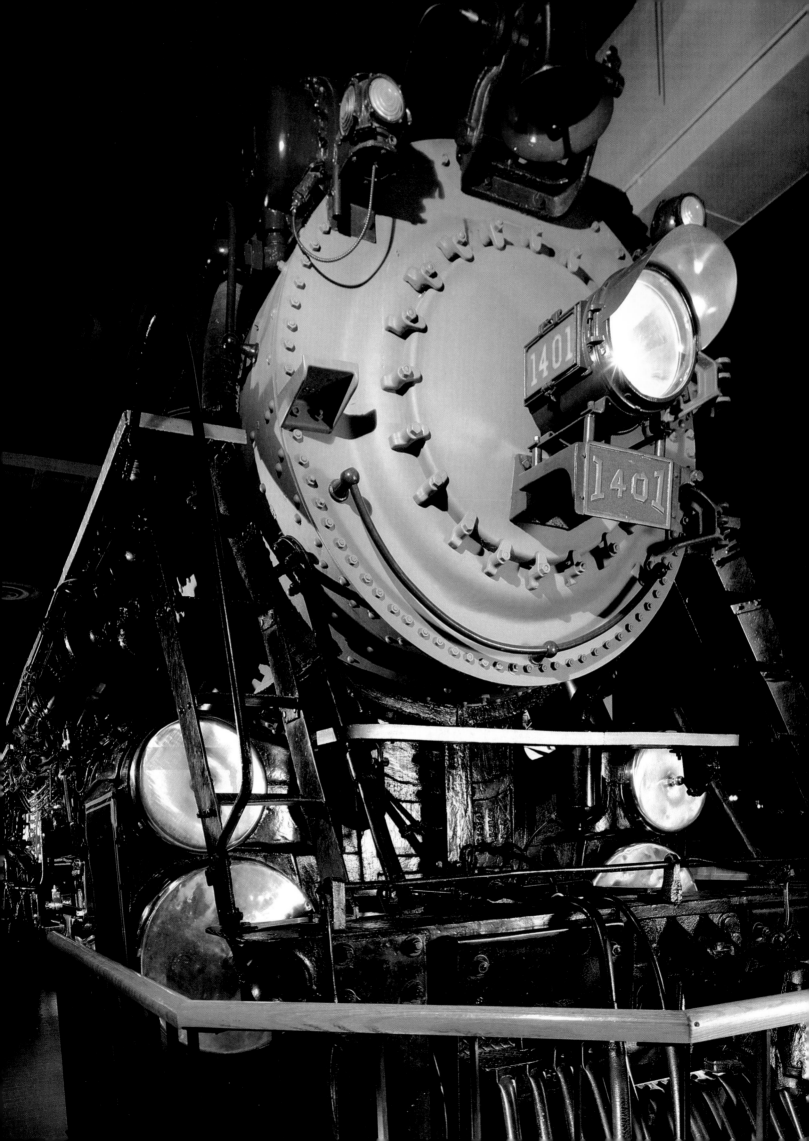

Below: *Called the Packard Deluxe Emblem or* Flying Lady, *this was the most famous of a series of radiator ornaments made by the Packard automobile company.* Left: *At a list price of $2,850 this 1923 Packard Phaeton was one of many eagerly bought by those with both a hankering after status and the pocketbook to go with it.*

Other exhibits in the Division of Transportation have their sounds, but they're not always turned on. I recall hearing the breathy pant of the 1931 Model A which stands before a period gasoline pump, perpetually getting refilled at 25 cents a gallon. Anyway, the sound evoked memories of the delicious smell of exhaust in country air. When the predominant aroma of one's world was a mixture of sun-warmed grass and pine needles and occasional whiffs of cowbarn on a hillside breeze, a snootful of automobile exhaust stirred one's heart with excitement.

The Packard was one of the grand cars of the 1920s and early '30s. It was splendidly powerful and responsive, and to be seen behind its wheel was the ultimate sign of status.

Driving a Packard made a man sit tall in the saddle, bow tie bristling, golf cap firmly squared against the breezes that rustled around the sparkling windshield with its side flaps. Ahead stretched the long hood, and at the very prow stood an emblem of the owner's choice. For a few extra dollars you could get the Flying Lady, for example. It was in-

BRAKE
SERVICE
Thermoid
CUSTOM BUILT
BRAKE LININGS

Gasoline

SINCLAIR
GASOLENE

Above: *This 15-passenger bus bumped its way along the Charles Street line in Baltimore from 1917 to 1922, offering passengers a slow and often jarring ride.* Left: *Looking like a movie set from a bygone era, this exhibit highlights the early days of motoring. The car is a 1931 Ford Model A Deluxe Roadster. It reflected the trend toward more stylish, sleeker automobiles. The two gas pumps date from 1922 (left) and 1918 (right).*

troduced in 1924, at first silver plated. It reminded everyone, especially the owner, of the Packard's undoubted nobility.

At the time of World War I, rapid transit in Baltimore consisted of, among other things, the 15-passenger White bus. It was built in 1917 and ground along Charles Street with many laborious shiftings of its four forward speeds as they eked power out of the 22.5-horsepower engine. The ride was hardly luxurious for the passengers, since the tires were solid rubber—two thicknesses on the rear wheels as a sop to comfort. But Baltimoreans suffered along with this bus until 1922.

One display in this museum uses the magic of smell. Around the corner from those vehicles is the Hall of American Maritime Enterprise, and as soon as you enter it, you breathe a mixture of tar, hemp, and tobacco. On the path of this scent, you will end up before the display of a colonial dockside warehouse.

There are actual hands of tobacco piled on the floor and tarry rope in coils. And nearby is a superb model of the tobacco ship—in this case the 18th-century American-built cargo vessel *Brilliant*. She is typical of the ships that nosed into creeks off the Chesapeake Bay to take on hogsheads of tobacco rolled down from the barns, and to unload in a credit exchange—no money was necessary—Chippendale furniture for the planter's great house.

The creeks are too silted for the real *Brilliant* to navigate today. And tobacco is bad for you, anyway. But the old, rich trade is still remembered by the fact that plantation houses always face the water, the link with the outside world, and that many a tobacco town around the Bay has a Rolling Road, marking the path of those hogsheads. And also by this model, beautifully made, with planking removed to show ship construction of the 1700s.

Walking away from little *Brilliant*, you hear

Opposite: *The four-cylinder engine of the 1902 Winton Bullet No. 1 helped make it one of the top racing cars of its day. Automobile manufacturer Alexander Winton broke several speed records in 1902–3 with this car.* Right: *This Model T Ford was one of 15 million manufactured between 1908 and 1927. This particular car was purchased for $600 in Rochester, New York, in 1913. Within the next 12 years, the price of Model Ts dropped by more than $300, putting them well within the reach of most Americans.*

*One of colonial America's most
important exports was tobacco.
It was stored in warehouses
like this one, opposite,
modeled after those of early
Tidewater Virginia. In the
same exhibit is a model of the
tobacco ship,* Brilliant, *above.
Ships like this carried tobacco
from colonial warehouses to
England.*

a new sound—voices singing in the room that houses the whaleboat. It's a forecastle song, obviously addressed to the youth of the land:

Come all ye young Americans
and listen to my ditty,
It's all about a whaling bark
belongs New Bedford city.

It goes on to introduce the captain and the boat crews (the harpooner of the larboard boat is "a gentleman good and true") and ends with a rousing chorus line:

We never will, we never will,
we never can deny
We want three thousand barrel of oil,
root, hog, or die!

Whale oil was the source of light in the mid-19th century, and wind alone powered the vessels that collected it. And so it's a strange parallel to find a similar song echoing from another gallery on the same floor of this museum—the Atom Smasher display, memorializing the early accelerators, the cyclotrons, the synchrotrons from which physicists gained their first knowledge of the atom and its seemingly numberless constituents. From these arcane devices we've learned to harness the energy in atomic fission, to build nuclear power plants to produce electricity . . . to light the lights of New England. And from the descendents of the primitive machines in the exhibit we may learn to make nuclear fission-powered lighting as obsolete as whale oil lighting. So it's fitting, too, to have this song, composed and sung by atomic scientists rather than whalers, which tells how "Once upon a midnight dreary / The cyclotron crew was weak and weary . . ." and in walks the boss and tells them to generate "Eighty million curies by half past nine!"

A curie, named after Madame Marie Curie, is a unit of radioactivity—not of whale oil. Times change, but people stay much the same.

Left: *Merle A. Tuve's 1933 high voltage particle accelerator towers over smaller devices in the Atom Smashers exhibit. In the foreground is a replica of C.T.R. Wilson's cloud chamber of 1912 which enabled physicists to see the tracks of colliding particles.* Opposite: *The world's first proton linear accelerator, completed at the Berkeley Radiation Laboratory in 1947, used parts from war surplus radar sets.*

The Smithsonian has no one building devoted to music, no opera house or concert hall. But so many performers have played at this museum that it has become a sort of forum for transient musicians. I have heard here college glee clubs, military bands, and bell ringers, to name a few. They enthrall crowds around the Foucault pendulum, whose constant sweep to prove that the earth is still turning is stilled for these events. I have heard Christmas carolers and a barbershop group touring upstairs galleries. And walking past this building on the Mall, I have been stopped in my tracks by the joyful, irreverent sounds of a Dixieland band.

The museum does provide one regular musical happening that was conceived and born within its walls. On the third floor, at the western end of the building, is a small gallery of musical instruments. Some are American folk instruments: dulcimers, banjos, a gourd fiddle of the type made by slaves in the early 1800s. Others are the famous orchestral items, dating back to the 1700s, that claim such huge value today: a viola da Gamba of 1718, its head carved as a human head; a Stradivari cello of 1701 with the French word *Servais* (named after the 19th-century virtuoso Adrien François Servais) etched on it; a serpent, that deep-toned woodwind shaped like a writhing snake dating from the late 18th and early 19th centuries; a long oboe da Caccia of the mid-18th century, and many, many more. Adjoining the display is a small auditorium where these wonderful antiques are played at stated times by Smithsonian musicians.

Listeners may not realize that the ancient instruments have been meticulously restored to playing condition. Nor do they realize, until they listen, how smooth and mellow the tones are. Music of the 18th century was written for soft, warm renditions, and it becomes more meaningful to hear it as the composers themselves heard it.

Among the Smithsonian's fine collection of musical instruments are these three banjos. Left: A handmade five-string fretless banjo was made in North Carolina in the late 19th century. Center: The S.S. Stewart Company of Philadelphia, a leading manufacturer of banjos, made this one about 1889. The ebony fingerboard is inlaid with mother-of-pearl; the shell is of rosewood. Right: Although built in the 1960s, this cherry banjo from North Carolina is modeled after the older fretless type.

Above: *In the mid-1970s the Smithsonian acquired this fiddle, which had been found in St. Mary's County, Maryland. It probably dates from the late 19th century, but is in the style of those made by slaves several decades earlier.* Opposite: *The Smithsonian owns 20 dulcimers, including the two seen here, both Appalachian or plucked dulcimers. The teardrop-shaped one on the left—a common design—comes from Kentucky and dates back to 1927. The more crudely wrought, straight-necked dulcimer on the right was made in Virginia and was purchased by the Smithsonian in 1895 for $5.00.*

European book dealers from the late 1800s until about 1940 re-bound many old science books in early Renaissance music manuscripts like these. The Smithsonian's Dibner Library owns these rare tomes, which originally date from the 15th and 16th centuries.

The sinuous shape of this obsolete bass wind instrument gives it its name—the serpent. The form was quite practical, bringing the fingerholes or keys within reach of the player. This particular serpent was made in London about 1805. Initially used as an accompaniment to church singing, the serpent was later played in military bands. After the invention of the tuba and other bass wind instruments in the 19th century, it gradually became outmoded.

A finely carved head tops the pegbox of this bass viola da Gamba. The instrument was made in London by Barak Norman in 1718, but the head was done by an unknown craftsman. Such heads, both human and animal, added graceful touches to many viols of this era.

Above: The Servais, *one of the few surviving
cellos made by famed instrument maker
Antonio Stradivari in 1701, ranks as one of
the finest treasures in the Smithsonian.* Right:
*Hugo Worch, a Washington, D.C., piano
dealer, donated many keyboard instruments to
the Smithsonian, making its collection one of
the country's largest. This Worch donation is a
harpsichord made in London about 1743.*

In 1982, George Washington's 250th birthday year, a special exhibit dealing with his life was set up in the Museum of American History. And in the first room you entered, the room devoted to the youth and development of this Virginia gentleman, music of a minuet wrapped itself around you, old music played on old instruments, sounding the way it did to Washington when he went through the paces himself—a towering, ruddy-faced figure, surprisingly light on his feet for so big a man.

His figure is hard to miss on the second floor. In fact, Horatio Greenough's mighty statue of Washington dominates the access to A Nation of Nations, seeming, in fact, to greet visitors with a raised right arm.

Greenough did this statue in 1840 at the height of the classical revival, so George Washington appears seated on a throne embellished with classical allusions, clad in a toga, sandals, and nothing else. The nudity of such a hallowed figure caused some consternation among some of the ladies of the capital when the statue arrived. But Greenough had suffered such pains even getting it to Washington from Italy that by then nothing could faze him.

It seems that when it was being loaded on a lighter for transferral to a cargo ship, it went through the bottom of the small vessel and sank it. Retrieved, the statue made it to the States, but when unloaded at the Capitol it went through the floor. Its original base is still there. The Smithsonian got it years later, and so far the museum floors have held up. So there sits Washington, stern of visage and enviable of muscle, epitomizing not the man, but the marble image Americans made him.

Washington appears in some three dozen portraits at the National Portrait Gallery. Many are "after" the great portraits of Gilbert Stuart, Charles Willson Peale, and his son Rembrandt Peale. The Stuart full-length portrait, called the Lansdowne, was the work of Gilbert Stuart in 1796, only three years before Washington's death. It's a huge, impressive painting, displayed at the second floor as an introduction to the Gallery of Presidents.

Full-length portraits were a British habit. American artists generally felt that they could better embrace the notion of democracy by painting the head alone—getting to the intellectual soul of the subject without any trappings of his place in society. But Stuart was impressed by the importance of painting Washington, and the Marquis of Lansdowne, for whom the painting was intended, was a British friend of America. So Stuart got Washington to sit for the head, then tacked it onto the body, for which someone else posed.

The painting tells me more about Stuart

Horatio Greenough. George Washington *(1732–99). 1840. Marble, 11 x 9 x 7' (3.35 x 2.74 x 2.13 m). NMAH, on loan from NMAA, transfer from the U.S. Capitol.*

than about Washington. He had studied in England under the great Benjamin West, the transplanted American who had become history painter to King George III, yet who never forgot his Pennsylvania origins and gladly played the part of guru for visiting American artists. Stuart had his mind set on portraiture, and after studying with West in London, moved to Ireland to practice his art.

He seems to have had distinct notions of how to make it as a portraitist. First, get an advance of half the fee. Then if you don't finish the job you will at least make something for your effort. When he sailed from Ireland to return to America, Stuart left a veritable gallery-full of unfinished portraits.

Gilbert Stuart never quite shook off that habit of not finishing his work. He had returned home to paint the great Washington—surely a steady source of income—and tried to make as many copies as he could, all eminently saleable. The head on the Lansdowne portrait is copied from the "Athenaeum Portrait" which Martha Washington had commissioned. Martha never got it because Stuart died before completing it, and his widow sold it. A confusing business—at least Stuart made it seem that way.

The grim, cold-eyed face that Stuart has left us is, of course, partly due to those damn false teeth. Washington had several sets, and the Smithsonian has a portion of one, on loan. They weren't made of wood, as some have suggested, but they were heavy, complicated devices that puffed out his lips. Also, the aging president was being initiated into the realities of democratic politics. In the vague concepts of government that all our leaders nurtured after the Revolution, few had foreseen the bitter infighting between factions that quickly broke out. Washington had wanted a forum for discussion and agreement. But by the time Stuart got to him, he was battling Congress the way every president since has had to do.

So all Stuart's quips and pleasant conversation cut no ice during Washington's sittings.

He didn't thaw. And that was a pity because he could be charming. French officers who joined the Washington mess during the Revolution were amazed at the informal, family-style arrangement—open, unabashed conversation between the commander and his juniors. Charles Willson Peale knew this side of Washington for he painted him many times. His son Rembrandt Peale did an oil of the president in 1795, which I think shows more of his humanity than Stuart's portraits do. It was at about this time that Stuart, hearing from Martha Washington of her husband's commitments to sit for the Peales, remarked that the president was "in danger of being Pealed all round."

During the Revolution, Charles Willson Peale served as a militia officer and presumably observed the General at close hand. At the time when conflict was inevitable and when Washington must surely have seen himself commanding the Americans, Peale came to paint him at Mount Vernon and found him watching some young men, friends and neighbors, heaving an iron bar across the lawn, trying to outdo each other. Peale said that Washington tried his hand and hurled the heavy bar far beyond the record mark. Then he said "When you beat my pitch, young gentlemen, I'll try again." He hadn't even bothered to take off his coat.

At the Museum of American History, we have a Washington uniform from the Revolution—the clothes of a big man, much trimmer of figure than I had supposed. We also have his sword and the white cotton campaign tent where he presumably sat with his staff officers, cracking nuts and emptying bottles of Madeira. It was then that his face would relax as he joined in the banter and the jokes.

Two other items appear in the third floor galleries devoted to ordnance and armed forces history, and both are extraordinary treasures of the Revolutionary War. One is the gunboat *Philadelphia*, and her story is a fine tale of courage and resourcefulness, of defeat which, in the long run, brought victory.

Gilbert Stuart. Martha
Dandridge Custis
Washington *(1731–1802).*
1796. Oil on canvas, 48 x
37" (122 x 94 cm). NPG,
owned jointly with the
Museum of Fine Arts, Boston.

Gilbert Stuart. George
Washington *(1732–99).*
1796. Oil on canvas, 48 x
37" (122 x 94 cm). NPG,
owned jointly with the
Museum of Fine Arts, Boston.

By the end of the American Revolution, George Washington was without a doubt the most widely known and lauded man in the country. Yet even during his lifetime many attributed to him near-legendary powers, enshrouding him in a cloak of myths and hero-worship. The Smithsonian's 1982 George Washington exhibit included a number of personal effects from his years in power, some of which are seen here. They lend a human touch to this often idealized man.

English brass double candlestick, c. 1770, used by Washington while writing his Farewell Address. The Lewis Collection.

The portable mess chest used by Washington during the Revolution.

124

Family legend maintains that
Washington wore this uniform
when he resigned his
commission as Commander-in-
Chief in December, 1783, at
Annapolis, Maryland.

One of the Commander-in-
Chief's field tents, this one was
ordered from a Philadelphia
firm in 1776.

Field glass with original case.
General Washington used it as
a spy glass or hand telescope.
The Lewis Collection.

For this was one of the hastily built vessels that General Benedict Arnold (back when he was a good guy, fighting for America) ordered to stop a British encroachment into New England from Canada, by way of Lake Champlain. Arnold's little fleet lost, but the British spent so much time getting ready to oppose it and then repairing their damage that the winter arrived in time to stop their campaign. Next year they surrendered at Saratoga to an American army that had gained the necessary time for beefing up.

The gunboat *Philadelphia*, in Arnold's words, "was hulled in so many places that she sunk [*sic*] in about one hour after the engagement was over. . . ." Oddly enough, generations of Vermont farmers knew pretty much where the vessel lay. She snagged their fishing lines. Finally, in 1935, she was raised, and here she is, an extraordinary relic, beautifully preserved by the cold waters of the lake.

I walked up the ramp that gives a view down into that hull, made of huge oak timbers, 54 feet long. A heavy 12-pounder gun is mounted in the bow. Nine-pounders are set amidships, and a little swivel gun is mounted on one gunwale. She carried a mast, and an adjoining model shows how she sailed into action that day in 1776 at Valcour Bay, her deck crammed with men to man the guns and to handle the vessel.

The second notable item is the Ferguson rifle. Only a handful of these remain in the world and one of them is here, yet for a while it was considered as a possible standard infantry weapon for the entire British army. Had it been adopted, I don't see how the Americans could have won their independence—at least in *that* war.

The rifle, invented by a Scottish officer serving the king, was a good, serviceable, accurate breechloader. When the trigger guard was turned, a worm gear arrangement opened a hole in the top of the breech so that ball and powder could be dropped in—strong, simple, workable. The soldier could then wind the breech closed and fire.

One of the delights of the American History Museum is that you can go from guns to glassware to quilts without having to leave the building.

Rounding a few corners from the Ferguson rifle will put you in the middle of pieces bearing such familiar American names as Steuben, Libbey, and Tiffany. Examples of fine wares from these glassmaking firms remind you that fancy glass design ranks as high art. Especially the Favrile glass of Louis Comfort Tiffany. He created quite a stir with his Art Nouveau style in that gold-colored, often iridescent glass.

More humble but of equal importance are the pottery pieces—the sturdy stoneware jars and jugs that played an active role in our history, and are so desired by collectors today.

Equally desired by collectors of our country's early furnishings are quilts, and the Smithsonian's collection includes about 300 American quilts and assorted quilt pieces from the 18th through the 20th century, encompassing a diverse range of quilting techniques and materials. No 17th-century quilts are known to have survived in this country—apparently after years of constant use they simply wore out and were discarded. What has come down to us through the years, both at the Smithsonian and elsewhere, is not really representative of the plain, functional quilt either. Instead we have many "show" quilts, elaborate pieces of handiwork probably tucked away awaiting the arrival of an important house guest. Viewing these lovingly crafted, thoughtfully preserved works of American folk art is a real treat, and most of the quilt collection, though not on exhibit, can be seen by appointment.

Two outstanding pieces of American craftsmanship, in different mediums, from the Museum of American History's collections. Left: Adelaide Alsop Robineau produced this vase in 1910, carving a delicate floral pattern into the porcelain. Opposite: Louis Comfort Tiffany created many forms in Favrile glass, such as this shimmering, iridescent vase, dated 1894. His work won awards in the United States and abroad and placed him in the forefront of the Art Nouveau movement.

Among the exquisite examples of American glass at the Museum of American History are those illustrated here. Below: *The engraved plate entitled* The Apotheosis of Transportation *was made by The Libbey Glass Company of Toledo, Ohio, for exhibition at the 1904 St. Louis World's Fair. The rare engraved tumblers,* opposite, *were made in the 18th century by German-born John Frederick Amelung, who opened the New Bremen Glass Manufactory near Frederick, Maryland, about 1785.*

The star was one of the most popular quilt motifs of the 19th century. This striking quilt from the Smithsonian's collection is called The Star of Bethlehem *or* Rising Sun. *Made by Betsy Totten of Staten Island, New York, about 1825, the central design is done in pieced work while the floral sections are appliquéd.*

This quilt is done in the red and green color combination that was popular in the mid-19th century. The widespread use of a technique called padded appliqué makes this an unusual quilt: the technique involved putting cotton wadding under the appliquéd fabric—the red and green areas in this case. The white grape wreaths and central fruit basket are stuffed with extra cotton inserted between the quilt top and lining. This elaborate piece of handiwork was done by Mary Palmer of Otsego County, New York, and her sister, Deborah.

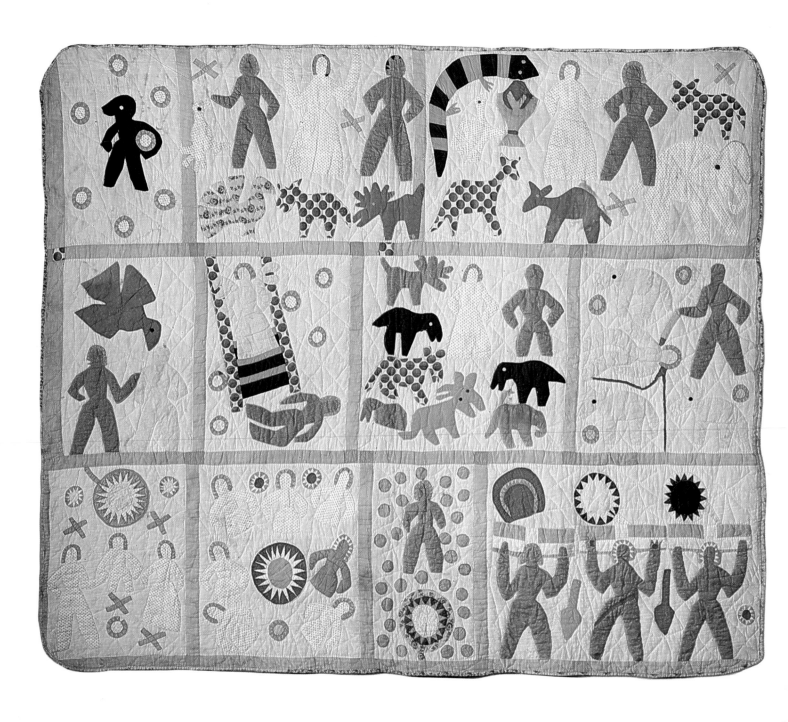

136

At the Mall entrance to the Museum of American History, a ripple of soft, old-fashioned music erupts at regular intervals. Startled sightseers have trouble at first recognizing "The Star-Spangled Banner." Instead of the martial beat, so sternly and fervently played at every official function from presidential appearance to hockey game, this version is relaxed and rather happy, indulging itself with a few fancy trills.

What you are hearing is the early 19th-century version of what has become our national anthem. It amuses me to think that Francis Scott Key's warmly emotional lines were set to the tune of an English drinking song, "The Anacreontic Song," and that today, bands and orchestras strive desperately to make it sound regal and powerful and so disguise its lamentable origins. Listen to this Smithsonian version, and you can picture bellowing it out in a pub, beating time with your beaker while watching the barmaid tap a new keg.

The occasion for this rendition is the periodic appearance of the old flag—the original Star-Spangled Banner. The protective cover that shields it from view is periodically lowered to allow us to catch a brief glimpse of it. For a long while it was constantly on view, but the dust damaged the frail remnants of the original flag, which was stretched out on a backing to show its exact, undamaged size: 42 by 30 feet. Cleaning it, conservators found tiny fragments of blue cotton in the dust. Someone realized that several generations of blue jeans have stood before the old banner, presumably rubbing together and so producing this microscopic blue lint.

The huge flag, specially made by Mary Pickersgill of Baltimore, flew over Fort Mc-Henry in Baltimore Harbor when a British fleet attacked the city in 1814 during the wretchedly ill-advised and generally disastrous War of 1812. I recently heard that Major Armistead, the commander of the fort, had asked for an ensign "so large that the British will have no difficulty in seeing it from a distance." The British force had just burned the White House and other government buildings. Now they struck at Baltimore; Fort Mc-Henry was the city's only hope.

It was a good fort, manned by good men under their stout-hearted commander, the above-mentioned Major Armistead. He raised his huge flag at dawn as a gesture of defiance to the British as they sailed away, and Francis Scott Key, detained on one of the British vessels, saw it flying in "the dawn's early light" and wrote his lines in a burst of patriotic inspiration. From 1815 on, the great flag belonged to the Armistead family, who kept it until 1907, when they loaned it to the Smithsonian. Their loan became a gift in 1912. In 1914, Mrs. Amelia Fowler was given the task of sewing the remnants onto a linen backing. She was an experienced seamstress and had learned her craft by restoring shot-torn battle flags in the Naval Academy's collection. She set to work with a small regiment of other seamstresses, spreading the old flag out on a long stretch of joined tables in what is now the Commons of the Castle. The Castle has, in fact, a photograph of the work in progress.

Most of the pieces missing from the flag seem to have been souvenirs, snipped away over the years. Everyone wonders about the

This appliqué and pieced work quilt depicts Biblical themes and was made about 1886 by an ex-slave from Georgia, Harriet Powers. Like some other quilts made by Afro-American women, the designs of this one resemble those of African textiles.

strange V-shaped patch of red in the middle of a white stripe. No one can explain it. Interestingly, however, that patch was there when Mrs. Fowler went to work, and she and her crew saved it. Why? No one knows.

Despite the "bombs bursting in air," there was apparently little damage to the flag from shell fragments. The iron casings of those mortar "bombs" generally shattered into a relatively few large chunks which did a lot of damage when they hit something, but which seldom *did* hit anything. As for the "rockets' red glare," the British rockets of the time were apt to be as dangerous for the British as for their enemies. You can see the Congreve rockets at the Air and Space Museum if you

venture into the Rocketry and Space Flight Gallery. Sir William Congreve developed them from rockets used against the British in India in the 1790s. But he didn't develop them enough. The theory was fine, as today's astronauts will attest, but in practice the British military rockets were apt to sizzle off in any old direction or perhaps just sit at their launching pads and blow up.

I have always thought that on that September night in 1814, perhaps a rocket managed to hit the great flag, and to memorialize that extraordinary event a militiaman patched the rip with a piece of his red woolen underwear—which, it being a very hot night, and the military mind being what it is, he would

have been wearing. It's as good an explanation as any I've ever heard.

Ragged and ravaged, restored and many times re-restored, cleaned of its blue denim dust and now safeguarded against further generations of the same, the Star-Spangled Banner is yet a splendid, emotional sight. It marks perhaps the true beginnings of the nation. As you face it, the great Washington statue on your left, you feel the sense of magic that provided us with such leaders during those perilous times.

Washington, Franklin, Jefferson. Have a look just outside one of the display rooms of the first ladies gallery and you will find Jefferson's portable desk, a wooden case whose top is hinged in the center so that it will unfold to form a writing surface. It was his own design, fulfilling his need for something he could carry around which would contain the rather messy necessities—ink, sand, quills, paper—for dashing off such phrases as "When in the Course of human events. . . ."

He did use this desk for the Declaration of Independence. With the lid folded down, the box is about 20 inches long by 14 wide by three deep. A drawer pulls out which contains those implements and paper. To use the desk, Jefferson could have put it on his knees, raised the top to a conveniently slanted position and unfolded it. There is a blotter set into wood. Sliding open the drawer, he would have pulled out what he needed and gone to work. He could have carried it like a briefcase, I suppose, but not with ink in it. I did notice quite a few splotches of spilled ink inside the drawer, but I imagine they came while he was fussing over "Life, Liberty and the pursuit of Happiness. . . ."

Three years before the Revolution, Jefferson married Martha Wayles Skelton, a 22-year-old widow of one of his Virginia friends. In a decade of conjugal bliss, she bore six children. Only two survived, Martha, or Patsy as her father called her, and Mary, known as Polly. Incessant child bearing, several mis-

carriages, the endless tragedy of losing children simply wore Martha out and she died in 1782, a year after Yorktown. Little is known of her for the future president, in his bitter grief, never wrote her name again.

So in the first ladies gallery, Patsy is represented as President Jefferson's hostess. She was a good friend to her father and knew him well, having been in Paris with him when he joined Franklin and John Adams to work out a commercial treaty. Jefferson stayed as Minister to France until 1789 when Washington brought him home to serve in the Cabinet. During those years in Paris, with many side trips to England, the lanky Virginian was accepted, indeed adored, by the witty, elegant intellectuals of prerevolutionary France. The Franco-American "set" of beautiful people found that beneath his official dignity Jefferson was as romantic as he was rational, that along with his brilliance was the innocence of a Piedmont upbringing. He was a *philosophe*, and also just a bit of a *sauvage*.

In 1793, botanist and physician Dr. Benjamin Smith Barton named this plant Jeffersonia binata *in honor of his fellow scientist and friend, Thomas Jefferson. It was later renamed* Jeffersonia diphylla, *the classification used today. The plant, a perennial herb of the Berberidaceae family, appears here in an engraving from* Curtis's Botanical Magazine, 1811. *The magazine is one of many old volumes owned by the Smithsonian libraries.*

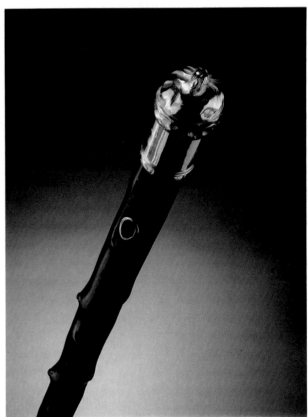

So he made friends with the Duc de La Rochefoucauld and Lafayette's aunt, the Comtesse de Tessé; with the Marquis de Chastellux who had fought with Rochambeau's troops at Yorktown and Talleyrand's former mistress, Madame de Flahaut.

Returning to the Museum of American History for a moment, glance at a walking stick bequeathed to Washington by Benjamin Franklin. (There's simply no getting away from that crowd and its association with both political and intellectual history.) The stick itself is a beautiful goldheaded crabtree piece, but its special value is the reminder of the donor. Franklin was in France for much of this time in the early moments of our democracy. He is remembered so often by Americans as a sort of "mad scientist." We reiterate the tale of his "discovery" of static electricity by flying a kite in a thunderstorm (if he really did this, he was most fortunate to have lived through this rather dangerous experiment).

Here at the Smithsonian we have a small display that owes its existence to Franklin's very real studies of static electricity. The "Electric Kiss" reveals two mannequins with lips pressed together. She is raised on a slight

Above: *This is Franklin's gold-headed walking stick, which he bequeathed to George Washington, whom he called "my friend and the friend of mankind." Left: Benjamin Franklin is believed to have worked at this press at Watts's printing shop in London in 1725–26.*

platform, her hands on the terminals of two brass conductors. A third mannequin, a scientist, by the foxy look of him, is turning a crank which obviously generates a bit of static electricity. The ardent lover figure, stretching on tiptoes, holds his lips close to the lady's. And at regular intervals there is a crack, and a spark dances between them. This, in essence, was what Franklin had learned. He had no idea of the knowledge that 200 years would add to his eccentric studies.

While Franklin was in France, hot air balloons began making the first flights ever which took living creatures into the sky. Franklin was charmed and delighted by the experiments that sent, first, farm animals into the air, and then two rather foolhardy Frenchmen, Pilâtre de Rozier and the Marquis d'Arlandes. They rose in a hot air balloon developed by two brothers, Joseph Michel and Jacques Etienne Montgolfier. Everyone who was anyone in Paris watched these ascensions. Of course Franklin was in the middle of it, loving every second. "But of what use is this balloon?" a French officer angrily asked him. And he is supposed to have replied (and I hope and suspect he did), "Of what use is a newborn baby?"

The impact of the balloon mania that swept the civilized world can best be seen in the balloon room of the Air and Space Museum. Every object here takes the shape of a balloon. There are pieces of furniture with that global motif carved on them. There are lamps and tables and gimcracks, all resembling balloons.

Franklin invented the lightning rod, the Franklin stove, and, in a way, the whole concept that Americans should think freely, without inhibition, should advance themselves with all the ingenuity at their command, should break mental restraints. He also wanted the wild turkey to be our national symbol. It is an intelligent, resourceful, freethinking bird, and it's totally American. Audubon struggled to get a decent painting of it, and when he succeeded, he produced it often, using the bird almost as a personal symbol. But Franklin's wish was not fulfilled. In 1782, Congress opted for the eagle as our national bird, as had many European countries and the legions of ancient Rome. At least ours is the bald eagle, a noble creature, even if it is a scavenger.

Symbols were immensely important to the new republic, and the American eagle was represented again and again in the decoration of buildings and objects in the early United States. Back at the Museum of American History, go venture into the section called We the People and discover this immense collection of American political memorabilia. Here is everything from Teddy Roosevelt's toothy

Above: *This bust of Abraham Lincoln on a silver plaquette was made for the centennial of his birth in 1909. Since then this same likeness has appeared on all United States pennies.*
Right: *To commemorate the 1901 Pan-American Exposition in Buffalo, several stamps with transportation themes were issued. Some, such as these, were accidentally printed "upside down." Such errors, called inverted centers, add to a stamp's value, much to the delight of collectors. These three are among the more than 14 million stamps in the Smithsonian's National Philatelic Collection.*

Over the years presidential campaigns have inspired hundreds of slogans, gimmicks, and gadgets as candidates have sought all manner of means to reach the widest possible audience. Here is an array of political paraphernalia spanning—with some gaps—the years from James Buchanan's bid for the presidency in 1857 (top left) to the campaign of 1912 more than 50 years later (bottom right). This collage is from the We the People *exhibit.*

Splendid spirited animals, opposite, *fashioned by skilled woodcarvers at the turn of the century for use on carousels now represent a fine example of American popular art. The old-fashioned ice cream parlor,* below, *at the American History Museum, with its authentic early 20th-century mirrored-back bar and Art Nouveau side panels and lamps, is a welcome stop for weary museum visitors.*

smile to John Kennedy's cabin in *The Caroline,* his personal plane used for campaigning. Here are buttons with photographs of LBJ or Nixon and peanut bags from Jimmy Carter's family industry, all collected by a devoted curator, Herb Collins, who used to plunge through the debris on the floors of convention halls just ahead of the sweepers, salvaging paper hats, noise machines, discarded banners.

These political memories fill many cabinets in the storage rooms of the museum. But a delightful sampling is offered in We the People. The whole section is a glittering historic treasure, made especially meaningful by those sounds that are the inevitable adjunct to this

museum's exhibits. For in this area is a depiction of an old-time torchlight procession, enacted by mannequins. And as you stare at it, you hear the songs that are sung at these moments of political hoopla: "Climb up with a cup of hard cider," exhorts a voice, "And drink to old Tippecanoe!" And another chorus goes through something about the State of Maine and James G. Blaine, and about his being good and true for the (what else?) "Red, White, and Blue!"

Silly? Yes. Musical? Not very. But the sounds are joyous here, and they help show us the way we were. And that's what a museum of history is all about. ✴

New Forms and
New Realms

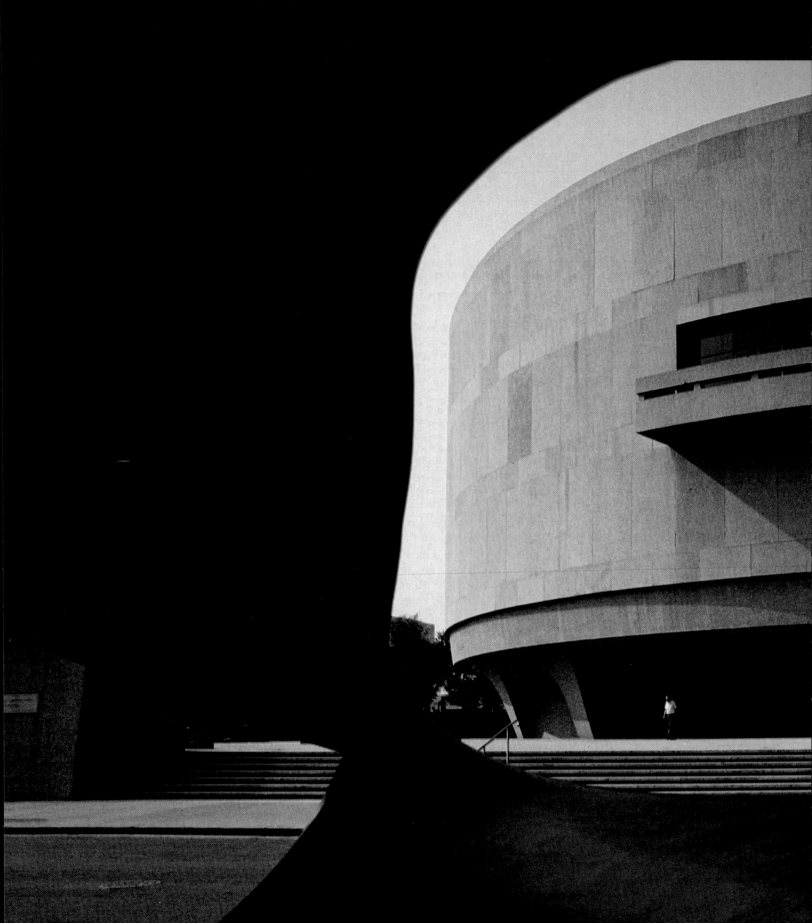

T hey are sisters on the Mall, both born in the 1970s, both modern, both different from the Federal architecture facing them, both eminently suited to hold their collections. Their collections are vastly different. The Hirshhorn Museum and Sculpture Garden opened in 1974 to house the immense number of paintings and sculptures amassed by Joseph H. Hirshhorn, the Wall Street entrepreneur who made a fortune in uranium. The National Air and Space Museum, next door, opened in 1976 to display the Smithsonian's store of air- and spacecraft and significant hardware that has been accumulating in corridors and corners of the Institution since Secretary Samuel P. Langley's experiments with flight at the turn of the century.

Seen from the outside, the Hirshhorn looks like an enormous flattened cylinder of concrete, solid except for a gallery that faces the Mall. The whole mass is raised off the ground by four immense piers. When you pass under it, you find yourself in an open court beside a wide circular fountain. So it's not really a cylinder but a ring, wider at one side than the other. An eccentric doughnut, if you will.

Inside are three floors of exhibits, one of offices and storage space. Large sculptures are outside in the sunken garden. Others stand all around the inner courtyard and the apron of concrete outside the building—but then, there

Right: *From beyond the Victorian rooftop of the Arts and Industries Building, the Hirshhorn Museum and Sculpture Garden and the National Air and Space Museum beckon us into the 20th century. For in these two museums are the tangible reminders that in our journeys of imagination and flight we have discovered new forms and new realms.*
Overleaf: *Architect Gordon Bunshaft designed a cylindrical building for the Hirshhorn Museum so that art lovers could walk through the galleries immersing themselves in the ever-changing tastes of the 20th century and end up where they had begun without retracing their steps.*

are sculptures outside almost *all* the Smithsonian buildings on the Mall.

Three sculptures stand outside the National Air and Space Museum, which is handily shortened to NASM. I like best the one facing the Hirshhorn: a gift from Venezuela called *Delta Solar* by Alejandro Otero. It's a stainless steel frame angling out of a still pool of water. From the frame hang scores of stainless steel triangular sails, and when the wind blows, the sails flutter and the water ripples and the whole impression is of a bright shimmer.

By any definition—as a museum or a piece of urban architecture—NASM is a wonderful building. Architect Gyo Obata won an award for it, and no wonder. By using sections of transparent wall and glass bubbles in the roof, he has given the impression that the sky itself is somehow trapped inside the structure. A tubular trusswork making use of the immense strength of the triangle supports the roof and allows heavy aircraft like the beautiful DC-3 of Eastern Airline's "Great Silver Fleet" of the 1930s to hang from the ceiling. You look up at the planes overhead and the scudding clouds beyond, through that glass roof, and you feel for a moment that the plane is moving, gaining altitude after takeoff or perhaps settling down to land.

Galleries, of course, alternate with the three great open bays of the building. It's a huge

Once a queen of Eastern Airlines' "Great Silver Fleet," this DC-3 now reigns over the National Air and Space Museum's Hall of Air Transportation. The first air transport to carry passengers profitably, the 21-seat DC-3 entered service in 1936.

structure, some 80 feet from floor to roof, taking up three city blocks at just about the place on the Mall where, in 1861, Professor Thaddeus Lowe launched his balloon, *Enterprise*. This name, incidentally, is repeated twice within the museum, for outside the Sea Air Operations gallery, where you enter the reconstructed hangar deck of an aircraft carrier, stands a superb model of the nuclear carrier *Enterprise*, perfect in every tiny detail. And in the space section at the east end of the museum is another intricate model, this time the spaceship *Enterprise* of the popular television series, "Star Trek."

But what in the world has this museum in common with the Hirshhorn? To me, they both capture the spirit of the 20th century, an age of civilization when the human race in all its characteristics and capabilities moved forward—and still moves—in giant leaps. We approached this century with a new confidence, looking to the future, not the past. We reformed politics; we invented devices to improve life; we tackled problems that had puzzled us for generations; we put away old rules and produced one new one: There is no ceiling. We entered the century with exuberance, and no two features of our life express it so clearly as our battle to conquer the air and our expression of ourselves in bril-

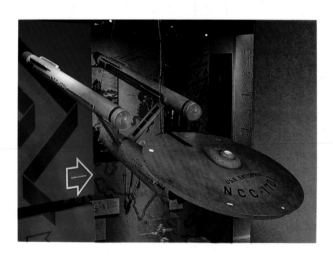

From the model collections of the Air and Space Museum, Enterprise *present. . .and future?* Opposite: *This 1/100 scale model of the nuclear-powered aircraft carrier U.S.S.* Enterprise *displays in intricate detail some of the real ship's complement of fighter and attack aircraft and helicopters. Model of the Starship* Enterprise, *left, was used in the immensely popular television series, "Star Trek."*

Above: *Smithsonian Secretary Samuel P. Langley's* **Aerodrome** *crashes into the Potomac River during an attempted flight on October 7, 1903. After another failure in December, Secretary Langley gave up his flight experiments.* **Right:** *Forerunner of today's colorful contraptions, this hang glider was built by German aeronautical pioneer Otto Lilienthal a few years before his 1896 death in a gliding accident.*

liant, uninhibited, imaginative paintings and sculptures of the 20th century.

In 1886, Auguste Rodin did his *Burghers of Calais*, the mighty sculpture that dominates the Hirshhorn Sculpture Garden. It memorialized an event in the Hundred Years War when Edward III of England agreed to lift his siege of Calais if the town's leading citizens were turned over to him clothed in sackcloth with ropes around their necks. So here are Rodin's burghers on their way to the gallows, presumably, although actually they were spared. He made them represent three ages: the old and spent, downcast in their defeat; the most respected middle-aged, carrying the key to the city; the young and angry, arms spread in rebellion and frustration.

Both this and Medardo Rosso's *The Golden Age*, done at the same time, express the artists more than the subjects. They attempt something far different from the smooth, idealized classic work of Hiram Powers over at the Museum of American Art. They try to look inward. Revolutionary!

At that same time, Samuel Pierpont Langley at the Smithsonian was studying problems of heavier-than-air flight, watching vultures at the National Zoo as they sailed past his specially constructed tower. In 1887, Langley was made Secretary of the Institution and set up a department of aeronautics.

In Germany, Otto Lilienthal was writing up the results of his long experiments with gliders. His most advanced, with curved wing surfaces, still soars overhead in the Early Flight gallery at Air and Space—a hang glider, an 1890s version of those seen today that have given us a new, skillful, graceful sport which I have no intention of ever trying to master.

Auguste Rodin. The Burghers of Calais. *1886. Bronze, 6'10½" x 7' 11" x 6'6" (2.10 x 2.41 x 1.98 m). Hirshhorn Museum and Sculpture Garden (HMSG).*

Lilienthal was killed in a glider in 1896. Three years later, Wilbur Wright of Dayton, Ohio, wrote to the Smithsonian for publications on the progress of flight experiments. And in that same year, Thomas Eakins painted the striking portrait of his wife that hangs in the Hirshhorn.

A Philadelphian and an admirer of Winslow Homer, Eakins studied art in Europe, then returned to set the old city of Benjamin Franklin slightly on its ear with his relentless pursuit of truth in painting. Homer went after the realism of man's struggle against nature (usually, in his case, the sea). He is called an objective realist. Eakins strove to make people come alive on his canvases, exactly as they were. He studied anatomy. He used nude models—including himself. In fact, he found himself fired from a nine-year teaching job at the Pennsylvania Academy of the Fine Arts for putting a nude male model in front of a mixed class.

Keats's Grecian Urn is supposed to say

"Beauty is truth, truth beauty," and Eakins bet his soul on that. His *Mrs. Thomas Eakins* is a complete personality, a true woman, and because of that, a beautiful one.

The Hirshhorn collection has the work of other important artists from Eakins' time—a time of great contrasts in American painting, as well as great artists out of whose seeming traditionalism developed a modern idiom in art. For example, contrast John Singer Sargent's work with Eakins'. Sargent, although an accomplished virtuoso, became known primarily as an international portrait painter, who had a knack for capturing the likeness and flattering his sitter at the same time. His portrait of *Catherine Vlasto*, while large in technique, is small in characterization when compared with Eakins' painstakingly realistic portrait of *Mrs. Eakins*. While the two men in Charles Hawthorne's *The Story* represent a realistically charming narrative portrait, the power of the painting, I think, is in the still life of the punch bowl and its fruit.

Medardo Rosso. The Golden Age. 1886. Wax over plaster, 16⅝ x 20½ x 11" (42 x 52 x 28 cm). HMSG.

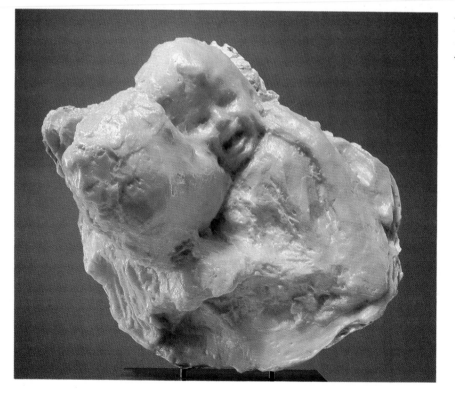

Gauguin's carving reflects his interest in the formal abstraction of primitive art that later influenced such 20th-century masters as Matisse and Picasso.
Paul Gauguin. Cylinder Decorated with the Figure of Hina and Two Attendants. *1891–93. Tamanu wood with painted gilt, 14⅝ x 5¼ x 4¼" (37 x 13 x 11 cm).* HMSG, *purchase with funds provided under the Smithsonian Collections Acquisitions Program, 1981.*

Left: *Thomas Eakins. Mrs.
Thomas Eakins. c. 1899.
Oil on canvas, 20 x 16" (51 x
41 cm).*
Below: *John Singer Sargent.
Catherine Vlasto. 1897. Oil
on canvas, 58½ x 33¾" (149
x 86 cm).*
Opposite: *Charles
Hawthorne.* The Story. *c.
1898. Oil on canvas, 48 x
30" (122 x 76 cm). HMSG.*

*The Hirshhorn painting collection begins with
Eakins, father of American realism.
Remembered most for his portraits, Eakins
strove to render his subjects truthfully, infusing
them with his penetrating psychological insight.
Sargent, who softened his aristocratic
Edwardian women with flattering touches, was
perhaps more popular with his subjects. While
Charles Hawthorne's* The Story *contains
elements of portraiture, it is the marvelous still
life with its heavy impasto that captures our
attention.*

s the century began, Wilbur and Orville Wright spent summers camped on the sands of a desolate stretch of the Outer Banks of North Carolina near Kitty Hawk. They swatted mosquitoes and tried out gliders, controlling the tilt of the wings by warping them so their angle to the force of the air could be varied. Their work culminated on a blustery December day in 1903 when they achieved controlled, powered flight. Their successful plane faces you as you enter Air and Space from the Mall. It hangs at about the height that Orville Wright reached that December day. It's not a replica. It's the same plane. I'm personally subject to a sensation in the scalp when I look up at it and realize that those strips of wood, curved and held under tension, and that primitive gasoline engine with its bicycle chain drive are exactly what the brothers built and used to take man's first wobbly steps into the air.

And I am unfailingly amazed, standing here, that about a dozen feet from the tail of the Wright *Flyer* is the rim of the Apollo 11 spacecraft *Columbia*. This was the vehicle in which Michael Collins (later to become first director of the new museum) orbited the moon while astronauts Neil A. Armstrong and Edwin E. Aldrin, Jr., took their lunar module *Eagle* to the moon's surface for that famous "giant leap for mankind." In those 12 or so feet are encompassed 66 years—easily within a person's life span. Yet the knowledge that bridges that gap between those two items in the Milestones of Flight gallery would seem enough to fill a millenium.

Flight seems now the ultimate symbol of the world's exuberant entrance into the 20th century. But at the time, the Wrights were barely appreciated, partly because the press had developed an understandable cynicism toward flight when so many attempts had failed, partly because there were so many other excitements. Factories seemed capable of turning out anything that civilization craved. A handful of motorcars now wheezed along

In this 1899 letter to the Smithsonian, Wilbur Wright wrote of his life-long interest in the "problem of mechanical and human flight." The Smithsonian had become involved in flight experiments with the appointment of Samuel P. Langley as Secretary in 1887.

Success at Kitty Hawk! With Orville Wright as pilot, the Flyer *leaves its launch rail to begin history's first powered, controlled flight of a heavier-than-air machine. Overleaf: A mannequin of Orville Wright peers through the forward-mounted elevators of the 1903 Wright* Flyer *in the Air and Space Museum's Milestones of Flight gallery.*

tire-shredding gravel roads as horses bolted and hordes of bicyclists pulled to the side to stare in admiration. Bicycling was a huge sport. So was baseball, not only to play, but to watch. And growing crowds flocked to college football in such numbers that huge stadiums and bowls would soon be built to hold them all. It was as a daring sport that aviation was first widely recognized, although governments weren't as slow as popular belief would have it to see the potential of the airplane.

The world's first military airplane, the Wright Model A of 1908–9 sits, oil-stained but serviceable looking, in Air and Space's Early Flight Hall. It carries the crossed-flag insignia of the army's Signal Corps for which airplanes seemed best suited if they were to be flown in some distant and unthinkable war.

Meanwhile, in spite of its underpowered Anzani engine, Louis Blériot's monoplane skimmed the Channel from France to England, linking, at last, two countries by air. He suffered none of the problems that had plagued the first balloonists to make the crossing, back in 1785. These two aeronauts, Jean Pierre Blanchard and American-born Dr. John Jeffries, barely made it after jettisoning ballast, food, pamphlets, clothing, finally even their bottle of cognac, and, as a last resort, the contents of their bladders. Their adventure is hilariously reenacted in a puppet show at the Air and Space Museum.

Also at Air and Space is a Blériot monoplane. It's not *the* Blériot that crossed the English Channel, but it's one that grew from that prototype. It was put back together from a pile of scraps out at the Paul E. Garber Restoration and Preservation Facility in Silver Hill, Maryland, and now it's one of the great

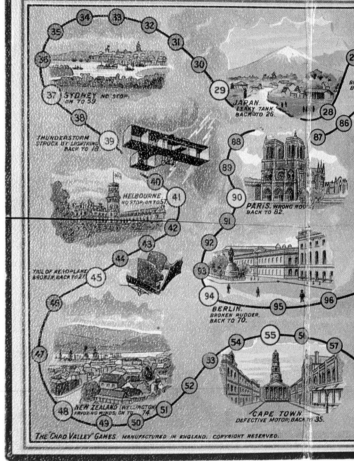

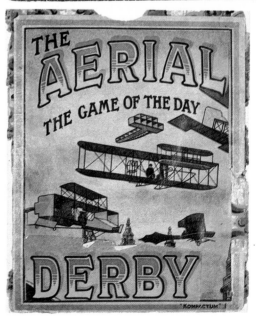

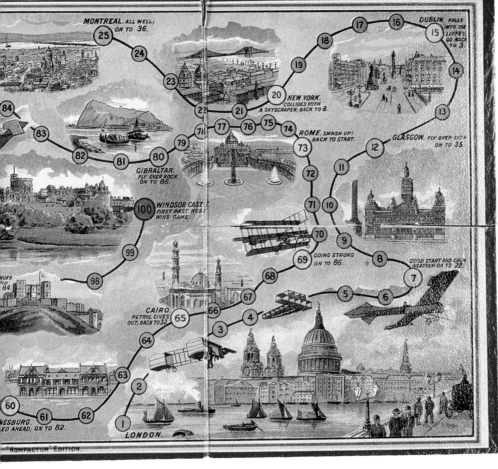

Aeronautical memories from the archives of the Air and Space Museum. Clockwise from top left: Pilot's license number one, issued to pioneer aviator and airplane manufacturer Glenn H. Curtiss; Louis Blériot and the Blériot Type XI in which he made the first flight across the English Channel, July 25, 1909; Raymonde de la Roche, who became the first licensed female pilot on March 8, 1910, in France; sheet music for the song, "I Wish That I Could Fly," published around 1860; and the Aerial Derby game, popular around 1910.

Above: *Pablo Picasso.* Head of a Woman.
1909, cast 1960. Bronze, 16 x 9⅜ x 10⅜"
(41 x 24 x 26 cm). HMSG.
*Cubist sculpture came into its own with
Picasso's creation of* Head of a Woman *in
1909. One of the most influential sculptures
ever, this piece marks the first attempt to apply
the principles of analytical cubism to three-
dimensional form.*
Opposite: *The Hirshhorn Museum's
Sculpture Garden, filled with many of the
sculptures that once graced the lawns and
terraces of Joseph Hirshhorn's estate in
Greenwich, Connecticut, provides a refuge
from the daily bustle of the adjacent Mall.
Aristide Maillol's* Action in Chains *dominates
this view of the snowy Sculpture Garden.
Maillol created this seven-foot figure—a nude
woman walking forward, her hands bound in
chains behind her back—in 1905–6.*

beauties of the museum, clean and bright and gleaming with varnish on all its wooden struts. That truly beautiful plane and others of its generation that took part in those early air meets (so delightfully depicted in the film *Those Magnificent Men and their Flying Machines*) culminated the innocent infancy of aviation. Many are either on display at Air and Space or are being repolished at the Garber Facility among all the other treasures of air and space that are awaiting their call to move up to the front. All reflect the exuberance of design that resulted from lack of experience. Anything was possible in that first decade of this century. *Anything* might fly.

Anything could be done in the world of art, too. Barbara Tuchman writes in *The Proud Tower*: "New movements in the arts were erupting everywhere. At the Salon d'Automne in 1905 and 1906 the *Fauves* (Wild Beasts) led by Matisse exhibited in riotous color and distorted line their credo of painting independent of nature. In 1907–8 Picasso and Braque, discovering essential reality in geometrical forms, created Cubism. . . . The time vibrated with a search for new forms and new realms . . . a wiping out of frontiers."

Picasso played around with various cube forms in his paintings, and then, in 1909, used the motif in sculpture. He did a cubist head of Fernande Olivier, a tall, lovely woman

Henri Matisse. The Serf. *1900–1903. Bronze, 36 x 13⁷⁄₈ x 12¼" (91 x 35 x 31 cm). HMSG.*

whom he later married. *Head of a Woman*, as it is called, became one of the most important masterpieces of modern art, opening the floodgates to a freshet of cubist sculpture from Picasso's contemporaries and influencing generations to come. Picasso's friend, Lithuanian-born Jacques Lipchitz, who was living in Paris, began devoting himself to cubist sculpture. His *Girl Reading* in the Hirshhorn is one of the most powerful works in this style.

In 1903, the year of the Wrights' mostly unnoticed success, a large, strange, brilliant woman named Gertrude Stein and her lanky, discursive, dyspeptic brother Leo moved into 27 rue de Fleurus, Paris. Leo had gone to Harvard, Gertrude to Radcliffe, where she was William James' prize pupil, then studied medicine at Johns Hopkins until she got bored with it and quit. Now Leo painted and Gertrude wrote.

Some of her writings—weird, experimental prose—were eventually published in a New York journal called *Camera Work*, which also dates from 1903. It dealt with photography, but its publisher, a Renaissance man named Alfred Stieglitz, wanted the avant-garde in prose in it, too.

He liked the way the moderns expressed themselves. With his photographer friend, Edward Steichen, Stieglitz set up a gallery at 291 Fifth Avenue. In a couple of years he was

Max Weber. Bather. *1913. Oil on canvas, 60½ x 24¼" (154 x 62 cm).* HMSG.

175

Lipchitz moved to Paris in 1909 and,
influenced by Picasso's cubist sculpture, began
creating some of his own, like the striking full-
length Girl Reading. Léger was a French
cubist who worked with Picasso and Braque
but whose art took on a more rounded form, as
we can see in Nude on a Red Background.
Both Lipchitz and Léger were to have con-
siderable influence on young American artists.
Left: *Jacques Lipchitz.* Girl Reading.
*1919. Bronze, 30¼ x 10⅜ x 10½"
(77 x 26 x 27 cm).*
Opposite: *Fernand Léger.* Nude on a Red
Background. *1927. Oil on canvas, 51¼ x 32"
(130 x 81 cm).* HMSG.

Stieglitz was a brilliant photographer who fought to have photography recognized as an art form. He was also sponsor and mentor of American experimental painters and sculptors, including Georgia O'Keeffe, whom he eventually married.
Left: *Alfred Stieglitz.* Georgia O'Keeffe *(b. 1887). c. 1925. Photograph, 9 x 7" (23 x 18 cm). Archives of American Art (AAA).*
Below: *Alfred Stieglitz.* The Terminal. *1893. Photogravure, 10 x 13¼" (25 x 34 cm). NMAH.*

Georgia O'Keeffe. Goat's
Horn with Red. *1945.
Pastel on paperboard, mounted
on paperboard, 31¹¹/₁₆ x
27⁷/₈" (80 x 71 cm).* HMSG.

filling it with paintings and sculptures from Europe. Rodin, Cézanne, Matisse, Picasso, and Brancusi were represented, and 291 gained a reputation as the place to visit if you wanted to see what these moderns were all about.

In Paris, Gertrude Stein's house had become a similar place. Leo had stopped painting and was buying the extraordinary works of the modernists. Gertrude turned her rooms into a combination gallery and salon. Pablo Picasso would show up frequently. His cubist works hung on the walls. He and Gertrude became good friends—even lasting friends, which was unusual for Gertrude.

Matisse was another habitué of 27 rue de Fleurus. He and Picasso became interested in African sculpture—exactly what we see in the Museum of African Art. Gertrude called it "very ancient, very narrow, very sophisticated." It influenced Picasso's style. He and Matisse were friends, then broke apart.

In the same summer as Blériot's flight, Alfred Stieglitz came to Paris, met Gertrude Stein and some artists, and became infected with modernism. He returned to the United States in 1911 determined to push the new styles at the Metropolitan Museum in New York for all he was worth.

The Met proved stuffy, so Stieglitz reproduced the works of Cézanne, Van Gogh, Matisse, and Picasso in *Camera Work.* Of course in his own gallery, 291, he had already been showing some of the new breed of American moderns. There was Max Weber, for example, whose painting, *Bather*, is in the Hirshhorn. It was one of the most advanced American cubist paintings at the time it was created in 1913. There was Marsden Hartley, who showed at 291 then went to Europe, checking in with the Steins and finally ending up in Berlin, where the large homosexual community made him feel at home. He was attracted to a young German army lieutenant, Karl von Freyburg, who was later killed. Hartley painted a series of war memorial canvases. At the Hirshhorn is *Painting No. 47, Berlin* with the initials "K.v.F" on a rectangle

near the bottom. You may have wondered what they stood for. Now you know.

But what proved to be the Stieglitz find that finally affected him most was his discovery of Georgia O'Keeffe. She was only 21 when she first went to 291 in 1908 to look at some Rodin sketches, and she was too shy to thrust herself forward into Stieglitz's consciousness. But when some of her drawings were finally thrust under his nose, he hung them in the gallery, then gave her a show to herself—the last show ever at 291—and in 1918 left his wife and moved in with Georgia. They were happily and lastingly married in 1924. O'Keeffe's *Goat's Horn with Red* at the Hirshhorn was done in 1945, a year before her husband died.

But let's get back to those pioneering days of flight—and of 20th-century art. Way back when the Wrights were still experimenting with gliders, a robust, magnetic artist and teacher named Robert Henri—he pronounced it "Hen-rye"—led an art movement of urban painters from nice, staid old Philadelphia, home of Eakins, to brassy, noisy, crooked New York, "the apotheosis of the raw," as Henry James called it. Raw or not, New York expressed the turn-of-the-century attitude, and Henri and at least four others recognized it.

The Hirshhorn has work by Henri, also by John Sloan, one of the leaders of "the Philadelphia Five" as they were called. My own favorite from this group is *Girl from Madrid*, partly because she's got beautiful black eyes, partly because her creator, George Luks, was perhaps the most colorful of the group.

He was a boisterous, hard-drinking man, so enchanted by pugilism that he dubbed himself such ringside pseudonyms as "Lame-em Luks," "Socko Sam," and "Chicago Whitey," and then, well in his cups, would pick a fight with a beefy stranger in a bar—the "I-can-lick-any-man-in-the-house" syndrome. Before things got out of hand, Luks would either skip out or make a joke of it and buy drinks all around, for he was not at all a physical hero. His close friends knew that he had covered most of the Spanish-American War (he was an artist-correspondent) from a Havana bar, and if he heard the distant rattle of rifle fire while nearing the front by train, he would hurl himself under the seat.

In 1933, George Luks was found propped up in a Sixth Avenue doorway, stone dead. No one knows what happened. Maybe a muscular fellow drinker called Socko Sam's bluff.

Rejecting traditional art influences, the Five recruited three new members and became the Eight. They showed their works in 1908, and their realism managed to offend New York to the extent that the whole movement was labeled the Ashcan School. John Sloan's *Carmine Theater* at the Hirshhorn does have an ash can, but that's the only one I've seen.

One of the Eight was Arthur B. Davies, brilliant, popular, a deeply respected setter of artistic trends. In 1913, Davies and Walt Kuhn, a former cartoonist with a broad streak of entrepreneur in him, organized an international exhibition at the 69th Infantry Regiment Armory in New York. It was a spectacular success, gathering together the best American modernists with some of the most important Europeans. Picasso sent Kuhn a handwritten list of his recommendations of European artists and sculptors who should be included. We have the note in the Archives of American Art; Picasso's spelling is atrocious. The names include Juan Gris, another Spanish habitué of the Stein salons, Marcel Duchamp, whose *Nude Descending a Staircase* caused the most furor at the show, and his fellow cubist, Georges Braque. In fact, the Europeans ended up stealing the show, overshadowing their American counterparts.

There was never another art show like it. Here was the ultimate sounding board for the new trends that had emerged with the Philadelphia Five, the Eight, Stieglitz's 291, the Gertrude Stein circle. Here in one place were all the forces that had been straining upward during the Era of Exuberance, expressing all the similar upheaval in every other facet of life—the questioning of every old

This handwritten note to Walt Kuhn from Pablo Picasso recommending European artists for the Armory Show is an example of the many treasures from the Archives of American Art that add a personal touch to the mute works of art on museum walls.

The common bond uniting the Eight was their opposition to the entrenched conservatism of the National Academy of Design. Artistically they were quite different from one another. For example, Davies invented a kind of mystical classicism that found little in common with Henri's concern with art as a reflection of everyday life.

Top: *John Sloan.* Carmine Theater. *1912. Oil on canvas, 25 x 31" (64 x 79 cm).* Above: *Arthur B. Davies.* Valley's Brim. *Before 1910. Oil on canvas, 18 x 30" (46 x 76 cm).* HMSG.

Right: *Robert Henri.*
Woman in White. *1904. Oil
on canvas, 77 x 38" (196 x
97 cm).*
Below: *Maurice Prendergast.*
Beach at Gloucester. *c.
1912–14. Oil on canvas,
30⅝ x 43⅛" (78 x 110 cm).*
HMSG.

Everett Shinn. The Door,
Paris. *1900. Watercolor and
charcoal on paper, 10 x 13¾"
(25 x 35 cm).* *HMSG.*

Ernest Lawson. Wet Night,
Gramercy Park. *1907. Oil
on canvas, 26¼ x 29" (67 x
74 cm).* *HMSG.*

Henri Matisse. Reclining Nude I. *c. 1907. Terra-cotta, 12⅝ x 19 x 10½″ (32 x 48 x 27 cm). HMSG.*

value, the hopeful scrutiny of every new idea.

The Smithsonian has a number of examples of this turbulent art world. Robert Henri did *Woman in White*; it's at the Hirshhorn; so is *Beach at Gloucester* by Maurice Prendergast, another member of the Eight. Arthur B. Davies did *Valley's Brim*. Marcel Duchamp's brother, Raymond Duchamp-Villon, did a sculpture, *Torso of a Young Man*, for the Armory Show—you can see it at the Hirshhorn, too. Matisse did *Reclining Nude I* at the same time as his *Blue Nude*, a painting of the same figure lent to the Armory Show by its owner, Leo Stein. And another fine piece at the show was Constantin Brancusi's *Sleeping Muse*. He

sent only the plaster of this marble head because it cost too much to insure the marble. The original was in his first one-man show— at 291. It was bought by Arthur B. Davies. And it's always a thrill for me to see it at the Hirshhorn.

In 1914, war interrupted every trend there was. Gertrude Stein and her companion, Alice B. Toklas, bought a Ford, named it Auntie, and began delivering supplies to hospitals. Gertrude had to learn to drive. She never mastered reverse, so she used to park in such a way that she could leave her space by going forward. She wasn't very popular with drivers whom she blocked in the process.

Constantin Brancusi.
Sleeping Muse. *1909–11.*
Marble, 7 x 11 x 8" (18 x 28
x 20 cm). HMSG.

Marsden Hartley. Painting
No. 47, Berlin. *1914–15.*
Oil on canvas, 39½ x 31⅝"
(100 x 80 cm). HMSG.

Among the many American artists represented at the Armory Show were Marsden Hartley, Walt Kuhn, and George Luks. These three paintings, all done after the show, reflect the influence of the European modernists.
Left: *Walt Kuhn.* The Tragic Comedians. *c. 1916. Oil on canvas, 8' x 3'9" (2.44 x 1.14 m).*
Above: *George Luks.* Girl from Madrid. *c. 1925. Oil on canvas, 30 x 36" (76 x 91 cm). HMSG.*

French artist Henri Farré portrayed the great French-born American pilot Raoul Lufberry in 1918. An original member of the Lafayette Escadrille, Lufberry shot down 17 German aircraft before he himself was shot down and killed on May 17, 1918.

The First World War quickly changed airplanes from sport machines to warplanes. A French artist named Henri Farré set about painting the air war, and some of his work hangs near the World War I exhibit at the Air and Space Museum. This gallery is certainly one of the most remarkable in the Smithsonian, for it recreates a dramatic moment at an American airfield near Verdun during the last days of the war. That was when a German Fokker D. VII, probably the most advanced fighter plane to emerge from the war, landed at the base and was captured, along with its pilot. No one knows whether he came in by accident or deliberately, for he was deeply depressed by the recent death of his brother and he must certainly have seen the chaos his country was already facing as the armistice neared. But his plane, new and perfect, was a treasure for the Allies at the time and remains so for the Smithsonian. Beside it is an Albatros fighter, an earlier German plane. This is another incredible product of restorers' magic, for it came to the Institution as a pile of dusty junk and has emerged as a clean, gleaming, brightly painted, tautly rigged little biplane, seemingly ready to go.

Farré's paintings of the earlier French planes and of the gallant, jaunty young men who flew them is beside the small exhibit of the Lafayette Escadrille. This group was

Captured intact by three American airmen on November 9, 1918, two days before the armistice that ended World War I, this German Fokker D. VII fighter today resides with other warplanes of its era in the Air and Space Museum's re-creation of a war-torn airfield "somewhere near Verdun."

Its fabric wing covering in tatters, its plywood fuselage rotting, this German Albatros D.Va fighter presented the Air and Space Museum's crew of craftsmen with one of their most difficult restoration projects. Today, in the World War I Aviation gallery, it gleams as it did when it entered service in February 1918. The Albatros D.V series of aircraft began to reach front-line squadrons in May 1917, just after the United States entered World War I. Despite jaunty songs, above, the United States was unprepared and had nothing to equal such advanced aircraft as the Albatros.

192

formed in 1916 of American volunteers who couldn't wait for the United States to declare war but wanted to play the game at once. For such as these, the air was the only field of battle—an element where pilots faced each other man to man, where the victor would salute the vanquished as he soared past him, where the man whose machine guns jammed would often get a sympathetic wave from his enemy and be left alone until he could defend himself. The Lafayette Escadrille was filled with them, former athletes from the Ivy League, rich men's sons, idlers with a craving for romance and chivalry.

One of the men who did most to get it started was Bill Thaw of Pittsburgh, a relative of the notorious Harry K. Thaw who in 1906 had killed architect Stanford White over the "girl on the red velvet swing," Evelyn Nesbit. The shooting, during a stage performance in New York, was the sensation of the decade. Evelyn Thaw—she had married Harry—became, according to Gertrude Stein, "the heroine of the moment." Fernande Picasso, the painter's wife, "adored her in the way a later generation adored Mary Pickford, she was so blonde, so pale, so nothing and Fernande would give a heavy sigh of admiration."

Blonde and pale, yes. Nothing? Well, not exactly, Gertrude. Evelyn grew up on the poor side of Pittsburgh, and she undoubtedly saw the baronial Thaw family out driving in their spanking carriages. She came to New York as a teenager, charmed her way into modeling jobs for illustrators and photographers, got a part in *Floradora*, and soon won the still-lusty heart of Stanford White, perhaps the leading citizen of Manhattan. He was more than twice her age, but he won her over

and, in her words, she "became a woman."

Stanford White's favorite photographer, Rudolf Eickemayer, made up a lot of platinum prints of little Evelyn, and the Museum of American History has many of them in the photographic display. There she is, again and again in pose after pose: smiling, sulky, aloof, ethereal, demure, brazen . . . beautiful.

While Gertrude and Alice B. were driving their Ford, and Bill Thaw, Vic Chapman, Norman Prince, Jim McConnell, Kiffin Rockwell, James Norman Hall, and the others were fighting Albatroses and Fokkers in their French Nieuports and SPADs, other Americans were girding up for the declaration of war that came in April 1917. When the Yanks finally started coming, however, the Army Air Service arrived with no planes. So the latest model SPADs, like the one in our Garber Facility, which still has its original fabric covering, complete with bullet-hole patches marked with little Maltese crosses, went into American action.

The United States did provide two notable pieces of hardware for those early days of aerial combat. One was the Curtiss Jenny, the training plane that produced thousands of pilots and then, after the war, gave many of them a hazardous living in the barnstorming business, so joyously described in the Exhibition Flight gallery. The second was the Liberty Engine, a good, sturdy, powerful aircraft engine that was used for years after that war—you can find one at the Garber Facility.

An experimental airplane that was to have been a contribution to World War I—the Martin Kitten—never panned out. Still, it's a dear little thing. It has an 18-foot wingspan, a two-cylinder engine that was supposed to give

Rudolf Eickemayer, Jr.
Evelyn Nesbit. c. 1901.
Photograph, platinum print,
9¼ x 7¼" (23 x 18 cm).
NMAH.

The brainchild of aeronautical inventor J.V. Martin, the tiny Martin Kitten, below, with its 18-foot wingspan, was offered to the U.S. Air Service in 1917. Underpowered, with poor handling qualities, it nonetheless boasted one of the first practical retractable landing gear systems. Right: An immortal of World War I, the Spad XIII flew with both French and American pilots. Of over 8,000 built, this Spad XIII is the only one left in the world with original fabric and markings. Captain Arthur Raymond Brooks of the U.S. Air Service piloted it during the summer and fall of 1918 and shot down three German aircraft. Numerous bullet-hole patches in the fabric attest to Capt. Brooks's good fortune in escaping a similar fate himself.

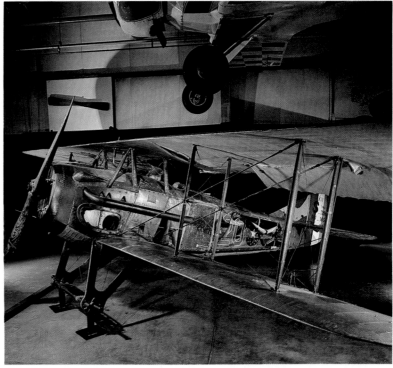

it 45 horsepower, and empty it weighs 350 pounds. Its inventor was a pioneering airman who constantly invented aeronautical devices, some of which worked well. The Kitten had retractable landing gear—a big breakthrough in 1917—and the system was strong enough to allow the little biplane to land with wheels partly down, which is more than today's jets can do. That was the good thing about it, aside from its looks. The bad thing was that when it finally was test-flown it was disastrously tail-heavy, had no lateral control, could climb to an altitude of about four feet, and that was it. But it's a beautiful, well-built little plywood machine, hanging from a rafter at the Garber Facility.

The Kitten wasn't tested until after the war, and by then Gertrude Stein's 27 rue de Fleurus was reopened, and expatriate Americans were flocking to it. Ezra Pound, the poet, came. Sherwood Anderson introduced young, hungry Ernest Hemingway, who in turn introduced even younger, already successful F. Scott Fitzgerald and his wife, Zelda. The National Portrait Gallery has fine sketches of Zelda and Scott, also a painting of Fitzgerald and a photograph of a war-injured Hemingway taken by Man Ray in Paris.

In *A Moveable Feast*, Hemingway describes visits with Stein at a time when he was writing in a cold hotel garret and was always hungry.

Left: *Harrison Fisher.* Zelda Sayre Fitzgerald *(1900–1947) and* Francis Scott Key Fitzgerald *(1896–1940). 1927. Sanguine conté crayon on paper, 23 x 14¼" (58 x 36 cm) and 22½ x 12⅜" (57 x 31 cm), respectively.* NPG, *gift of their daughter, Mrs. Scottie Smith.*
Below: *Jo Davidson.* Gertrude Stein *(1874–1946). 1923. Terra-cotta, 31" (79 cm).* NPG, *gift of Dr. Maury Leibowitz.*

But at nombre 27, "there was a big fireplace and it was warm and comfortable and they gave you good things to eat and tea and natural distilled liqueurs. . . ." He loved her paintings and envied the Picassos, and she read his stories and told him that he "might be some sort of new writer. . . ." They were good friends for a while, then grew apart.

It was in 1923 that the sculptor Jo Davidson did his bust of Gertrude Stein. It, too, is in the Portrait Gallery, and it has her in a Buddha-like pose, as though she were seated cross-legged. Hemingway says she reminded him of an Italian peasant.

During the '20s, art moved from cubism to surrealism. Among the surrealists, Joan Miró had perhaps the most fertile imagination. When you first glance at *Circus Horse* in the Hirshhorn, you are inclined to enjoy a sense of fun and gaiety, but then an uncomfortable realization creeps over you that things are not what they seem—not as humorous or delightful. His subjects almost appear to be hallucinations and part of an uneasy world.

It was at this strange, sunny yet restless time between the wars that Stuart Davis, who had contributed to the Armory Show, began to be noticed in the art world for his experimental abstract paintings. Whatever the style of the day, Davis kept plugging away with his abstractions, which combined a tablespoon of cubism with a dash of the literal and also a dollop of words—from which he sometimes gathered fresh abstract meanings. In 1928 and 1929, Davis lived in Paris where he painted *Rue des Rats No. 2*, a street scene with a surrealistic horse on the side of a building. Picasso had a lot of influence on him, of course, and so did American jazz. People say his *Rapt at Rappaport's* is the painter's equivalent of jazz. I don't know exactly why, except that when I look at it at the Hirshhorn I feel it has a sort of tempo—a beat. Maybe it's because he's got that title—those alliterative words—right on the painting, flashing across the canvas with the urgency of a news bulletin on your TV screen.

Man Ray. Ernest Miller Hemingway *(1899–1961). 1923. Photograph, gelatin silver print, 9 x 6¹⁵/₁₆" (23 x 18 cm).* NPG.

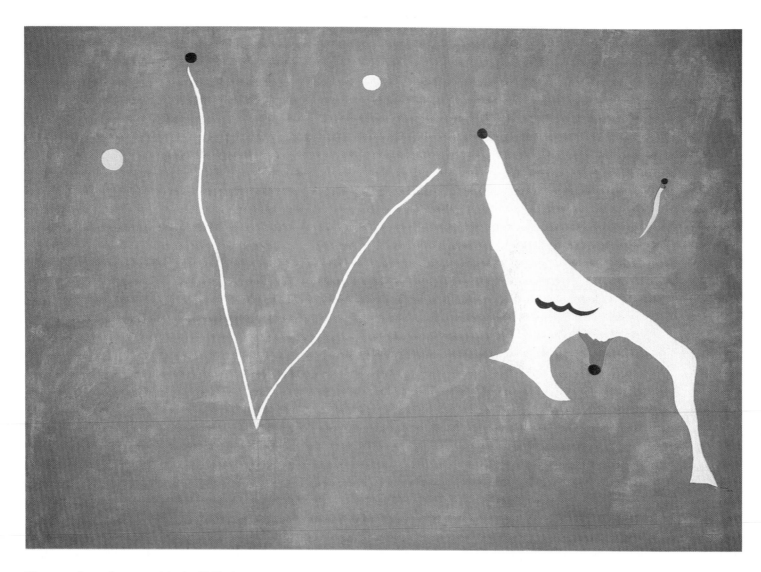

The surrealists, who emerged in the 1920s in Paris, inhabited a world of fantasy where the imagination played freely, unhampered by reason. Prominent among them were Joan Miró, Max Ernst, and Jean Arp.
Above: *Joan Miró.* Circus Horse. *1927. Oil and pencil on burlap, 6'4¾" x 9'2⅜" (1.95 x 2.8 m).* HMSG.

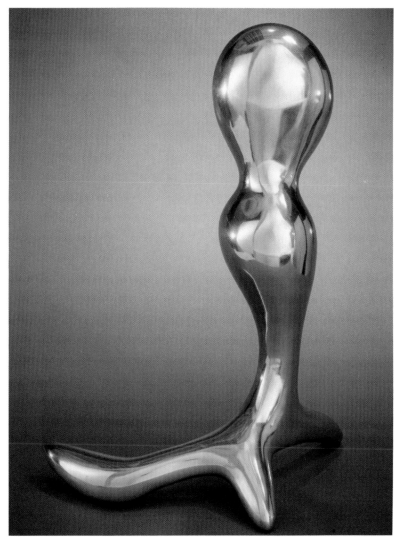

Above: *Jean Arp. Alu with
Claws. 1942. Polished bronze,
22¼ x 14½ x 12⅛″ (57 x 37
x 31 cm).*
Left: *Max Ernst.
Moonmad. 1944. Bronze,
36½ x 11¾ x 12″ (93 x 30 x
30 cm). HMSG.*

During his roughly 50 years of painting,
Stuart Davis changed his style repeatedly and
yet remained essentially Stuart Davis. Here we
see his progression from a painting with both
literal and surreal elements to one that is
almost entirely abstract and influenced, he said,
by American jazz.

Above: *Stuart Davis.* Rue
des Rats, No. 2. *1928. Oil
and sand on canvas, 20 x 29"
(51 x 74 cm).*
Opposite: *Stuart Davis.*
Rapt at Rappaport's. *1952.
Oil on canvas, 4'4" x 3'4"
(1.32 x 1.02 m).* HMSG.

And what about that parallel world of flight? In 1922 the Fokker T-2, a huge, ungainly monoplane on the second floor of the Air and Space Museum, crossed the country nonstop for the first time. The land had been traversed before, of course. Back in 1911, a daredevil pilot named Calbraith Perry Rodgers (descendant of Commodore Perry) flew a Wright plane from coast to coast. It advertised a grape drink and was named for it: *Vin Fiz*. And it crashed so many times that only three pieces of the original remained by the time Cal completed his trip, 49 days after he started. *Vin Fiz* looks pretty now, however, back at the museum in the same gallery as the

Fokker T-2, which made it in one piece and in just under 27 hours.

In 1924, the Douglas World Cruiser, right next to the Fokker T-2, made the first trip around the world. It was one of two planes to survive that trip. Four started.

In 1926, Dr. Robert H. Goddard launched the first liquid-propellant rocket at a Massachusetts farm. It rose 41 feet in the air as though, to paraphrase Goddard, it just wanted to go somewhere else. That little flight opened the way to space.

And in 1927, Lindbergh made his flight to Paris in the *Spirit of St. Louis*, another plane that speeds my pulse as I look up at it and re-

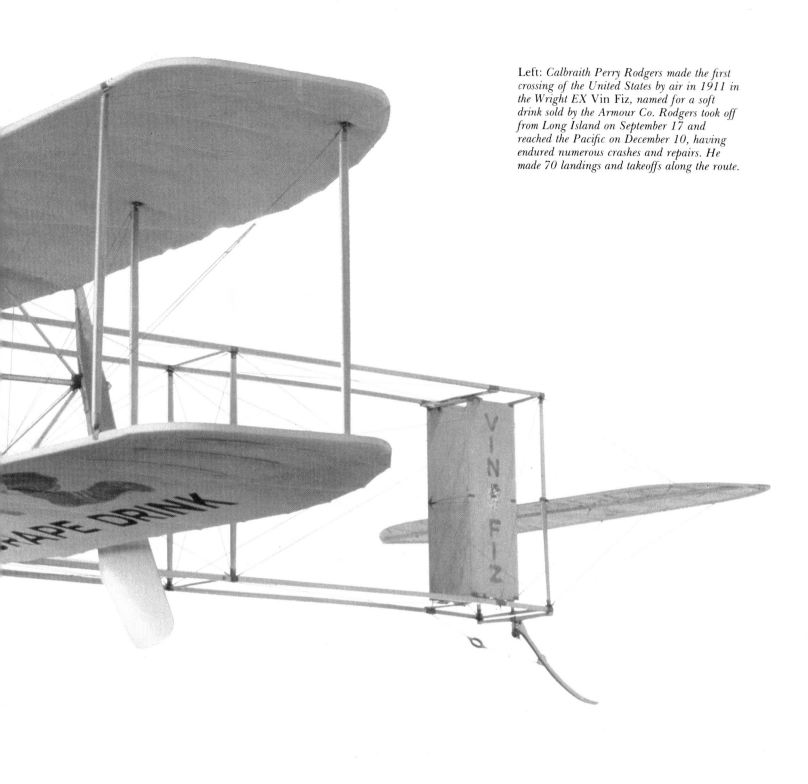

Left: *Calbraith Perry Rodgers made the first crossing of the United States by air in 1911 in the Wright EX Vin Fiz, named for a soft drink sold by the Armour Co. Rodgers took off from Long Island on September 17 and reached the Pacific on December 10, having endured numerous crashes and repairs. He made 70 landings and takeoffs along the route.*

Left: *U.S. Air Service pilots Oakley G. Kelly and John A. Macready accomplished the first nonstop flight across the country in the Fokker T-2, on May 2–3, 1923. The T-2 made the flight from Long Island to San Diego in 26 hours, 50 minutes, at an average speed of 92 miles per hour.*

On April 6, 1924, the Douglas World Cruiser *Chicago,* below, *and three sister ships of the U.S. Army Air Service took off from Seattle, Washington, to attempt the first flight around the world. On September 28,* Chicago *and one other World Cruiser returned victorious to Seattle, having completed their epochal flight in 175 days.*

The four World Cruisers were still together when they anchored in the harbor at Sitka, Alaska, at the end of an early leg of the flight.

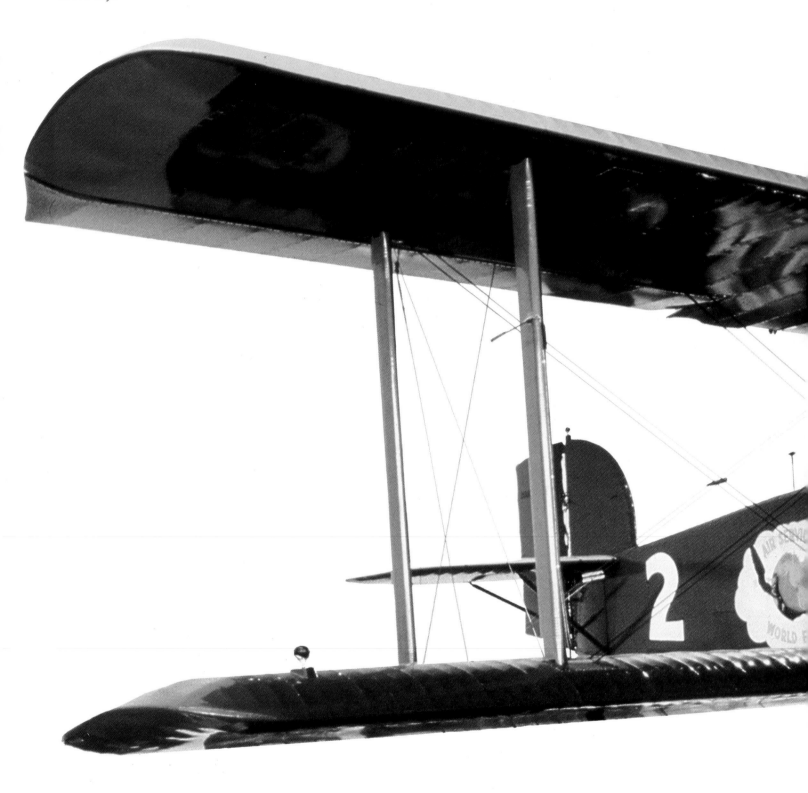

Charles A. Lindbergh's solo flight across the Atlantic *in the* Spirit of St. Louis, *opposite, on May 20–21, 1927, won the adoration of the world. His goal was the $25,000 Orteig prize,* left, *for the first nonstop flight from New York to Paris. Cramped in his tiny cockpit,* center, *for 33 hours, 30 minutes, Lindbergh monitored his few instruments, managed fuel flow, fought bad weather and his worst enemy—sleep.*

alize its authenticity. Lindbergh penciled marks near the valves that controlled the gasoline flow, the marks showing how far down the level had gone after so many hours. And when he was writing his second book about the flight, *The Spirit of St. Louis,* he asked permission to visit his old plane, then in the Arts and Industries Building, and copy the notes. Paul Garber, who was then an avid collector for the Smithsonian and was the man responsible for getting the *Spirit* into the Smithsonian collection, met the General and held a stepladder for him. The visitors had gone and it was still and half-lit, and while Garber was waiting below he sat down and let his mind drift back to the great Lindbergh flight, the incredible feat of staying awake, the strange night landing, almost blind, at Le Bourget field outside Paris.

And then, as Garber tells it, a voice called him from above and he looked up and saw Charles Lindbergh's head sticking out of the cabin of the *Spirit,* just as though he were trying to get his wheels safely on the grass after those grueling 33½ hours.

Lindbergh opened the way for more records, even though the Depression had arrived. Amelia Earhart won us all over with her brains and modesty and quiet courage. Clearly, she hated the hoopla that surrounded her and wanted to prove herself as able to cross continents and oceans as any man. And so she did, in the early '30s in the superb aircraft, the Lockheed Vega, red with gold trim, that is displayed in Air and Space. It took her across the Atlantic solo in May 1932, and then across the continent three months later.

Left: *The* Spirit of St. Louis *today occupies an honored place in the Air and Space Museum's Milestones of Flight gallery. Built by Ryan Airlines, the* Spirit of St. Louis *is a heavily modified Ryan M-2 monoplane powered by a 223-horsepower Wright Whirlwind engine. A large fuel tank mounted in front of the cockpit blocks forward vision.* Overleaf: *The nose of the aircraft bears painted flags of the countries visited by Lindbergh during a 1927–28 tour.*

Round the World Flight
in the Lockheed Electra.

Five years to the day after Lindbergh's flight across the Atlantic, Amelia Earhart flew this Lockheed Vega 5B from Newfoundland to Ireland in the first solo, nonstop, trans-Atlantic crossing by a woman. Later in 1932, she flew the same Vega from Los Angeles to Newark alone and nonstop; again she was the first woman to accomplish the feat. In 1937, she and Fred Noonan set out to circumnavigate the globe in a twin-engine Lockheed Electra. On one of the last legs of the flight, they disappeared in the South Pacific. No trace of airplane or crew was ever found.

Courage

Courage is the price that Life exacts
   for granting peace.
The soul that knows it not
Knows no release from little things:
Knows not the livid loneliness of fear,
Nor mountain heights where bitter
   joy can hear
The sound of wings.

How can life grant us boon of living,
   compensate
For dull gray ugliness and pregnant
   hate
Unless we dare
The soul's dominion? Each time we
   make a choice, we pay
With courage to behold the resistless
   day,
And count it fair.

        —AMELIA EARHART

One of the most famous airplanes in history, the Lockheed Vega 5C Winnie Mae, below, was piloted by Wiley Post on a series of spectacular record-setting and experimental flights between 1930 and 1935. Named for the daughter of F.C. Hall, Post's employer, Winnie Mae set the first record in 1930 with a dash from Los Angeles to Chicago. In the next year, with navigator Harold Gatty, Post flew around the world in 8 days, 15 hours. In 1933, he made the flight solo in 7 days, 18 hours. Post then modified the airplane for high altitude, long-distance experimental flights. With the assistance of the B.F. Goodrich company, Post developed the first practical high-altitude suit, below right, the ancestor of today's space suits. Post's high flights with Winnie Mae led to the discovery of the jet streams and the phenomenon now known as jet lag. Post perished with famed humorist Will Rogers in the crash of another airplane at Point Barrow, Alaska, on August 15, 1935.

At almost the same time, Wiley Post, an extraordinary, inventive pilot, went about stretching the boundaries of flight with the assured competence that the Wrights showed when they got us up there in the first place. Thus, not quite 30 years after the Wrights' first flight, Post went around the world solo. He also developed a pressure suit and probed the stratosphere, breaking various altitude records. He named his modified Lockheed Vega, white with blue trim, *Winnie Mae*. It's in the Flight Testing gallery.

Near it is his space suit. The story goes that Post had to make an emergency landing once while wearing it, and when he walked up to a nearby individual, absorbed in what he was doing, the poor man nearly fainted at the sight of what he thought was a Martian. Look at Post's space suit, and then look at the display of space suits worn by the first explorers of the Moon in the museum's "Apollo to the Moon" Hall, and notice all that the new models owe to the old.

The worse the Depression got, the more exciting the air races became. They often were low-altitude affairs with fast and dangerous little planes flown by some very dashing characters. Roscoe Turner was one, with his waxed moustache and self-designed sky-blue uniform. Turner flew with a mascot, a lion cub named Gilmore, who finally grew so big he couldn't fit into the cockpit. Gilmore was eventually retired and after he died he rated being stuffed. We have him now, along with Turner's lovely, sleek RT-14 Meteor, winner of the Thompson Trophy races in '38 and '39, at the Garber Facility.

Turner also piloted the Boeing 247 D that is now in the Hall of Air Transportation (pages 242–243). This twin-engine plane (the engines are named "Nip" and "Tuck") was designed as a new, fast air transport to take over from the old trimotors and byplanes. Turner and Clyde Pangborn flew it in a London to Melbourne international race and came in third, behind a British-built racing plane and a KLM Airlines Douglas DC-2. The DC-2 was the immediate ancestor of the DC-3, and its performance in the race tells you why you've heard more about DC-3s than Boeing 247s.

Of course lots of money helped good technology to win races. So Howard Hughes, seeking new records in the 1930s, put the best

brains to work designing what I consider the most beautiful aircraft in the museum. You find the Hughes racer in a circular alcove in the Flight Technology gallery, which in itself is an extraordinary tour de force with its explanations of engines, air foils, and above all the endless compromise of design so that a plane can be both fast and profitable or effective as a weapon or safe or have endurance. Hughes wanted speed, and the racer is what he got. It looks as though it had been carved out of a bar of wet soap—a work of art.

The Depression was hard on artists, for in the United States art is considered all very well until the going gets tough. Starving mod-

Howard Hughes, above, designed and built the Hughes H-1, left, to break the world's speed record for aircraft, a feat he accomplished on September 13, 1935, at an average speed of 352 miles per hour. In 1937, Hughes flew the same airplane across the country in 7 hours, 28 minutes, a record that stood until after World War II.

ernists were glad to be put to work for WPA art projects like painting murals on the inside walls of the "Farley post offices"—the endless series of new post offices that sprang up all over the country while Roosevelt's postmaster general, James A. Farley, was in the government. Such abstractionists as Stuart Davis and Willem de Kooning went about painting scenes of American life that could be understood by anyone with a letter to mail or a stamp to buy (for a couple of pennies).

There was, in fact, a general turn toward American themes by American artists. Reginald Marsh and Ben Shahn painted cities; Thomas Hart Benton and Grant Wood tended to get into the country. Edward Hopper had never painted anything but his own private brand of realism with sharp contrasts of light. He ignored the influences from Europe and just kept on being an isolated American force. His *Eleven A.M.* at the Hirshhorn is an example—spare and lonely and very American.

World War II ended the Depression (a drastic cure, indeed) and freed the modernists to get back to surrealism. They were reinforced by refugees from Europe with the result that a number of branches or "schools" of artistic expression developed. One of these immigrants was an artist named Piet Mondrian whose emphasis on line and color in geometric shapes inspired painting that became known as "hard edged." Contrast this style of painting with the work of artists who collectively became known as the abstract expressionists—Arshile Gorky, Jackson Pollock, and Willem de Kooning. An example is de Kooning's *Queen of Hearts* at the Hirshhorn, done in the '40s. Gorky's *Composition* is also there, painted between 1938 and 1940.

Abstract Expressionism really blossomed in the mid-1940s. World War II was dying out; modern technology, aiming toward space flight and the computer age, was being born. Americans prospered and so did American art, with Gorky and de Kooning catching the

Above: *Ben Shahn.*
Brothers. *1946. Tempera on
paper mounted on fiberboard,
38¹⁵/₁₆ x 25¹⁵/₁₆" (99 x 66 cm).*
Opposite: *Edward Hopper.*
Eleven A.M. *1926. Oil on
canvas, 28¹/₈ x 36¹/₈" (71 x
92 cm).* HMSG.

lively intellectualism of the time. They were popularly castigated as "primitives" and "brutes," but their work kept in touch with our changing culture. It reflected existentialism and the new interest in psychology—the creative powers of the unconscious mind. We now look at this artistic movement as one of the most important of this century.

Sculpture had tended to cling to traditional forms in the '30s and '40s, but some bright new sculptors were coming along as the war ended: David Smith, Louise Nevelson, and others. Alexander Calder, whose work had been known for some time, began doing his playful, free-spirited mobiles. In Britain, Henry Moore was taking off on objects found in nature, on people, on family groups. Picasso, now a grand old man, stirred with new interest in abstract sculpture. His wire constructions had an effect on all American sculpture—new materials and new techniques to express new ideas.

Benton's painting marks the beginning of his lifelong preoccupation with local Americana and his elevation of the common man to heroic scale. During the '30s, when artists inspired by American subjects developed three movements—urban realism, social realism, and regionalism—Benton traveled into rural America in search of its agrarian past.
Thomas Hart Benton. People of Chilmark. 1920. Oil on canvas, 5'5⁹⁄₁₆" x 6'5⅝" (1.67 x 1.97 m). HMSG.

Immigrant artists Mondrian and Lachaise had a great impact on American art. Mondrian took objective abstraction to its logical extreme by limiting his lines to vertical and horizontal strokes and his palette to the three primary colors, red, blue, and yellow, and the three noncolors, black, white, and gray. Lachaise created voluptuous sculptures of female figures as a loving tribute to his wife—a most petite woman.

Opposite: *Gaston Lachaise.* Heroic Woman. *1932, cast 1981. Bronze, 7'4" (2.24 m) high. Purchase with funds provided under the Smithsonian Collections Acquisitions Program, 1981.*
Below: *Piet Mondrian.* Composition with Blue and Yellow. *1935. Oil on canvas, 28¾ x 27¼" (73 x 69 cm). HMSG.*

Immigrant artists Arshile Gorky and Willem de Kooning developed the New York school of abstract expressionism after World War II, establishing New York as the art center of the world. Jackson Pollock emerged a little later and, before revolutionizing American art with his drip paintings in the late '40s, created paintings like Water Figure.

Above: *Arshile Gorky.* Composition. *c. 1938–40. Oil on canvas, 34 x 56⅛" (86 x 143 cm).*
Left: *Jackson Pollock.* Water Figure. *1945. Oil on canvas, 72 x 29" (183 x 74 cm).*
Opposite: *Willem de Kooning.* Queen of Hearts. *1943–46. Oil and charcoal on fiberboard, 46⅛ x 27⅝" (117 x 70 cm).* HMSG.

Balthus. The Golden Days. *1944–46. Oil on canvas, 4'10¼" x 6'6⅜" (1.48 x 1.99 m). HMSG.*

Max Ernst. Belle of the Night. *1954. Oil on canvas, 51 x 35" (130 x 89 cm). HMSG.*

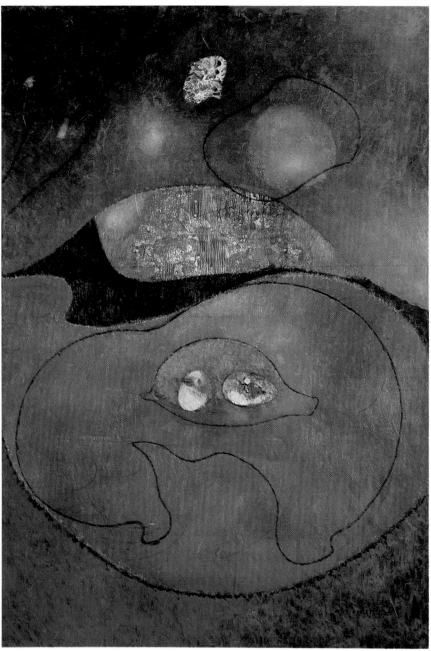

Above: *In the late 1930s Balthus began creating languid and sensual paintings of young girls awakening to sexual consciousness. In* Golden Days *he establishes a mood both erotic and detached.* Left: *Max Ernst, one of the leading surrealists, found unusual ways to create special effects in his paintings. The blue and white shapes in* Belle of the Night *have a strange, almost moon-rock texture that adds to the eerie quality of the painting.* Opposite: *In paintings such as* Delusions of Grandeur, *Magritte lured his observers into a disconcerting and uneasy world by deliberately choosing nondescriptive titles and placing familiar objects in unusual juxtaposition.*

René Magritte. Delusions of
Grandeur. *1948. Oil on
canvas, 39⅛ x 32⅛" (99 x
82 cm). HMSG.*

Joseph Hirshhorn collected many sculptures by European artists, among them Picasso, Alberto Giacometti, and Henry Moore.
Left: *Henry Moore.* Rocking Chair No. 2. *1950. Bronze, 11⅛ x 12⅜ x 3¼" (28 x 31 x 8 cm).*
Below: *Alberto Giacometti.* Dog. *1951, cast 1957. Bronze, 17¼ x 36¼ x 6⅛" (44 x 92 x 16 cm).*
Opposite: *Pablo Picasso.* Woman with Baby Carriage. *1950. Bronze, 80⅛ x 57 x 24" (204 x 145 x 60 cm).* HMSG.

229

Alexander Calder and David Smith, who
gained prominence as early as the '30s, are
widely recognized as the pioneers of 20th-
century American sculpture. Like Russian-born
Naum Gabo, they began to work with materials
new to sculpture and to use space as a vital
element in their constructions.

Above: *David Smith.* Aerial
Construction. *1936. Painted
iron, 10 x 30⅞ x 11½" (25 x
78 x 29 cm).* HMSG.

Above: *Alexander Calder.*
Stainless Stealer. *1966.*
Stainless steel and aluminum,
10 x 15 x 15' (3.05 x 4.57 x
4.57 m).
Left: *Naum Gabo.* Linear
Construction No. 2. *1949.*
Plastic with nylon thread, 15 x
11 x 11" (38 x 28 x 28 cm).
HMSG.

Known as the "Peashooter," the diminutive Boeing P-26A was the first all-metal monoplane adopted by the U.S. Army Air Corps and was the front-line fighter of the mid-to-late 1930s.

In the world of aviation, the war meant a solidifying of all that had been learned in the '20s and '30s. Hanging at the west end of the Air and Space Museum is usually (it sometimes gets rotated back to the Garber Facility) a tiny, chunky little monoplane with fixed landing gear and open cockpit, with the old Army colors, olive drab and gold. This is the Boeing P-26A, first line fighter of the early '30s. It was called the "Peashooter," and when the newsreel at the local movie theater showed a formation of these little planes, all neatly in position like West Point cadets on parade, many a youth in the audience decided he'd like to be one of those debonair pilots, goggles gleaming in the sun, white scarf tucked into leather jacket.

I wanted that. When I joined up I had the old vision still implanted in my head. Of course I never flew a P-26A because this was war, and the 1930s were gone forever. A few of these pretty little planes actually saw combat, flown by Filipino pilots in the first days of the Japanese attack. That was the end of them. I had to be content with a newer plane which was a little better than a P-26A, but not much. It isn't on display.

The World War II gallery at Air and Space is effective and remarkable—the mural alone is almost an entire exhibit. Keith Ferris painted this scene of a B-17 raid with such documented accuracy that families have appeared to stare at it and spot their son, brother, husband. The great treasure, I guess, is the Macchi 202, the Italian fighter. This is the only known survivor. But I, personally, look up at the Japanese Zero—the "Zeke"—with special feelings of my own. It's hard to realize that I am right beside one of them.

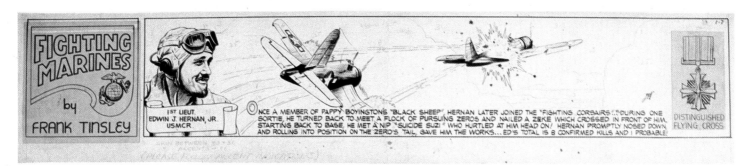

A Messerschmidt Me 163 Komet, top, *awaits restoration at the Air and Space Museum's Garber Facility. This stubby rocket-propelled fighter saw combat in the last days of World War II. A top speed of 600 miles per hour and high rate of climb made it a potentially formidable opponent of slower Allied aircraft. However, mechanical problems and a very limited fuel supply reduced its effectiveness. An Italian Air Force cap insignia and U.S. Army Air Force bombardier's wings,* left, *recall the human side of the WW II air war, as do the comic strip,* above, *and still life of flying memorabilia,* opposite. *Against a leather flying jacket are a pair of goggles, flying helmet, U.S. Distinguished Flying Cross medal, gauntlet, and cockpit clock.*

236

Air Force Captain Charles E. "Chuck" Yeager, left, *became the first pilot to break the "sound barrier" on October 14, 1947, flying the rocket-propelled Bell X-1,* Glamorous Glennis, below.

They were always bright, glimmering, dainty shapes in the sky, always above us, turning together when they saw us and diving on us, the gun flashes lighting their wings. For me, seeing this one is laying a ghost.

In the middle of the war I was with a handful of pilots who watched the Bell XP-59A, the first American jet, being tested. We have one, in Flight Testing at Air and Space. It was noisy and awkward, with frighteningly slow acceleration. We sneered at it. But we did so with the instinctive resentment of people who see the future arriving to shake up all the things they understand. We all knew our days were over, that a plane would soon crack the sound barrier, that man would make it to the moon. We figured, in our bull sessions, that a moon landing would be made around the late 1960s. Not bad.

Of course, while we were laughing at the XP-59A, the Germans were flying jets in combat. The sisters of the ME-262 jet fighter in the Jet Aviation Hall brought consternation to European skies in late 1944 and early 1945. Another harbinger of the future was the German ME-163, a *rocket*-propelled fighter so far ahead of its time that it didn't really work very well. (It carried only eight minutes of fuel.) Still, it saw service, presumably frightening its own pilots a little less than the Allied bomber crews it pursued. Swept-winged, tailless, bat-like, one sits on its handling dolly at the Garber Facility.

Among the Milestones of Flight is Chuck Yeager's orange Bell X-1, another rocket plane, named *Glamorous Glennis* for Yeager's wife. In it he flew faster than sound in 1947. He made the flight with a broken rib which he concealed from everyone. It hurt badly

Although the Bell X-1 Glamorous Glennis *made one takeoff from the ground, most of its 78 test flights were conducted after it was carried aloft and dropped by a modified B-29 bomber. The greatest speed achieved by the X-1 was 957 miles per hour.*

The North American X-15 rocket-propelled research aircraft were the highest and fastest flying airplanes ever built. Designed to fly at the upper edge of the atmosphere, they were equipped with both aerodynamic and reaction control systems, or "thrusters," like those used on spacecraft. Air-launched from a B-52 bomber, opposite, the three X-15s made 199 flights, during which they reached altitudes of over 67 miles and speeds of over 4,500 miles per hour. The workhorse of the program, X-15 number one, now hangs in the Air and Space Museum's Milestones of Flight gallery.

getting into the cockpit from the B-29 which dropped him, and he had to do many things with one hand that should have required two. But he made the flight. And from then on, space travel was only a matter of time.

And so we reach it at the Smithsonian: the X-15 flew six times faster than Yeager and touched the edge of space. Our Vanguard satellite, the size of a cantaloupe, finally followed our first satellite, Pioneer I, into orbit. The Vanguard at Air and Space was picked up off the ground when our first shot with the Vanguard failed and the rocket exploded. Then, close on the heels of pioneer cosmonaut, Yuri Gagarin, was Alan Shepard who got us into space; John Glenn had us orbiting; Edward White made our first space walk from Gemini 4; and then Apollo 11 landed us on the moon. You can see all of these spacecraft and more at Air and Space.

Some of the space treasures are huge and obvious. Skylab in the Space Hall dwarfs practically everything else in the building. Roughly 58 feet high and 21 feet in diameter, its main section had to be cut into three great slices to be brought into the museum. Its Airlock Module sits beside it on the floor and you can look at its surgical blue-white interior through a plastic window.

The Skylab itself is so big you can walk through it, and millions do. There always seems to be a line. Standing on the great spacecraft's eating and sleeping deck you can imagine the crew, weightless in orbit, sleeping upside down like bats—they did it sometimes. One Skylab astronaut called down to Houston one morning to remind his earth-bound colleagues that "we aren't like other men. We put our trousers on two legs at a time." And

Overleaf: *The Hall of Air Transportation spans the early days of open-cockpit biplanes to the aircraft that triggered the explosive growth in passenger travel: the Boeing 247 and the DC-3. Their direct descendants are the wide-bodied, comfortable jets that today speed air travelers around the globe.*

Top: *Known as the "father of modern rocketry," Robert H. Goddard poses with the world's first successful liquid-propellant rocket. Parts of this rocket are in the collections of the Air and Space Museum, as are Goddard's notebooks from which this photograph was taken. Launched on March 16, 1926, the little rocket traveled only 184 feet. Nonetheless, it heralded the coming of the Space Age. Above: Americans were chagrined on December 6, 1957, when the first U.S. attempt to launch a satellite failed as the launch vehicle exploded on the ground. Burned and battered but still beeping, the three-pound satellite was recovered from the wreckage. Today it nestles in Uncle Sam's hand in the Air and Space Museum's Apollo Hall.*

Left: *Rockets tower in the Air and Space Museum's Rocketry and Space Flight gallery. In the center is a Jupiter-C rocket like that used to launch the first successful U.S. satellite,* Explorer I, *on February 1, 1958. A Vanguard rocket like the one on the left propelled the second U.S. satellite,* Vanguard I, *into orbit on March 17, 1958, after an earlier Vanguard launch had failed. On the right is a Scout, typical of the vehicles routinely used to boost communications and scientific payloads into space.* Above: *Astronaut Alan B. Shepard, Jr., spent 15 minutes in space in the cramped interior of his Mercury spacecraft* Freedom 7 *during the first U.S. manned space flight, May 5, 1961.* Top: *A typical Mercury program space suit.*

looking up through the grill-work deck that separates the living area from one of the huge working areas, I remember the extraordinary films of Skylab astronauts performing weightless acrobatics, effortlessly tumbling, twisting, spinning from one wall to the other. Dreams of flight come alive. Nearby is the lunar module, LM-2, one of two remaining from the Apollo program. It's been covered with glittering, exotic plastic films, aluminum, and heat-resistant black nickel-steel alloy sheets to look exactly like the Apollo 11 lunar module that landed on the moon in July 1969. In the Apollo Hall is a main engine for a Saturn 5 moon rocket. It is surrounded by mirrors so that the whole complement of five engines that powered the monster rocket seems to be there. The engine developed over one-and-a-half million pounds of thrust. Launching one of those rockets was about the noisiest thing we humans have ever done, not counting nuclear weapons tests. Why, the propellant pump of the engine put out more power than the four main engines of a Navy destroyer.

It's almost a physical relief to go from that glittering hardware, built to pummel the senses with power, to the Art Gallery and on upstairs to Rowland Emmet's *S.S. Pussiewillow II*, endlessly waffling through space as its determined astronaut with handlebar moustache peddles away, and the little fringed

"Houston, the Eagle *has landed." The whole world was on tenterhooks as it waited for this radio message, surely one of the most momentous in history. At the Air and Space Museum, a lunar module cockpit simulator,* top left, *captures on screens in the triangular windows the moment when Edwin E. Aldrin, Jr., joined Neil A. Armstrong on the moon's surface, July 20, 1969. Meanwhile Michael Collins, later first director of the museum, circled the moon in the Apollo 11 command module* Columbia, bottom left. *In the museum's exhibit memorializing the event is the lunar module LM-2,* opposite, *used in the Apollo program's ground tests but never actually flown. A postage stamp,* top, *commemorates Armstrong's first steps on the moon.*

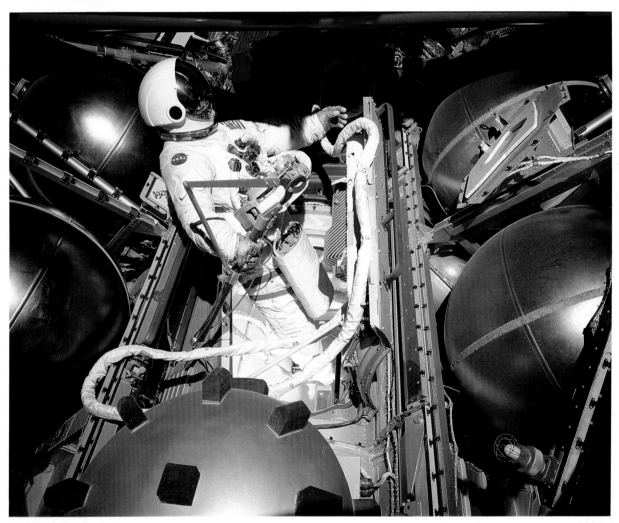

Glittering in its gold-hued Mylar plastic-film covering, an unflown, backup Skylab Orbital Workshop dominates the Air and Space Museum's Rocketry and Space Flight gallery, left. *Part of the Skylab's Airlock Module can be seen at the right of the photograph, and in the foreground stands a checkered German V-2 rocket. Over these hang two German World War II anti-aircraft missiles.* Above: *A spacesuited Skylab astronaut conducts an experiment outside the Airlock Module in the gallery's Skylab exhibit. A Skylab mission patch,* top, *recalls the heady days in 1973 when three crews visited the giant space station for a total of 171 days. Skylab was launched on May 14, 1973, and was destroyed in a fiery reentry into the earth's atmosphere on July 11, 1979.*

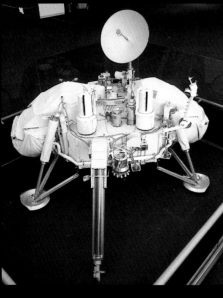

During the last three decades, unmanned spacecraft have served as extensions of our senses, probing our solar system and gathering more information about it than had all of previous astronomy. **Top:** *The back-up for the Mariner 10 spacecraft that sped by Venus and Mercury in 1974, transmitting detailed images of Venus' heavy cloud cover and the first close-up look at the surface of Mercury.* **Above:** *Two Viking spacecraft identical to this Viking test craft landed on Mars in 1976 to sample its atmosphere and soil and send back images of its surface. On-board biological experiments found no signs of life. The last Viking fell silent in November, 1982.* **Opposite:** *Voyager 1 transmitted this image of Jupiter's Great Red Spot, a permanent storm system larger than earth. Io, one of the planet's four major moons, orbits above the Spot and Europa, another moon, can also be seen.*

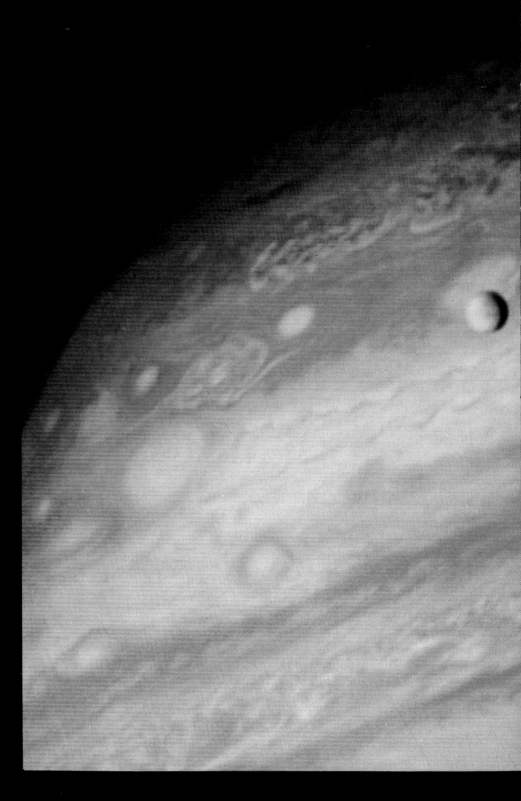

Jackson Pollock, who invented the phase of abstract expressionism called action painting, created paintings like Number 25 *by spreading his unprimed canvas on the floor and dripping diluted paint in broad gestures that vibrated with emotion. Hans Namuth's photograph,* **below,** *shows Pollock and wife Lee Krasner in 1950. After watching him at work, Frankenthaler developed Pollock's staining technique to produce wonderfully fresh and luminous paintings like* Basque Beach, *which in turn influenced the Washington, D.C. color abstractionists, Noland and Louis.*

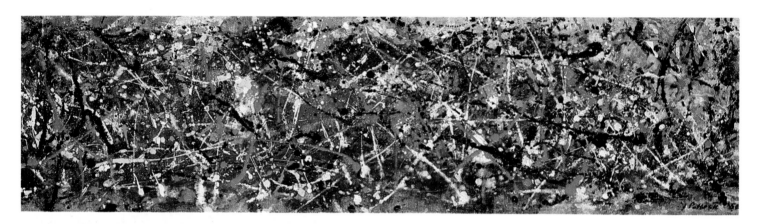

Top: *Jackson Pollock.*
Number 25. *1950. Encaustic on canvas, 10⅛ x 38″ (26 x 97 cm).* HMSG.

lamps dip and sway, and the flower petals open and shut, and the butterfly wings flap lazily. What a way to go.

Space, the concept of infinity, inspired some important art (not that Emmet's isn't; it is to me, all right!) by color-field painters like Morris Louis and Kenneth Noland. Their canvases with large areas of color appear vast and boundless to the eye. Through their dramatic use of color and abstract symbols, these artists are concerned with expressing one dominant, all-encompassing statement. As a contrast to the highly intellectual and, some thought, elitist art of the early abstract expressionists, the color-field painters flourished, especially in Washington, D.C., where both Louis and Noland began painting stained canvases in the '50s. Staining—eliminating the undercoat of priming and applying paint directly on the canvas, allowing it to absorb pigment directly—was something that had originated with Jackson Pollock. He, more than any other painter, radically rejected conventional easel painting with his drip method—flicking, dribbling, or pouring almost liquid color onto his canvas laid on the floor—existing for itself as a system of color, line, and rhythm. But it was Helen Frankenthaler who developed this technique and directly influenced Louis and Noland. The fluid, expansive, and flowering images that staining allowed is evident in Louis's *Point of Tranquility.* When school children are touring

*Kenneth Noland. Beginning.
1958. Synthetic polimer on
canvas, 7'6" x 8' (2.29 x
2.44 m).* HMSG.

Morris Louis. Point of
Tranquility. *1958. Acrylic on
canvas, 8'5¾" x 11'3¾"
(2.58 x 3.45 m). HMSG.*

the Hirshhorn they are often asked what Noland's *Beginning* reminds them of, and they inevitably reply, "the world spinning." Actually, the red-hot orange center is tied in closely with what Noland chose as his title: it's the beginning of the formation of the world. I like it.

The art of the '70s was more pluralistic than before, with a number of different tendencies prevailing. In an effort to get away from the illusion and metaphor of abstract expressionism, artists like Richard Estes focused on what was real. Look at his *Diner* at the Hirshhorn—it's so real you might think it's a photograph. Alongside this photo-realism or super-realism is the magic, intimate realism of William Bailey's *Still Life with Rose Wall and Compote*.

Illusion, however, did play a part. Al Held's *Volta V* falls under "abstract illusionism." As I understand it, it is an extension of abstract expressionism—but with a trick, geometric slant. The next time you visit the Hirshhorn take a look at this hard-edged painting—you'll find it's almost a trompe l'oeil.

Helen Frankenthaler. Basque Beach. *1958. Oil and charcoal on canvas, 4'10⅝" x 5'9⅝" (1.49 x 1.77 m). HMSG.*

Robert Motherwell. Elegy to the Spanish
Republic #129. *1974. Acrylic and charcoal
on canvas, 8 x 10' (2.44 x 3.05 m).* HMSG,
*gift of Joseph H. Hirshhorn by exchange and
Museum purchase, 1981.*
*One of the leading color abstractionists was
Mark Rothko, whose calm, hazy rectangles melt
and bleed into an ordered, atmospheric
environment. Robert Motherwell created a
fresh, dramatic poetry in his Elegies, a series of
almost 150 paintings, created between 1949
and 1976, that express his profound reaction
to the Spanish revolution.*

Mark Rothko. Blue, Orange,
Red. *1961. Oil on canvas,*
7'6¼" x 6'9¼" (2.29 x 2.06
m). HMSG.

Henry Moore and David Smith represent, respectively, high-water marks of British and American 20th-century sculpture. Moore used traditional methods in creating his figurative sculptures, working in plaster and then casting in bronze. Smith, who preferred to work with his materials directly, used plates and welded boxes of steel and stainless steel to create his essentially nonfigurative sculptures.
Left: *David Smith.* Cubi XII. *1963. Stainless steel, 109⅝ x 49¼ x 32¼" (278 x 125 x 82 cm).*
Opposite: *Henry Moore.* King and Queen. *1952–53. Bronze, 63½ x 59 x 37½" (161 x 150 x 95 cm).* HMSG.

Left: *Red Grooms.* Loft on 26th Street. *1965–66.* *Painted plywood, cardboard, paper, and wire, 28¼ x 65¼ x 28½" (72 x 166 x 72 cm).* Below: *George Segal.* Bus Riders. *1964. Plaster, metal, and vinyl, 5'9" x 3'4" x 6'4" (1.75 x 1.02 x 1.93 m).* HMSG.

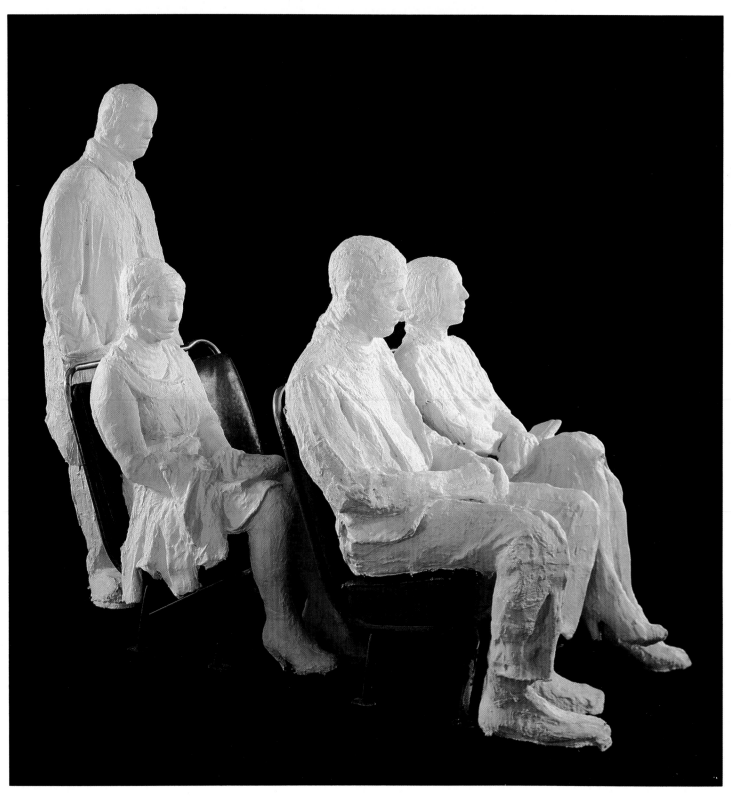

A new literalism emerged in the '60s, in part
as a reaction to the ambiguity of abstract
expressionism. We see its beginnings in the real
objects mounted onto the canvas of
Rauschenberg's Dam. It becomes more firmly
established by the time of Segal's Bus Riders
and Grooms's Loft on 26th Street several
years later. In the '70s it's taken to its extreme
in paintings like Estes' Diner, whose mastery
of detail has a photographic quality.
Above: *Richard Estes. Diner. 1971. Oil on
canvas, 3'4⅛" x 4'2" (1.02 x 1.27 m).
HMSG, purchase 1977.*
Left: *Robert Rauschenberg. Dam. 1959. Oil
and collage on canvas, 6'3½" x 5'1½" (1.92
x 1.56 m). HMSG.*

The soft, dreamy, almost magical realism of William Bailey's still life objects forms a definite contrast to the hard new realism of Estes' paintings.
William Bailey. Still Life with Rose Wall and Compote. *1973. Oil on canvas, 3'4" x 4'⅛" (1.02 x 1.22 m).* HMSG, *gift of Mr. and Mrs. Robert Schoelkopf, 1979.*

266

Left: *Beneath the bubbled roof of the Air and Space Museum lie the treasured machines that have helped us conquer the air and go far beyond. In the background is the National Archives Building.* **Below:** *Albert Einstein, engraved in glass after a photograph by Yousuf Karsh. National Air and Space Museum.*

Now, in the '80s, thirty-odd years after the '50s of Pollock and the others who recklessly shook a stodgy world with their art, we seem to be in a quieter time. Maybe it's the same with flight, too. The 1950s saw the arrival of the Jet Age and the Space Age, both revolutionary bursts of technological creativity. The big jets made air travel routine, and the Sputnik and Pioneer I spacecraft heralded the space Shuttles, the Mariners, the Vikings, and the Vanguards that have taken us away from the earth and revealed the awesome beauty of the solar system. Perhaps we're on a plateau now, in art and in flight, wanting for another burst. Creativity seems to work that way, with great leaps forward, flurries of action, vast upheavals followed by periods of refinement, adjustment to the new. We can't see what the next big steps will be. We only know that the rules will be changed again.

How possible it suddenly sounds when we recall the turn of the century, the time of Pablo Picasso and the Wright brothers, the raising of man's roof. ✳

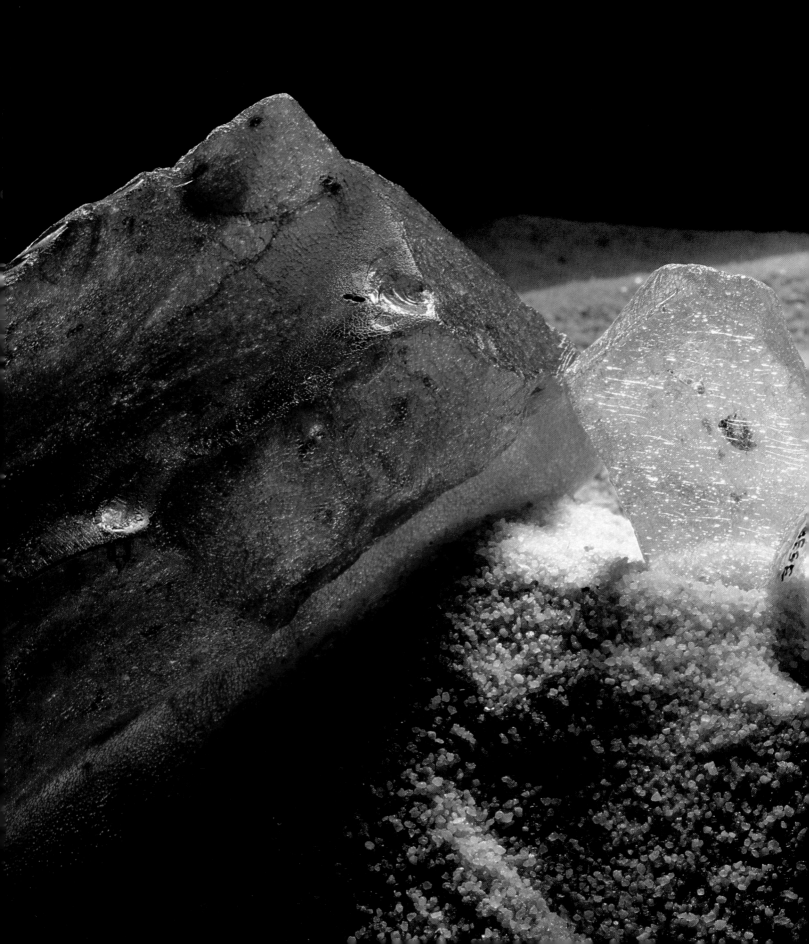

Splendors of
Nature

In the years that I have worked at the Institution I almost invariably get lost in the National Museum of Natural History. I have no shame, now, in asking a guard where the jade collection is, for example. And my self-esteem is fortified when the guard thinks, starts twice to tell me, stumbles over the directions and gets them slightly wrong. It matters little, since I know that if I aim at the jade with certainty in the first place, I will surely be ensnared by other delights along the way and forget my purpose. That's what a *good* museum does to you. And this one has been doing it for a good long time.

An official bulletin of 1913 describes the two-year-old Natural History building. Its photographs show a bison mounted in the rotunda, handsome display cases filled with ethnological material, long aisles lined with glass-protected tables bearing minerals and gems. An exterior shot shows a horse and carriage parked on Constitution Avenue (then B Street, Northwest) behind what appears to be an electric car.

The gray granite in the photographs seems stark and forbidding to us today. We are used to seeing the building draped with bright banners telling what special exhibit is offered inside. But a photograph of the central hall of the north wing shows walls and partitions richly hung with paintings—the art that was kept here in those days.

Then there's *Diana of the Tides*, a huge painting that is shown overlooking a large hall of fossil vertebrates. It had disappeared by the time I began wandering the museum. But, when that hall was redone in 1979–81 to become a new dinosaur hall, Diana reappeared. She had been covered over years ago and all but forgotten. I took an interest in her and found out a little about her.

An Englishman named John Elliott painted *Diana of the Tides* in time for the museum's opening. He was the son-in-law of Julia Ward Howe, who wrote *The Battle Hymn of the Republic*, and he painted in the illustrative style we associate with Maxfield Parrish and, to some extent perhaps, N.C. Wyeth (father of Andrew Wyeth). At that time books for young people had brilliant, splashy illustrations, often classically symmetrical—a huge Grecian urn on a marble stand overlooking a cobalt blue lake with bright mountains behind, reaching toward the tumbling clouds. Elliott's *Diana* is a little like that—four huge white horses pull her out of a foaming sea, and there are mountain cliffs beside the beach and a violet sky. She dwells in a world of mystery and excitement.

I found that Elliott was indeed infected by Parrish, having met him at the Cornish, New Hampshire, art colony of sculptor Augustus

"All creatures great and small"—or almost all—are somewhere to be found in the Natural History museum, including more than seven million beetles, a few of which are seen here, left, *and the world's largest stuffed specimen of an African bush elephant,* opposite, *which greets visitors entering the rotunda.* Overleaf: *Recovered from the shore of the Baltic Sea, these amber samples are over 38 million years old.*

Saint-Gaudens. Elliott was given a commission to paint the ceiling of the Boston Public Library. The head of the Library's trustees was Frederick Prince, a former mayor, and the grandfather of Norman Prince of the Lafayette Escadrille of World War I. During that war, Elliott painted young Prince and some of his squadron mates—we have those portraits at the Air and Space Museum. As they say, it's a small world, after all.

When the new dinosaur hall was completed, *Diana* disappeared again. To a storeroom somewhere? To tell the truth, she was walled up so that she could pop out at another generation of museum redesigners and have her long and, I suppose, pretty unimportant story retold. Perhaps the new discoverers will feel, as I do, that *Diana*, and the old book illustrators with their formal, yet untamed, world—squeaky clean and throbbing with challenge—evoke a special time in American history. We might as well label it the Time of Theodore Roosevelt, for I can't picture that period without the intrusion of his image. This was a time to meet a challenge head on and attack it as though it were the crest of San Juan Hill; to fight zestfully for the right; to proclaim your final triumph with delight.

He did like guns, and hunting also, and put them to work for science and for the Smithsonian. "Our aim being to cure and send home specimens of all the common big game—in addition to as large a series as possible of the small mammals and birds—it was necessary to carry an elaborate apparatus of naturalists' supplies. . . . We had hundreds of traps for the small creatures; many boxes of shot-gun cartridges, in addition to the ordinary rifle cartridges which alone would be

necessary on a hunting trip. . . ."

So, with barely concealed relish at the prospect of all that shooting, Theodore Roosevelt described the massive expedition he led into East Africa in 1909, at the end of his second term in the White House. As a final presidential gesture he had proclaimed 21 forest reserves for the U.S. Forest Service that he had created. And now he was free to roam the game trails with his son Kermit and a number of friends and naturalists. Preservation and hunting may seem unlikely companions among a person's interests. Not necessarily. Roosevelt was not alone in loving both and in feeling that both added weightily to his serious avocation, the study of natural history.

The Smithsonian sponsored Roosevelt's African safari, and he rewarded it with more than 12,000 specimens. In his account of the expedition, *African Game Trails*, Theodore Roosevelt lists 512 creatures "shot with the rifle" by Kermit or himself. Added to these were thousands of small mammals, fish, reptiles, insects, and plants taken along the way by the entire team. No wonder a newspaper cartoon of the day showed the Castle wellnigh buried under cases labeled "T.R." with a caption: "The East African express is arriving." As it happened, the specimens could be fitted into the Smithsonian's third building, the Natural History building of the United States National Museum, as it was so carefully called, completed in 1911.

This was a time for Peary to dash toward the North Pole and for Amundsen and Scott to race for the South. It was a time for youngsters to join the brand new scouting movement and for their elders to save the great trees of the West. It was soon to be a time when those gallant young men would fly primitive airplanes for France. Their commitment—all too often leading to their death—came straight from the hero of their youth: it was based on moral assurance, enthusiastic concern, eager participation.

The Natural History building was built at a time when the Smithsonian was gaining an average of about a quarter-million new items a year—most of them natural history specimens. The new edifice on the Mall eased the cramp like the next size in shoes, for it had wide spreading wings with what seemed like ample space for storage as well as display. The Smithsonian's art collection, now housed in the National Museum of American Art, was moved into the Natural History building along with the well-established Bureau of American Ethnology.

Theodore Roosevelt's African animals seemed a drop in the bucket. Yet the fine new building kept attracting specimens like a magnet, and its space was exhausted by the early 1960s when almost a million new items showed up, on the average, every year. Some collections were huge. The Lepidoptera collection alone contained more than three-and-a-half million specimens of butterflies and moths. New wings were built, new floors for storage added. The art collection moved to its own gallery in the old Patent Office; the National Museum of American History rose on the Mall to further ease the pressure. But the major relief seems to be the Museum Support Center on the outskirts of Washington. In 1983 its four massive storage bays, each almost the size of a football field, began to take the overload from the Mall museums. Natural History is the building that benefits most.

This great building with its splendid dome crowning the rotunda—where the world's largest stuffed specimen of an African bush elephant greets visitors—is, along with the Museum of American History, one of the Mall's most bewildering and fascinating mazes.

Just meandering along, with no fixed route in mind—even if I could remember one exactly—I might bump into a Steller sea cow. This great sirenian (member of the order Sirenia) used to inhabit Alaskan and Russian waters, but this largest of all sea cows was hunted to extinction within 25 years of its discovery in 1741, by sailors from sealing and sea otter vessels. The blue whale may be following, at a slower pace, down this dismal route of untimely extinction.

In the Life in the Sea gallery, where we keep our life-size model of a big blue, I walk through under the gracefully curving bulk of this great whale. Up on the wall near the whale's head is a fourteen-and-a-half foot black marlin, a model (as are most mounted fish) of the 1,560-pound fish caught by Alfred C. Glassell, Jr., off Cabo Blanco, Peru, in 1953. For many years it was the largest bony fish on record ever caught with rod and reel. It may be yet.

Entering the rotunda from Life in the Sea, I pass the immense African bush elephant and wind my way back through the Asian and African galleries into the Ice Age. Here I make the acquaintance of North America's own elephants, the extinct mastodons and mammoths. If there's anything that you learn in the Museum of Natural History it is that the constellations of living species are always changing. In some eras even more extinction was going on than in our own rapacious

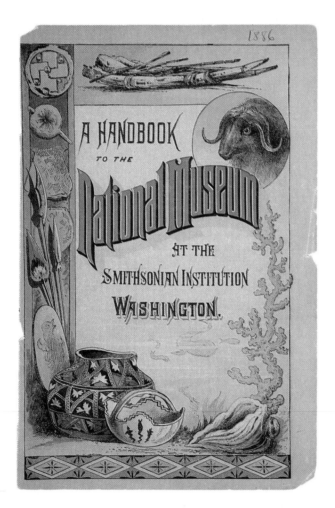

By the time this guidebook to the National Museum—now called the Arts and Industries Building—appeared in 1886, more than two million specimens had filled the building to overflowing, indicating even at this early date the need for a new facility.

times. One of those epochs about two million years ago in which many of today's familiar mammals including our own *Homo sapiens* evolved, is termed the Pleistocene. Scientists speak of a great wave of extinctions here that accelerated at the end of the last Ice Age.

And it was those very early Americans, descendants of the Asian patriarchs who crossed by the Bering land bridge, who last saw the mammoths alive on this continent. Today the anthropologists are hot on the trail of these ancients who tracked the New World pachyderms that survived until the glaciers retreated for the last time, leaving an open, essentially modern continent.

The Smithsonian's anthropologists inhabit offices on the third floor of the Natural History Museum, that is whenever they are at home. The field is their hearts' home and they bring back the artifacts and documentation from cultures and civilizations as far removed as those of the ancient American Indians and of today's few remaining Micronesian navigators. Their work eventually makes its way down to the display halls on the first and second floors or is pored over elsewhere for research purposes. I especially like the Hall of the Native Peoples of the Americas. Here are the adaptations, cultural and environmental (can the two even be separated?), of peoples from Alaska to Mexico, from Massachusetts to Oregon. I always stop at the exhibit of the Eskimo in his kayak, shielded from Arctic spray in his parka of seal gut, the strips sewn with tiny, uncountable, waterproof stitches. A little farther along, you can peer into an Arapaho tipi, the "Centennial tipi" acquired for display at the Philadelphia Centennial Exposition of 1876. It may be

the oldest complete Plains Indian tipi around. Outside the entrance hang the owner's shield and weapons, decorated with feathers and leather fringes. He sits inside, facing the entrance across the fire, holding a long pipe. To his left is a male guest. His wife and a female guest are to his right. One of his children beckons to us from the doorway.

As I continue down the hall, rounding corners, poking into niches, a thousand articles of daily life—clothes, weapons, tools, pots, baskets, religious objects—speak to me of myriad ways of life, some of them so long lost that these are the only relics of an existence.

Somewhere between the carved ivory figures of Ellesmere Island and gorgets from the earthen platforms of the Mound Builders, I'm swept along with a rush of visiting youngsters. These teenagers, and I'm not really surprised, are too interested in their buddies, sweethearts, and the group itself to pause for long before any exhibit or artifact.

Yes, the generations are changing. The museum has always been a Happy Hunting Ground for these little roving bands of adolescents. But I wonder if today they ever thrill to the old trumpets and challenges of the past. I wonder, well . . . what they might think of Theodore Roosevelt.

Big, gleaming teeth. Thick neck. Glinting spectacles. Exuberance. Energy. Force. Rightness. No, I don't remember him—he's one of the few American institutions I am too young to recall. But my generation grew up in his recent shadow. I read his autobiography in school, assigned as an inspiration toward vigorous courage and zestful involvement. The writings of his friends Rudyard Kipling and Owen Wister were read aloud to me. I tried,

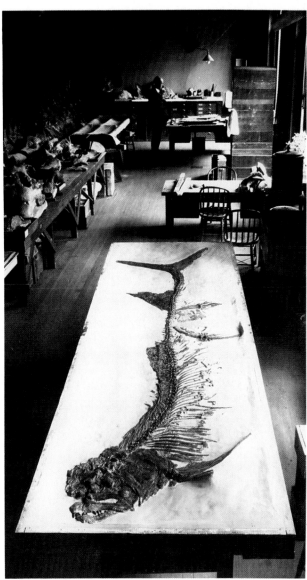

Fossil bones, such as those of this large fish, were treated and assembled at this vertebrate paleontology laboratory, photographed in 1926.

A newspaper cartoon dated August 25, 1909, pokes fun at the burial of the Smithsonian Castle by a shipment of specimens from the Roosevelt African expedition.

mightily, to do my best in sports, taking heart that Theodore Roosevelt, too, had been a wispy, underweight little boy. I learned about birds and insects and could walk quietly in the woods. I hunted woodchucks and squirrels. I fished New England lakes and streams. I wanted to be a natural historian—and more!

Being at that bloodthirsty stage so many boys seem to go through, I thrilled particularly to stories of Theodore Roosevelt hunting big game animals, beloved .405 Winchester model 95 in hand. Bears especially. There was much publicity given to Roosevelt on the trail of bears "out West." One thinks of bears and Roosevelt together, partly because he looked sort of bearish; partly, I suppose, because of the teddy bear named after him (we have one of the originals, made by the Ideal Toy Company in 1903, over at the Museum of American History). Standing in the North American Mammal Hall and looking at the grizzly bear diorama, or in the evolution exhibit looking up at the awesome polar bear towering over me on his hind legs, I still feel a little of the old childhood thrill. I like to think of Theodore Roosevelt as a matchless example of unflinching courage. Of course, he had that rifle when he faced his bears. Eskimo hunters had only spears or bows and arrows when they hunted the polar bear or other large game. They knew very well what a fearsome adversary the white bear was, and carved little images of him in ivory, which were sometimes used as a charm to insure success or provide protection when hunting this fierce mammal.

By going out Connecticut Avenue to the National Zoological Park, you can see real, live polar bears, all three of them. They often sit sleepily in the sun, seemingly jovial and harm-less enough. But if you watch for a while, one will get up suddenly, fluidly, and plop into the water with effortless strength and speed, and you know it wouldn't do to be in there with them. Not at all. Or you can watch the Atlas lions. Basking or playing on their hillside, they seem to give the lie to talk of their nearness to extinction. Go see them on a cold day, when they are active. They sometimes bat each other ponderously with giant paws, or mouth each other, expressing their feelings with those grunts and roars that come from deep within their chests.

At the entrance to the museum shop of the Museum of Natural History you can see the fine display of a charging tiger, the great animal caught in mid-flight, claws unsheathed and ready to sink into its unseen prey. That's rather a sobering picture of tiger-might. But at the zoo, the famous white tigers may well be playing with their toys in the water-filled moat, splashing each other like kids as they hurl them about.

Those white tigers, whose grandparents were acquired in the 1960s from an Indian maharajah, constitute a special treasure of the zoo. So do the pandas, of course. They have been an unmatched attraction, though their fame probably rests as much on their amatory awkwardness as on their rarity.

Some time ago, on a cold day, I went to report on a VIP visit to the pandas and, waiting for the official cars to arrive, sought warmth in the nearby elephant house. There I met Shanthi, then only three—perhaps the most charming three-year-old I ever knew. She and her big friend Ambika were performing elephant salutes in unison, each raising her trunk to her forehead and lifting one huge foot.

Garbed in safari attire, Theodore Roosevelt struck this dignified pose during his celebrated African trip.

About 1903, the Ideal Toy Company got President Roosevelt's permission to name their new line of stuffed "teddy bears" after him. This lovable toy, now at the American History Museum, is one of the first bears made by Ideal.

Left: *Collections at the Natural History Museum attest to the incredible diversity of life on earth. The Lepidoptera collection alone has more than three-and-a-half million moths and butterflies, of which a small sampling is illustrated here.* **Above:** *The division of fishes preserves most of its specimens in jars filled with an alcohol solution.* **Top:** *Ornithologist and Secretary S. Dillon Ripley catches up on research in his own laboratory at the museum. He has made significant contributions to the bird collection since the 1940s.*

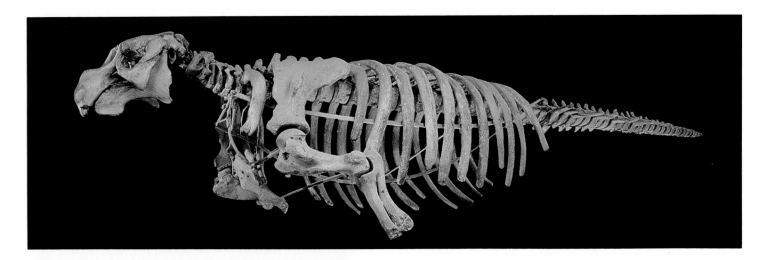

The Steller sea cow, above, once hunted ruthlessly to extinction, looms over the hall of Osteology. This specimen was assembled from the bones of several different individuals which were discovered by Smithsonian scientists on Bering Island in 1880–90, more than 100 years after the last of this species had disappeared. Another extinct species, the American mastodon, left, disappeared about 10,000 years ago from the woodlands of North and South America. This specimen in the Ice Age hall towers over the skull of a fossil beaver, which is displayed, by way of comparison, with a modern beaver.

The Anthropology Department has an extraordinarily diverse collection of artifacts used by early man in America. Left: *The six-inch carved wooden feline figure was made for ceremonial functions by an obscure people living in Key Marco, Florida, about 1200–1500. Although it looks somewhat Egyptian or Meso-American, no relationship between these cultures has ever been discovered.* Opposite: *For centuries, the Southwestern cultures have lived in adobe pueblos, practiced simple farming, and made pottery, such as this Sikyatki ceramic vessel,* top left, *from Arizona, c. 1300. Shell ear spools from the mortuary temple mound at Spiro, Oklahoma,* top right, *date from c. 1250, and were worn for personal adornment and to symbolize status. Recovered from a burial mound in Ohio, built by the Hopewellian Mound Builders, this stone disk,* center, *with its dramatic image of a hand, is similar to later ones, which were used as paint palettes, although the exact purpose of this one is unknown. It dates from roughly the first or second century.*

Overleaf: *An array of spear points from the Agate Basin site in Wyoming gives anthropologists clues as to how early man hunted 10,000 years ago. Such points were attached to wooden spears, which were then hurled at bison already entrapped in canyons or small waterholes.*

43126
Mound Naples Ill
J.C.Henderson

The artifacts illustrated here
offer glimpses of life as it once
was lived by several North
American Indian cultures.
Above, left to right: A mid-
19th-century Sioux horse's
bridle or headstall used for
ceremonial occasions; a
feathered gift basket decorated
with clamshell beads and
abalone-shell pendants by the
Pomo Indians of northern
California; pottery birds from
the Zuni of New Mexico, left,
and from a Pueblo tribe, right,
for use possibly as toys or for
religious purposes. Left: The
carved wooden owl mask is
worn by the Tlingit of Sitka,
Alaska, in their ceremonial
dances.

Above, left to right: *A beaded pouch fashioned by either the Seminoles of Florida or the Creeks of Oklahoma for carrying small items such as tobacco, face paint, or travel food; a water jar decorated with a parrot motif by the Acoma of New Mexico—a particularly fine example of the potter's art, dated about 1885; shaman's rattle from the Tsimshian Indians of British Columbia, carved to illustrate a legend about the coming of toads and frogs with the rain. Right: An "olla" or water cooler made by the Pima of Arizona.*

Tucked in behind the galleries of Indian cultures is a small yet splendid exhibit of some of the gifts given to the United States by Thailand (Siam) over the last 100 or more years. Above left: President Franklin Pierce was presented this teapot inlaid with gold and black enamel in 1856. Above right: Beautiful handwoven silks represent a traditional form of Thai craftsmanship. Left: Its inscription commemorating the 1873 coronation of King Chulalongkorn, this vessel cover made of black lacquer and mother-of-pearl inlay depicts the Hindu god Indra's elephant. Opposite: This early 20th-century robe of 12-carat gold thread was worn on ceremonial occasions by the Thai ambassador to the United States before it was given to the Smithsonian in 1947.

Above: *Fine pieces of ivory carved by Eskimos and now in the Natural History Museum's collection include, clockwise from top: a tube adorned with carved human figures used for storing sewing needles; another needle case in the shape of a flask; a float handle used in hunting sea animals; a handle for a woman's workbox; a thread spool or reel; another float handle; a harpoon foreshaft.* **Left:** *Ivory cord attachers with carved animal and human faces held lines to kayaks. Smiling men and frowning women were images commonly found on sea hunting equipment.*

Left: *Common to Eskimos throughout the Arctic, waterproof garments such as this parka, made of either seal or walrus gut, were often worn by men when they went hunting in kayaks. The gut was soaked, scraped, inflated, dried, and, in this case, bleached in the sun. It was sewn with the seams on the outside, probably for waterproofing, and decorated with fur and with crested auklet feathers and beaks.* **Below:** *Eskimo men made a variety of wooden articles for themselves and their wives. The serving dishes and ladle illustrated here are decorated with mythological creatures, hinting at the pervasive influence of the spirit world on the Eskimos' lives. The man who carved the seal box may have used it for lance points, tobacco, or trinkets.*

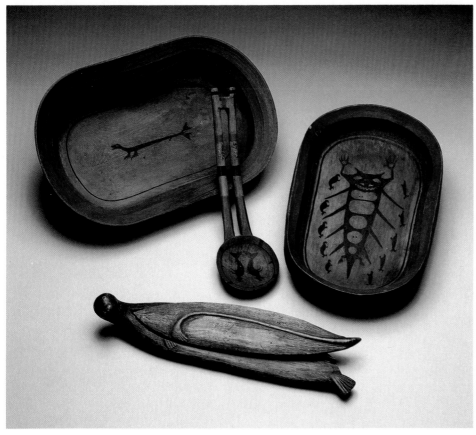

Their keeper, sharing a general Smithsonian feeling that the pandas get a disproportionate amount of attention, was determined to lure a few glances away from the panda compound and toward the elephant yard. So he had been teaching them this gesture of greeting and respect.

The VIPs arrived, the Secret Service cooped up all the journalists in a sort of corral so that we could watch the VIPs watch the pandas, cameras whirred as the pandas appeared and sat down to munch bamboo. I looked around toward the elephant yard and there were Shanthi and Ambika, trunks raised, feet lifted, as nice as could be.

I was the only one who saw them. Quietly I returned the salute.

Shanthi is pretty well grown now. I doubt if I'd know her. That's the way it is at the zoo—you can't label certain creatures as your favorites because they are always growing and changing and finally dying. But I will always be delighted by memories of the otters endlessly playing in Beaver Valley, of ostriches mating in the spring—an epochal sight!—of a certain patriarchal Barbary ape who stalks through his "turf" with the assurance of a gangland chief, looking neither right nor left as females and youngsters clutch each other and scamper out of his way. I love the stories of the elephant who was given a trayful of experimental hydroponic hay for her lunch, and wore it on her head like an Easter bonnet, of the boss gorilla who watched soap operas on television. Or of Ham, the chimpanzee who preceded all of our astronauts into space with his 1961 Mercury flight. He died in January 1983, in North Carolina where he had gone to live after his long stay at the zoo. We still have his spacecraft and flight couch in the Air and Space collections.

I wander into the free flight aviary, a soaring structure of arches and netting where you can stroll about under a variety of relatively unfettered birds. One of my favorites is the Inca tern, which raises its young almost every year from its nest tucked away in a rocky crevice within sight of curious visitors like me. Inside the aviary I am calmed by the soft cooing sounds of the Chinese necklace doves, and delight in the graceful soaring of silver gulls swooping high over my head.

These birds are treasures, and so are certain splendid places in the zoo. Recent improvements—they go on all the time—include a magnificent bird house, a newly renovated Reptile and Amphibian House, an ultramodern Monkey House where, as a zoo director noted, the monkeys are insulated by glass from the noise and smell of humans, a separate, new Ape House, Beaver Valley, William M. Mann Lion/Tiger Complex with its

Striking an impressive pose, a polar bear at the National Zoological Park rears up on hind legs to survey its surroundings. The three polar bears at the zoo spend a lot of time in the water, especially in summer, to escape the midday heat of Washington, D.C.

The diversity of life at the National Zoo can be
seen in this parade of animals and places.
Clockwise from top left: *A pygmy
hippopotamus; an Asiatic elephant; a
sunbittern with young; a short-tailed bat; two
young white Bengal tigers.* Opposite,
clockwise from top: *Three gray seals; the
great flight cage, home of about 20 species of
birds; Hsing-Hsing, male giant panda; green
tree python hatching from an egg; infant
golden lion tamarin; American flamingos.*

moat, and the Education Building, the zoo's headquarters where children of all ages learn to love their fellow creatures.

If you become discouraged about Washington, about the dealings of political leaders, about the lobbying of special interest groups, about the carefully maintained self-importance of so many people, go visit my friends at the zoo. About human importance, political clout, pomposity . . . about all that, frankly, they don't give a damn.

Theodore Roosevelt again played a minor role in helping to get the National Zoo started. Theodore Roosevelt, as a devoted hunter, was quick to realize—with horror— that his game targets were diminishing. He formed the Boone and Crockett Club of rich and influential friends and acquaintances to preserve wilderness and wildlife. It would be a cheap shot to say that he did this in order to have something to hunt. As one of his foremost biographers, Edmund Morris, says, "Ironically, he had always been at heart a conservationist. At nine years old he was 'sorry the trees have been cut down,' and his juvenile hobby of taxidermy, though bloody, was in its way a passionate sort of preservation." As founder and first president of the Boone and Crockett Club, he set up a committee which threw its weight behind the zoo concept by supporting legislation creating the National Zoo in 1889.

Since its earliest days, the Smithsonian had been given wild animals—a photograph shows bison grazing on the Mall outside the Castle— so an early population was on hand for the new zoo. Breeding certain endangered species, however, has more recently become an important purpose of the Institution, and as the pandas have shown, breeding in captivity isn't easy. So, in the 1970s, when the Smithsonian obtained a 3,140-acre chunk of glorious Blue Ridge Mountain scenery already owned by the government, we gratefully snapped it up. Here at the Conservation and Research Center at Front Royal, Virginia, a number of exotic animals and birds, some just hanging on the edge of extinction, are given the room and the care to help maintain their species. Père David's deer from China, Eld's deer from Southeast Asia, European bison, scimitar-horned oryx (an African antelope), Persian onager (a wild ass from Iran) have huge paddocks to call their own in a superb environment. All of these hoofed animals are given plenty of privacy. And they breed. Front Royal now provides zoos worldwide with these and other endangered species.

Smaller, more delicate species—maned wolves, crab-eating foxes and others—are cared for indoors in the cold mountain wintertime and sometimes watched by closed-

This young double-wattled cassowary hatched from an egg that was laid at the National Zoo, then shipped to the Conservation and Research Center at Front Royal, Virginia. The National Zoo often sends bird eggs to Front Royal where sophisticated incubators and brooders help to ensure healthy chicks. The cassowary is quite rare in captivity, though still plentiful in remote parts of its native New Guinea and northern Australia. Overleaf: *Two zebras—a mother and her foal—are caught in a restful pose at the National Zoo.*

Left: *Persian onagers, an endangered species in their native Iran, graze in spacious outdoor quarters at the Conservation and Research Center in Front Royal where more than 20 of these animals are being bred successfully.*
Above: *Researchers work at the Front Royal facility during the spring and early summer studying the breeding habits of some of the animals. Here they observe a male Père David's deer.* **Top:** *Front Royal's resident mammalogist, Larry Collins, tries to stay on friendly terms with a young Matschie's tree kangaroo so that he can study its habits at close range.*

A young girl at the Insect Zoo tentatively admires a hissing cockroach, one of several insects children can hold here—under the supervision of trained volunteers.

circuit television when they produce young, since their extreme sensitivity wouldn't stand for human intrusion. And I am happy to say that *they* are breeding, too. One reason for this establishment's success is its seclusion, its freedom from human observation.

The Institution has another zoo—a small one—right within the Natural History Museum. This is the Insect Zoo, a Smithsonian inspiration. You enter the room to a pleasant sound—the amplified chirps and creaks of insects. And then you are faced with cases of live insects and their relatives. You can watch them gnaw their way along a leaf, wreaking the destruction that sometimes haunts gardeners. You can see the stages of their growth. You can witness the daily feeding of a tarantula. The great, hairy creature is brought out in its plastic box. The lid is carefully removed—enough for a grasshopper to be shoved inside—and then closed again. The danger doesn't come from the tarantula, which, according to its young volunteer guardians, bites about as badly as a ferocious wasp or a feeble hornet, but from the fact that if the creature gets out, onlookers will move back suddenly and perhaps knock over a case. When I've watched the feeding, the tarantula paid no attention to his proffered meal. He was as finicky as a spoiled cat. However, I'm told that, in my absence, he usually does eat at the appointed time.

There is another living exhibit at the museum, to my mind the best of all the galleries. Entering the Life in the Sea gallery from the rotunda, you face a green-yellow wall of glass, a source of shimmering illumination that lights the faces of the constant crowd standing, enthralled, before it. This is the world's first captive coral reef—alive, self-sustaining. That glass wall is the side of a 3,000-gallon tank, 12 feet long, 6 feet high. Waves crash into it on the left in an apparently irregular rhythm, spilling random amounts of water as they would in nature. The foaming surges sweep against the steep left-hand face of the reef—the ocean side. Bubbles whirl down and

Among the more than 40,000 orchid plants grown in the Smithsonian's greenhouses are these two delicately shaped specimens: below, Oncidium barbatum *from Barbados;* bottom, Telipogon sp. *from Colombia.* Overleaf: *The lush interior of one of the eight greenhouses maintained by the Smithsonian's Office of Horticulture on the grounds of the United States Soldiers' and Airmen's Home in northwest Washington, D.C.*

across the coral. Fronds wave languidly in the current, and brilliant little reef fish dart about feeding on whirling particles.

The reef is topped by a zone called the reef crest that is partially exposed at "low tide." Animals that can endure a lot of wave action and sunlight live here. On the other side, the reef slopes gently down on the right, then wide pipes lead to an extension of the tank where part of the water—500 gallons—lies still, practically unaffected by the waves. This, of course is the lagoon. Small fish live here and emerge, under the cover of darkness, to feed. That way, they avoid being attacked by a barracuda or a snapper.

Above the whole display are mounted 14 metal halide lamps, blazing in a simulation of tropical sunlight. They come on, one by one, in the morning and turn off gradually at sunset time. Temperature is carefully maintained. So is the salinity of the water.

In fact, the maintenance of the coral reef display is in itself an adjoining display. Around the corner from the tank wall, a picture window opens onto a working laboratory where people can watch lab assistants checking their graphs and gauges and making necessary adjustments. And beside that window is a movie screen where the whole process of gathering the coral and the reef life is explained. Probably nowhere else in the Smithsonian is the James Smithson tenet, "increase and diffusion of knowledge," made so obvious to us laymen.

The originator of this tank—and of a new one containing a cold-water environment with kelp and lobsters—is Dr. Walter H. Adey. He had tried several times to keep coral alive in an aquarium and finally learned that life could be sustained by an "algal lawn"—a film of different kinds of algae on the reef's surface. The organisms grow by utilizing the filtered light for photosynthesis. They absorb wastes. And then, in turn, fish feed on the algae, completing the food cycle.

Adey's lawn can be applied anywhere. Barren stretches of open ocean could be made

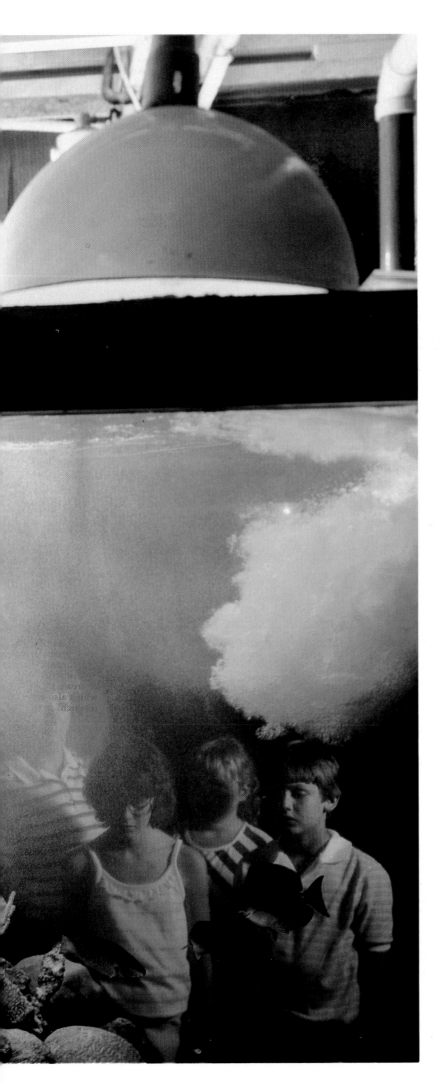

productive by using the technique. Says Adey, "Large scale harvesting devices can be applied to millions of miles of now unused ocean." On a museum scale, the Adey system has been duplicated (under his supervision) at the St. Louis Zoo and at the Pittsburgh Aqua Zoo.

The tiny organisms of the coral reef live, breed, and form the food chain of their small, wet world. Their concerned deities, the lab assistants, leave them pretty much alone, only interfering in the ecosystem to remove the occasional fish that has grown too big for that confined environment.

In the same museum we can see how the same sort of organisms lived much the same way millions of years ago. These fossil creatures appear to have been similar to the species down in the reef, but they lived out their eons and then became extinct, and all we have is their remains in rocks—their fossils. Trilobites, for example, once must have been as common as crabs in the Chesapeake. They were bottom crawlers and swimmers with bodies that had, as their name suggests, three longitudinal lobes and a number of segments, some with pairs of legs. You might say they just about owned the world half a billion years ago, but they're long gone now.

The coral reef exhibit, left, *fascinates visitors in the Life in the Sea hall, and, as the first such living ecosystem ever installed in a museum, it has drawn the widespread interest of marine biologists as well. Overleaf: Brought back from Mayaguana Island in the Bahamas, this specimen of lettuce leaf coral is a particularly fine example of the species, found in abundance throughout the shallow waters of the Caribbean.*

A spectacular array of ancient giants fills dinosaur hall, opposite. Diplodocus, *center,* looms over the skull of Triceratops, *foreground. A reconstruction of* Stegosaurus *is at far right, while above it are* Edmontosaurus, *foreground, and* Albertosaurus, *rear. Suspended overhead is a pterosaur.* Right: *Outside the museum, the ever-tolerant* Uncle Beazley, *a 22-foot-long fiber glass model of* Triceratops, *continues to delight scores of clambering children.*

Dinosaur hall, with its 90-foot-long *Diplodocus longus,* is the Smithsonian's spectacular exhibit of the Mesozoic era—which you will find graphically defined on the 27-foot-tall Tower of Time that greets visitors to the hall. *Diplodocus* was excavated in 1923 by renowned dinosaur collector Charles Gilmore for the Carnegie Museum of Pittsburgh. The big bones, representing parts of two individuals, came to the Museum of Natural History through an exchange of specimens and were assembled to make one enormous, reasonably complete skeleton. You can motor to the discovery site, Dinosaur National Monument, near Vernal, Utah, and watch paleontologists quarrying more of these great reptiles. But in 1923, all 36 crates of *Diplodocus* bones, 25 tons of them, had to be hauled in freight wagons nearly 200 miles to the nearest railhead. *Diplodocus* presides over smaller, but often fiercer, reptiles, some displayed as skeletons, some reconstructed in habitat groups. A massive skeleton to one side of the hall is *Triceratops,* a horned 20-odd-foot-long beast of a kind that flourished at the end of the dinosaurs' day on earth. Outside, on the Mall, stands a life-size fiber-glass reproduction of a *Triceratops.* He's called "Uncle Beazley" and he has patiently endured thousands of children climbing over and between his great horns.

Back in the hall, over them all soars another restoration, the pterosaur—not a bird, not a plane, but a flying reptile with a 40-foot wingspan. Museum experts fabricated it from knowledge gained from some strategically located fossil bones, plus a large amount of educated guesswork. I like its scientific name, *Quetzalcoatlus northropi,* referring first to the sacred plumed serpent of the ancient Toltecs

of Mexico and then to that experimental plane, the Northrop Flying Wing (we have one in the Air and Space collection).

The whole room is a treasure. But near the entrance to it, almost overlooked, are three panels that tell the story of the museum's greatest fossil treasure, the Burgess Shale. The center panel depicts underwater life in that distant Cambrian period, the time of the trilobites. These appear, also worms and algae and sponges. Also other things we don't really know much about.

They are presented as though they were under water, going about their business on a sloping mud bank at the foot of a submerged cliff. Now, occasionally, we are told, the mud bank would collapse on them, roiling them up and trapping them, carrying them down the sloping seabed to a region where they were isolated from oxygen and scavengers, enclosed in soft mud that did not destroy even the softer-bodied creatures.

The two flanking panels show the fossils that reappeared half a billion years later, with traces of those early creatures etched on black shale. It's not the sort of exhibit that will make your toes twitch with excitement unless you're a paleontologist. But in their significance the Burgess Shale fossils rank with the Rosetta Stone and Dead Sea Scrolls.

In 1909, while Theodore Roosevelt was on safari, Dr. Charles Doolittle Walcott, Secretary of the Smithsonian, took a summer trip to the Canadian Rockies, an area where he had enjoyed good luck in finding traces of the Cambrian, the period that he, a noted paleontologist, had become so expert in that he seemed to his colleagues to "own" it. The story goes that his horse stumbled, he dismounted, and

saw a piece of dark shale. With his usual instinct he cracked it open, and there were fossils that he, a careful scientist not given to easy enthusiasms, found "very interesting."

For in the shale were soft-bodied creatures that had never before been found as fossils. Also, there were enigmas—a little three-inch animal that had inched across the sea bottom and had five eyes and grabbed its food with a single, claw-like apendage; another smaller thing that had walked on seven pairs of stilts and had small rod-like things waving above its back. They look as though they belonged in some other galaxy, but no. They were once ours, fellow earthman.

The seabed where these creatures—some 140 species—had lived uplifted through the millenia to become a slab of shale in the Canadian Rockies about 7,000 feet up. Walcott knew that there was a wide belt of the Cambrian in the region, so he had his eyes open for likely looking rock. The Burgess Shale was thick enough for him to set up a sort of quarry operation to which he and his expeditions—including his sons—returned year after year. Go see—and stand in awe.

One of Walcott's sons, incidentally, was shot down while flying for France. Not in the Lafayette Escadrille, but in another squadron of

Left, top: *Charles Doolittle Walcott, paleontologist and Secretary of the Smithsonian, digs for fossils at the Burgess Shale in Canada, a site he discovered in 1909. Two Burgess Shale fossils, stilt-legged* Hallucigenia, center, *and* Opabinia, bottom, *bear little resemblance to modern phyla. Above: Charles Walcott's wife Mary painted these wildflowers while accompanying her husband on a scientific expedition to western Canada:* Menziesia glabella *Gray on the left;* Campanula rotundifolia *Linnaeus on the right. Opposite: This mass of tiny fossils is from the Glass Mountains of west Texas. Smithsonian scientists G. Arthur Cooper and Richard E. Grant have been working with such fossils for years. Seen here is the triangular shell of a brachiopod, surrounded by a mass of bryozoans, marine invertebrates of the Permian period.*

young Americans in what was called the Lafayette Flying Corps. Though personally stricken by the death of his boy, Walcott maintained a strong interest in flight during his years as Secretary.

About a year after Roosevelt's African safari and Walcott's discovery of the Burgess Shale, a very rich and rather spoiled young American couple, Evalyn and Ned McLean, were on a pleasantly free-spending holiday in Paris and were visited by the famed jeweler, Pierre Cartier. He showed them a fabulous dark blue diamond, the Hope, which, he said, had a history of bad luck. That was enough to intrigue young Mrs. McLean. She didn't take the bait immediately, but when Cartier persuaded her later to take it for a weekend and wear it around, she was hooked. Ned McLean bought it for $180,000, meticulously paying it off for a number of years. When Evalyn Walsh McLean died, her jewels had to be sold to pay off debts and claims. Harry Winston, the New York jeweler, bought them all. In 1958 he

gave the Hope to the Smithsonian because he felt the United States should have a first rate gem collection. And so you find it in its central glassed vault in the Hall of Gems—the fabled, glittering Hope diamond.

The stories about it are marvelous. Here is the general idea: The Hope originally was part of the eye or forehead of an Indian idol. A merchant ripped it out and apparently sold it to Louis XIV, the Sun King. The merchant was torn apart by wild dogs, and the Sun King died in agony and disgrace. Louis XVI and Marie Antoinette inherited the stone, then believed to be part of the French crown jewels. They died on the guillotine. A Dutch diamond cutter recut the stone, producing what is now the Hope. He died of a broken heart after his son stole the Hope. The son then killed himself.

There's more. There was a French princess who got ripped to shreds by a mob; a diamond broker who went mad; a Folies-Bergère beauty who got shot; a Russian or East

Left: *Since ancient times, the opal has been admired for its beauty, but not until rich fields of this gem were discovered in Australia in the late 19th century did it gain widespread popularity and commercial appeal. These black and white opals from the Smithsonian's collection are fine examples of those found in Australia.* Opposite: *Probably the most famous diamond in the world, the Hope is renowned both for its long, somewhat embroidered history and its remarkable dark blue color. It was given to the Smithsonian in 1958 by New York jeweler Harry Winston.*

European prince who was stabbed. All presumably because of something to do with the notorious diamond.

Sad to say, the stories are largely bunk. Cartier may have spun some of them, and Mrs. McLean, who loved a drama in which to star, undoubtedly polished and embellished them. Certainly there are gaps in the gem's history, but no special run of bad luck seems to have dogged it. The Hope family lived happily with it for generations, although the last to inherit it, Lord Francis Hope, did go broke—but this was because of his lusty penchant for the gaming tables, not because of a hex brought on him by the diamond.

Evalyn Walsh McLean lived with her fabled trinket in amiable informality, wearing it almost constantly except for the times she supposedly pawned it with her friendly hock shop to get a little pin money. She lent it to brides for their weddings ("something borrowed, something blue. . . .") and gave it to her baby son to cut his teeth on. When visiting Walter Reed Army Hospital during World War II, she allowed wounded soldiers to toss it from bed to bed. And the story is told of her misplacing it one day, then suddenly, and dramatically, remembering where it was. She opened the window, shouted "Mike!" and in the door bounded a huge Great Dane with the priceless necklace around his neck, the blue diamond thumping against his chest.

Part of the magic of the Smithsonian display of great jewels is the juxtaposition of these fabulous treasures with the raw stones that come from the earth. Most of the latter are in the adjoining Hall of Minerals. But only 20 feet or so from the Hope is a superb diamond in the rough. It gives you an idea of what to look for next time you visit Johannesburg or the deserts of Western Australia.

But the chances are you won't look for these wonders because you know that the market is all sewed up. And you probably won't go on an African game safari—at least not the gun-toting kind—because you are concerned about keeping the few remnants of African game alive and well. You probably won't even scale the passes of the Canadian Rockies, splitting rocks to see what you can find. It's all been found, you say to yourself.

So the time of Theodore Roosevelt is over. The enthusiastic probing of the earth's wilds and wonders, the arduous expeditions with pith helmet and double-barreled elephant rifle, the squelching through tropical swamps in big leather boots with soft folds at the ankles, the pack trips through the mountains with geologist's hammer and a skillet for sourdough—all these are done with.

And yet. . . . Go to NASM. Go see the moon rocks. You can touch one at NASM, but

Fine quality emeralds occur naturally as a gem variety of the mineral, beryl, left. Their transparent, rich green color comes from traces of chromium. These well-formed crystals are from Colombia, where the world's finest emeralds have been mined for over 300 years. One of the most exquisite pieces in the National Gem Collection is this necklace, opposite, adorned with 336 diamonds and 15 emeralds. According to legend it was worn at the Spanish court in the 15th century during the time of the Inquisition. Although a few of its stones date back to this era, experts question the legend because some of its gems are much more modern. The exact date and history of the necklace remain a mystery.

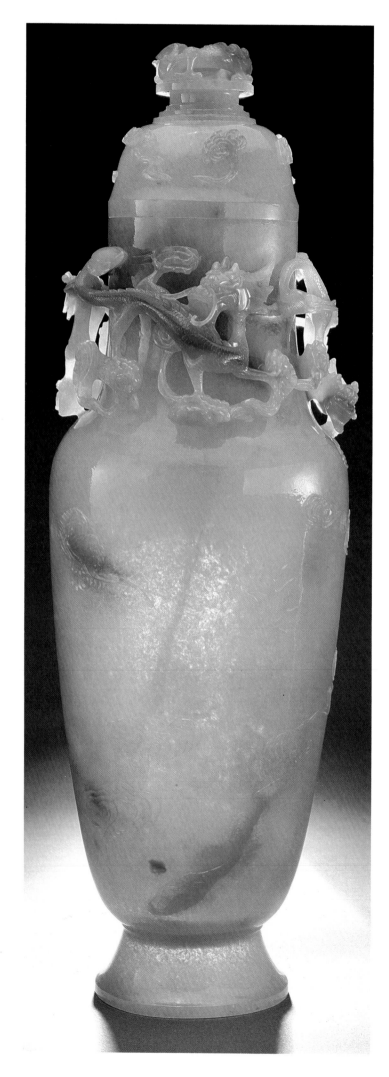

Above: *These richly hued bowls were carved from semiprecious minerals by George Ashley of California. Clockwise from top: Agate, malachite, agate, chrysocolla, binghamite, nephrite, and center, jasper.* **Left:** *A polished cross section of a liddicoatite crystal reveals striking geometric design and color patterns. Liddicoatite is a member of the tourmaline family and is found only in Madagascar.* **Far left:** *This 14-inch high Jade Dragon Vase is carved of a rare quality of jade in a traditional Chinese style. Though the carving is modern, its exact origin is unknown. It was given to the Smithsonian by Marjorie Merriweather Post.*

Overleaf: *Two specimens of pyrite, the one on the left covered with multifaceted quartz crystals, illustrate some of the more popularly known minerals in the gem collection.*

Vastly abundant, as commonplace as the beach sands of which it is often the primary constituent, quartz sometimes grows in spectacular groups of multihued, large crystals. Opposite: *Lavender-hued rose quartz crystals encircle a Brazilian quartz specimen.* Below: *Mexican amethyst crystals, another variety of quartz, reveal the orderly molecular structure common to all minerals.* Bottom: *Called the Candelabra, this piece from California consists of three minerals: white quartz, blue-capped red elbaite, and tan albite.*

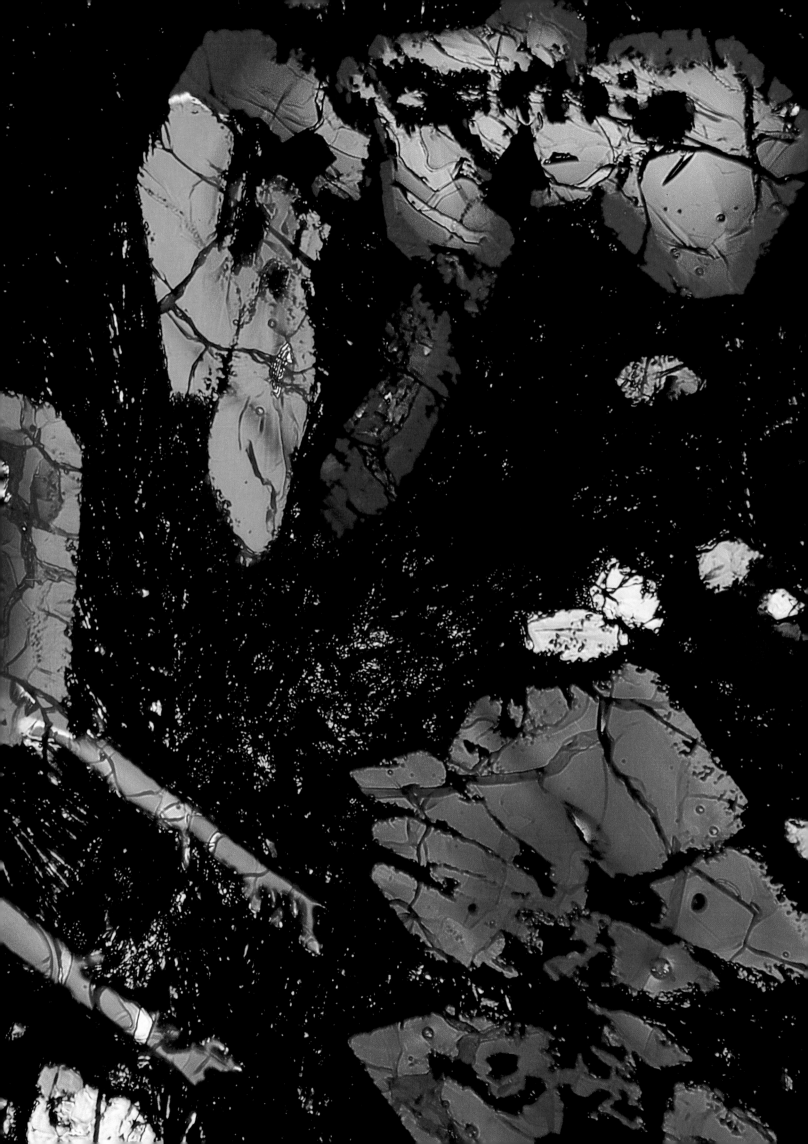

frankly, it feels just like a rock. You'll learn more from the exhibits in Natural History. Study the meteorites.

Think about the Allende whose age may be greater than that of our solar system. Brian Mason, a curator of meteorites at the Smithsonian, has recently come into possession of many exciting new finds from Antarctica. Somehow they got deep-frozen down there and concentrated in fields of blue ice. Because of these new specimens the history of our solar system and of our universe is becoming a little clearer right this very minute.

Since I've just hinted at it, and almost let the cat out of the bag earlier, maybe it is time to reveal the best-kept secret in the place, the Smithsonian in general and the Natural History museum in particular. However big and enthusiastic the crowds out front, the real, scientific heart of the museum beats behind the scenes—with a small army of geologists, mineralogists, botanists, ornithologists, paleontologists, and anthropologists all engrossed in their particular fields.

I well remember a moment in company with Richard Grant, a paleobiologist and Smithsonian's "King of the Glass Mountains."

Opposite: *A photographer's polarized light imparts dazzling color to a magnified gray mass of lunar rock brought back to earth by Apollo 15 astronauts and believed to be about 3.3 billion years old.* Right: *Colored spotlights heighten the pattern of an iron meteorite (siderite) that has been polished and acid-etched to reveal its crystalline metallic structure.*

We and his assistants watched as a metal tray of delicate fossils, cast by nature in hard but brittle silica, emerged from the acid bath. The corrosive liquid had dissolved a limestone deposit that had both imprisoned and protected the delicate remains. Grant and other Smithsonian researchers, building on the pioneer work of Dr. G. Arthur Cooper, have long mined the Glass Mountains of Texas to learn of life in ancient seas.

There is still excitement in discovery. There is still room on the earth for enthusiasm. Even out in the Mexican mountains there are rare and valuable species of wild corn that need to be saved from the encroaching plow. Many of the big breeders of hybrid corn will tell you just how valuable a new wild species can be when it comes to saving a whole crop, for instance, from a new blight. And there are plenty of wild animal species that need rescuing, along with their habitats—the challenge is immense. There are even coral reefs to build.

In a way, the challenges may be greater, and are probably much tougher. They are certainly quite different. Yet I can't help feeling that if Theodore Roosevelt were alive today, he would still find it a bully world. ✴

Princess From the
Land of Porcelain

Chinoiserie doesn't quite qualify as a portmanteau word. Yet its commodious recesses can hold all the curios, both ridiculous and sublime, from the Celestial Empire. In centuries past, Chinese artistic influence spread toward Japan, and with the Mongols through Central Asia, India, and Persia as far as Mother Russia. Kublai Khan sent a cultural armada with gift crockery to East Africa. His treaties of friendship didn't last nearly as long as the dishes—whose shards are still found scattered upon far shores.

Gradually, chinoiserie completely conquered Europe, including Britain, and thus many colonial outposts as well, including our American ones. The influence has persisted for centuries. In Europe especially, artists explored the designs, ornaments, and philosophies of the East. They also paved the way for a growing appreciation of Turkish, Egyptian, Indian, and Japanese art. So, we find, chinoiserie goes right in our bag with all the fans and screens, metalwork and jade, calligraphy and swords and ceramics from the Far East, closer parts of Asia, and even North Africa. Those caravans really got around.

We also gain the impression that Oriental objects aren't always possessed by their owners, the owner often being owned by his objects. But, then, reciprocal possession is always a fact of life with the great collectors and collections. Take, for example, Charles Lang Freer of Detroit, Michigan, and the museum on the Mall in Washington, D.C., which bears his name and the fruits of his acquisitive labors.

I never found Freer, or his collections, especially accessible until I pondered that word chinoiserie. To enter Freer's halls is to enter his special world by a door not only into the long hidden East but into the exotic artistic milieu of turn-of-the-century Europe. Freer and his special era both perished shortly after World War I. Stuff right out of Galsworthy and Henry James.

Freer's own gallery is neither the richest nor the largest when it comes to Oriental art. The Victoria and Albert in London has acres and acres more. The Metropolitan in New York certainly holds more, and Baltimore's splendid Walters Gallery rivals us in terms of the number of artifacts on display. But for aura, mystique, and faithfulness to an era, it's hard to top the Freer. The man himself calculated it that way, hedging in his bequest to the country with ironbound rules and regulations, protocols and procedures to assure that his personal influence would last and last.

In the process, the prim old Freer takes on sensuality—the kind that clings to the Peacock Room, the fixture of many a European schloss and chateau where the master traditionally installed his mistress and arranged his dalliance. Many visitors sense this voluptuous undercurrent from times-gone-by.

The pictures and captions that accompany this chapter speak well enough for valuables that can sit for a photograph. But Charles Freer and his era—his time capsule—comprise a special treasure that is totally intangible. It is an aura, a feeling of a long ago and faraway time. And it's carefully ensnared in the legacy of the Freer Gallery.

Any avid collector with taste and resources is apt to collect a few people along with many objects. Thus in our roundabout way we come to James McNeill Whistler, his name forever associated with a portrait of his mother. But he was also a man who had an eye for Ori-

Overleaf: *James McNeill Whistler.* Caprice in Purple and Gold, No. 2: The Golden Screen. *1864. Oil on wood panel, 19³/₄ x 27″ (50 x 69 cm). FGA.*
Whistler painted his mistress and model, the redheaded Irish beauty Jo, as she gazed at Hiroshige prints, surrounded by Oriental objects.

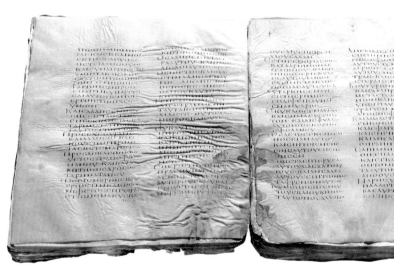

On his travels to the Far East, Freer usually stopped in Egypt. The Cairo dealer with whom the bearded Freer is drinking coffee, above, *may well be Ali al-Arabi, who sold him four Biblical Greek manuscripts—the* Epistles of St. Paul, *the* Books of Deuteronomy and Joshua, *the* Four Gospels, *and the* Book of Psalms. *Extremely important to Biblical scholars, they probably originated in a Greek monastery in the fourth or fifth century.* Left: *The* Books of Deuteronomy and Joshua, *written in dark brown ink on thick parchment made mostly of goatskin.* Top left: *In the seventh century, painted covers were added to the* Gospels *manuscript, showing the Evangelists in the order in which they appear within: Matthew and John (almost obliterated) on the front cover, Luke and Mark on the back.*

ental style, design, and color, which helped him forge an alliance with Freer.

Funerals are always splendid places to begin a good story. We can get acquainted with the living while we reminisce about the dead—in this case James Whistler. Charles Freer had made the necessary arrangements and served as a pallbearer at the small funeral of his good friend in London. The year, 1903.

It was quite in keeping with Whistler's life that few people showed up to see him off on his final venture. Proud, combative, lightning-fast with a lawsuit and snail-slow to forgive, the great artist never suffered friends gladly. Acquaintances, yes, by the score; sycophants, yes: never too many for his taste; elegant personages to crowd his salons and be entertained by his restless wit, yes indeed. But friends, no. Freer was one of the few.

Whistler had burst upon Victorian London like a sharp gust in a calm—a slight, swaggering figure, sporting a monocle and a slender, overlong cane. As an artist he was no easy member of any school, but hewed to his own rules and flew at his critics in a rage. He scoffed at the academicians of the British art world as he did at generally accepted standards of behavior. He affected long hair, jet black except for an odd feather of white, which he carefully preened into prominence—a sort of highlight to match the bright sheen of his tight patent leather shoes. "A mean, nagging, spiteful sniggling little black thing," an English novelist called him.

Yet even the nobility waited on him, arriving for one of his famous Sunday breakfasts (brunches, we would call them) to eat his strange, American buckwheat cakes, and cooling heels for two hours while the diminutive maestro sloshed in a hot bath. He practically invented la vie bohemienne.

What in the world was a nice, normal American millionaire from Detroit like Charles Freer doing with a man like that?

Whistler's style of painting was affected by the Pre-Raphaelite movement that was all the rage in London at that time. But he was also much enamored of the Japanese prints he had come across as a student in Paris in the early 1860s. Freer met Whistler and asked his advice about collecting art. Whistler told him to look for Japanese and Chinese objects and paintings. Freer was grateful; Whistler was flattered. Although he made a big thing of eschewing friendship (he was writing a book, *The Gentle Art of Making Enemies*), he liked this unpretentious industrial baron who showed such enthusiasm combined with good taste. Whistler, for all his popinjay manners, bristling conceits, and studied eccentricities, took art very seriously and professionally. When someone asked him for help in that area, he

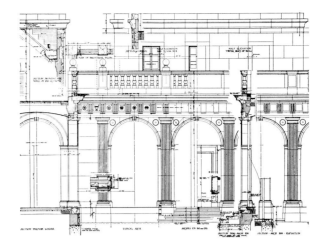

gave it honestly and generously.

Freer had lived out the Horatio Alger theme, starting with little, working hard as a youth, becoming noticed by an older man of influence, moving onward and upward. He rode the railroad boom of the 1870s and '80s. He arranged the merger of 13 railroad car companies which became the American Car and Foundry Company (still a biggie on the stock exchange). By 1890, he was rich enough to travel and to indulge his interest in art, and by 1900 at age 46, he was able to retire and devote himself completely to his collection. He had bought some Whistler etchings and later arranged to buy at least one copy of every new one Whistler produced. He also bought, a year after Whistler's death, the artist's most spectacular and controversial achievement: the Peacock Room. This Victorian dining room, completely assembled at the Freer, is the focal point of the gallery and one of the great treasures of the Smithsonian.

The tale of the Peacock Room opens with one Frederick R. Leyland, who, like Freer, was a self-made man. He had all the careful dignity of one who had hauled himself upward into social prominence and financial power. Leyland had risen from office boy in a shipping firm to become head of his own shipping company. As haughty and saturnine as he may have been, he—again like Freer—had a deep interest in collecting art and his tastes were refreshingly nonacademic. He was devoted to the art of the Pre-Raphaelites.

Frederick Leyland had bought a home in London, a town house he wanted to redo to resemble the residence of a Venetian merchant prince. Architect Norman Shaw and his workmen soon swarmed over the place, enriching it with pendant lights, carpeting, panels for a staircase. Whistler was asked to paint designs on those panels, and he did so— they're now at the Freer. Then he was asked for advice about the decor of the dining room.

Leyland wanted the dining room to show off his collection of blue-and-white porcelain and to provide a space on one of the end walls for Whistler's *Princess from the Land of Porcelain*, which he had acquired. Leyland also wanted to use leather wall coverings. He had bought some very old Spanish leather and prized it. Some said it had belonged to Catherine of Aragon—the first wife of Henry VIII. Anyway, with all those requirements, the dining room was turned over to Tom Jeckyll, a young architect and noted wrought-iron designer working with the team. He saw a chance to get ahead and worked very hard on the project. Then Whistler was eased into the picture as an adviser.

He immersed himself in the project of the dining room. He painted it, trimmed the car-

Above: *Every evening as he sat down to dinner, Leyland faced these bridling peacocks—Whistler's crafty last word on their quarrel. The peacock on the left had become Whistler, poor but proud; the one on the right Leyland, greedily clutching his gold and silver.*
Far left: *James McNeill Whistler.* Portrait of F. R. Leyland: Arrangement in Black. *1873. Oil on canvas, 75⅞ x 36⅛" (193 x 92 cm). FGA.*
Whistler labored many months over his Velázquez-like portrait of Leyland. The legs gave him so much trouble that he finally had a nude model pose for him. Leyland called the portrait "my own martyrdom."
Left: *Henri Fantin-Latour.* Portrait of Whistler. *1865. Oil on canvas, mounted on an aluminum panel, 18⁷⁄₁₆ x 14⅜" (47 x 37 cm). FGA.*
This is actually a fragment of a much larger painting, most of which has been destroyed.

pet, painted over the leather, repainted, lost himself in it. And all with only sporadic supervision from Leyland who was away on business most of the time.

Friends of the artist came to call and found that the room, with work in progress, was now a Whistler salon. The artist, spotted with paint, his hair twinkling with bits of gold leaf—for he had decided to liven up the turquoise blue he had chosen for the leather with gilded peacocks—greeted guests exuberantly, even dancing among the paint pots with one blue-blooded lady. An American journalist dropped by and found him "flat on his back, fishing-rod in one hand and an enormous eyeglass in one eye, diligently putting some finishing touches on the ceiling, his brush being on the other end of the fish-pole. Occasionally he would pick up his double glasses, like some astronomer peering at the moon, and having gained a near and better view of the effect, he would again agitate the paint brush at the other end of the long pole."

Mysteriously, the Peacock Room became Whistler's room. When Leyland finally was alarmed enough at the reports to come and have a look, he blew up at Whistler for going so far beyond "advice." Whistler told him he would be forever famous as the owner of the Peacock Room; Leyland asked for Whistler's fee to get rid of him—he was already facing a pile of bills (gold leaf, for example) and the ruin of his antique leather—and Whistler named two thousand. Guineas, that is—a guinea being the pound and a shilling that professional people traditionally were paid. Leyland offered him a thousand pounds— plain old pounds—which was how tradesmen were paid. Whistler went wild at this neat and effective insult—just the sort he liked to fire off at other people himself. He had done a wall panel for one end of the room—opposite the site where the portrait would hang— which showed two peacocks battling each other. The story goes that while cleaning up his mess and gathering his gear he found time

to touch up one of the peacocks with gold coins, making it a symbol of arrogant wealth, and to add silver coins under its feet—supposedly the extra shillings that Leyland had withheld from the fee.

How Leyland allowed Whistler to get away with that final artistic sally is unclear, for Leyland was in no mood to let him stay around. Even Mrs. Leyland, whom Whistler adored, deserted him. Apparently she overheard him dismissing her husband as a parvenu, and she threw him out for good. He didn't see the Peacock Room again while Leyland was alive.

Leyland, for all his anger, kept the dining room just as Whistler had left it, the *Princess* at one end, the fighting peacocks at the other—where Leyland was supposedly reminded of the Whistler touch every time he dined. After Leyland's death in 1892 the portrait was sold, and the house, with the room unchanged, finally went to Mrs. James Watney (Watney's Ale).

After Whistler died, Charles Freer went after the painting, then the room. Fortunately, the construction technique allowed it to be disassembled and reassembled easily. It was set up in Detroit, then, after Freer's death in 1919, in the Washington museum that he had bequeathed to the nation.

Left: *Whistler wanted to create the proper setting for* Rose and Silver: The Princess from the Land of Porcelain, *his portrait of Christine Spartali, daughter of the Greek consul-general in London in the 1860s, which Leyland had hung over the mantelpiece in his dining room. What began as a little touching up to the room turned into a radical transformation that has since become the focal point of the Freer Gallery—the Peacock Room. When asked if he had thought to consult Leyland on the changes, Whistler replied, "Why should I? I am doing the most beautiful thing that has ever been done, you know—the most beautiful room!"*

Entering the Peacock Room today, after going through the bright, skylit oriental galleries is like coming into a shady glen on a warm and sunny day. Green is the most restful of all colors to the human eye, and turquoise is really more green than blue—at least to my unqualified eye. The feeling of the room is dark and shadowy, but not gloomy, for the golden peacocks dance in the vision, strutting on closed window shutters and the broad panelling of that end wall where the two birds are caught in a moment of combat. The pendants of the ceiling seem almost fluid. They originally held gas lamps, later electric ones.

I always feel I have taken a giant step backward in time, and of course I have, for the Peacock Room is the 1870s, more ornate and yet more serene than anything I have experienced in the 20th century. I have stepped into a time of elegantly bustled and parasoled ladies, and gentlemen with pipestem trousers and intricate whiskers. I can almost hear costers shouting their wares outside those shutters, and I find myself wondering where the street arabs will sleep tonight. I know, however, that all's well with the Empire, for Mr. Disraeli is safely in charge, and Gilbert and Sullivan are at work on their sixth opera, *Patience,* a tuneful and hilarious gibe at the Pre-Raphaelites.

I remember *Patience,* with its long-haired poets carrying drooping flowers in limp fingers. Embracing the Pre-Raphaelite craze, one of them describes himself as:

"A Japanese young man—
A blue-and-white young man. . . ."

and in the context of this room the words make abundant sense. Blue-and-white por-

Katsushika Hokusai. A Courtesan. *Edo period, late 17th–18th century. Color and ink on paper, 27¹⁵/₁₆ x 9⁷/₁₆"* *(71 x 24 cm).* FGA.

336

celain was to line these walls, and as for Japanese, look at Whistler's figure, *The Princess from the Land of Porcelain* and then visit the display of Japanese painting and see Hokusai's *A Courtesan* from the Edo period. The geisha has a distinctive sigmoid curve: hips thrust forward, shoulders back, neck forward. And the *Princess* has almost exactly the same (rather unhealthy) posture.

It was really Whistler's friend, Oscar Wilde, who Gilbert and Sullivan were teasing in *Patience*. Also Algernon Swinburne, of course. But Oscar was deeply involved in the Whistler salons, and the two traded quips which were eagerly reported in the press:

OSCAR (after a Whistler *bon mot*): Jimmy,
    I wish I had said that.
JIMMY: You will, Oscar, you will.

So Freer sought the American art and artists of his time. But the great bulk of his collection of more than 26,000 works of art is Oriental, going back some three or four thousand years, and the building that holds them is sort of Italian Renaissance on the outside and delightfully Oriental in its sense of lightness on the inside. The Freer is a famous research establishment—a facility where Oriental art scholars can lose themselves in esoteric projects without hindrance. And what objects for study and just plain viewing! Charles Freer became an extremely informed collector and a connoisseur of the traditional arts of Asia. As you will soon discover for yourself, he found treasures from China, Persia, Pakistan, India, Turkey, Japan, and Korea.

Mori Sosen. A Peacock. Edo period, late 18th century. Color and ink on silk, 39¹¹⁄₁₆ x 15⁵⁄₁₆" (101 x 39 cm). FGA.

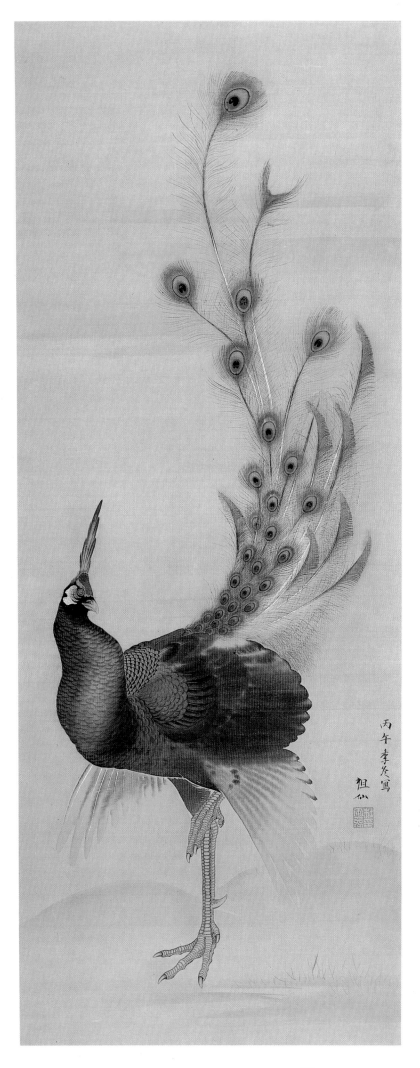

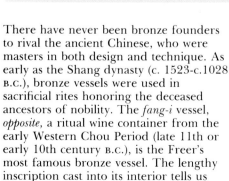

This little acrobat balancing a bear on top of a pole is another special bronze from the Freer. Dating from the fifth century B.C. during the early Warring States period, this piece was cast at a time when figural sculpture was unusual in China, a time when the Chinese were more comfortable depicting animals than humans.

There have never been bronze founders to rival the ancient Chinese, who were masters in both design and technique. As early as the Shang dynasty (c. 1523-c.1028 B.C.), bronze vessels were used in sacrificial rites honoring the deceased ancestors of nobility. The *fang-i* vessel, *opposite,* a ritual wine container from the early Western Chou Period (late 11th or early 10th century B.C.), is the Freer's most famous bronze vessel. The lengthy inscription cast into its interior tells us that it was commissioned by the annalist Nieh-ling, who was serving in the palace of the Duke of Chou during the reign of King K'ang. The ceremonial bronze weapons, *above,* dating from roughly 1000 B.C., are thought to be relics from the tomb of Marquis K'ang, Prince of Wei. The top weapon is a battle-ax (*ch'i*), the bottom one a dagger-ax (*ko*). Both weapons have iron blades—and yet there is no record of iron being used in China until 400 years after these were made. Freer experts have determined that this particular iron is of meteoritic origin: it fell from the sky, making the blades unique now and in their own time.

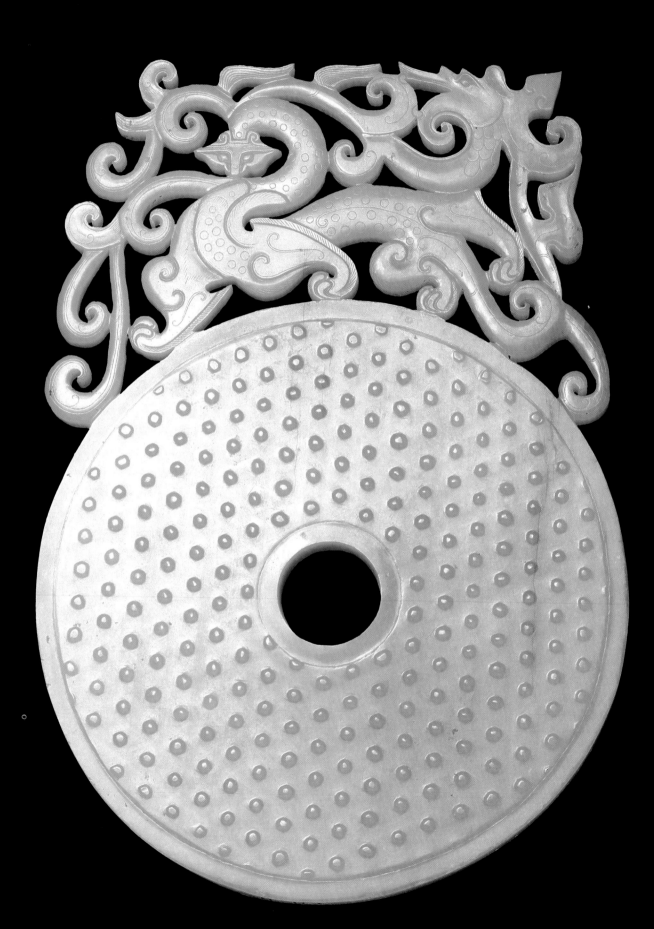

A symbol of beauty, intellect, and purity, jade has been worked in China for almost 7,000 years. Because jade is too hard to carve and has to be worn away by abrasion, early craftsmen painstakingly ground moistened quartz sand into it with simple tools made of wood, bamboo, bone, or gut. Among the earliest jade pieces are plain perforated disks, or *pi*, which are thought to have been used in heaven worship and as funerary objects. The Freer's Han (206 B.C.-A.D. 220) *pi*, *opposite*, shows the type of embellishment that later artisans began to add to the very simple disks—dragons and felines and curling plumes and tails. Jade artisans introduced a new flamboyance and reached an extremely high level of technical refinement during the Ch'ien-lung period of the Ch'ing dynasty (1736–95), the time of the covered bowl, *above*. Fashioned from a single boulder in the shape of an archaic bronze vessel *ting*, the relatively simple bowl is adorned with intricately worked dragons on the handles and legs and a lion on the lid. *Left:* The dragon in China is not the ferocious beast of our Western folklore, but is regarded as benign, prestigious, and a symbol of the Emperor. This embroidered silk dragon is a detail from an 18th-century Ch'ing dynasty throne cushion that gives us some idea of the sumptuousness of imperial furnishings of the time.

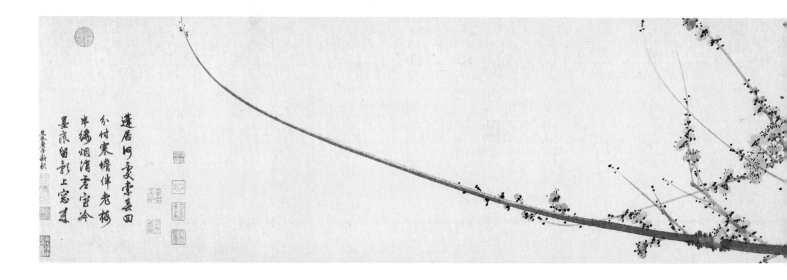

Above: *Tsou Fu-lei.* A Breath of Spring.
*Yüan dynasty, dated 1360. Handscroll, ink on
paper, 13⁷/₁₆ x 88" (34 x 224 cm). FGA.*
Flower painting as a genre has existed in
China since the tenth century, and with
time certain flowers have acquired
symbolic meaning. The plum blossoms in
A Breath of Spring are the harbinger of
spring, bursting into bloom before the last
snow has melted. They represent
endurance, loftiness, and purity.
Left: Peony and Lotus. *Ming, Ch'ing
period, 17th century. Silk tapestry, each 16¹/₂ x
25 ³/₈" (42 x 64 cm). FGA.*
The top panel symbolizes prosperity,
wealth, and honor with a phoenix—the
most aristocratic of birds—standing
proudly before peonies—the most
gorgeous of flowers. The other panel
shows the lotus rising fresh and untainted
from the murky waters in which it grows,
thus symbolizing purity and integrity.

Right: A flowering pine tree winds its way
up this little bottle from the Yung-cheng
period (1723–35) of the Ch'ing dynasty.
Pine tress are often depicted as windswept
and ancient, symbols of longevity. Pine,
bamboo, and plum trees, which stay green
year round, are called "the three friends
of winter."

Chiang T'ing-hsi. *Morning Glories and Birds*. Ch'ing dynasty (1644–1912), 17th century. Folding fan, ink and color on paper, 7¼ x 19¾" (18 x 50 cm). *FGA.* An array of morning glories emerges from behind a rock on this fan painted by the imperial court painter Chaing T'ing-hsi. Perching on a branch are two birds, one of them watching a ladybug.

343

Left: A pattern of flowers and fruits covers this 16th-century cloisonné incense burner from the Ming dynasty. The shape of the vessel is derived from an ancient bronze *ting. Below:* This 13th-century brass canteen from Syria, inlaid with silver, is rich in Christian and Islamic imagery. The rounded side of the canteen depicts scenes from the life of Christ, while the outer frieze of the flat side (not shown) consists of Western medieval and Oriental figures. On the side walls are fabulous animals in human garb, almost all of them with snouts and menacing aspects. These may refer to the zoomorphic dances performed in Iran and various parts of the Arab world from pre-Islamic to modern times. *Opposite:* In the early 15th century, Chinese potters at the Ching-te Chen kilns began imitating the 13th-century metal canteens from Syria. This large blue-and-white flask (almost 19 inches in diameter) follows its metal prototype closely in size, shape, and proportions, but its spout and handle are different. Although the eight-pointed star in its domed center is derived from the Star of Islam, the flask is essentially Chinese in its decoration.

Left: The Chinese began making their famous blue-and-white porcelains in the early 14th century when cobalt blue pigment was imported from the West. The Freer's 14th-century plate depicts a fish swimming in eelgrass, a popular motif in the Yüan dynasty that may allude to the Taoist hermit Ch'in Kao, who rode away on a carp. *Far left:* This stem-cup, just over three inches high, represents the peak of refinement in Chinese porcelains. It is decorated in the *tou-ts'ai* method: blue outlines under the glaze, enamel washes in red, green, and yellow over the glaze.

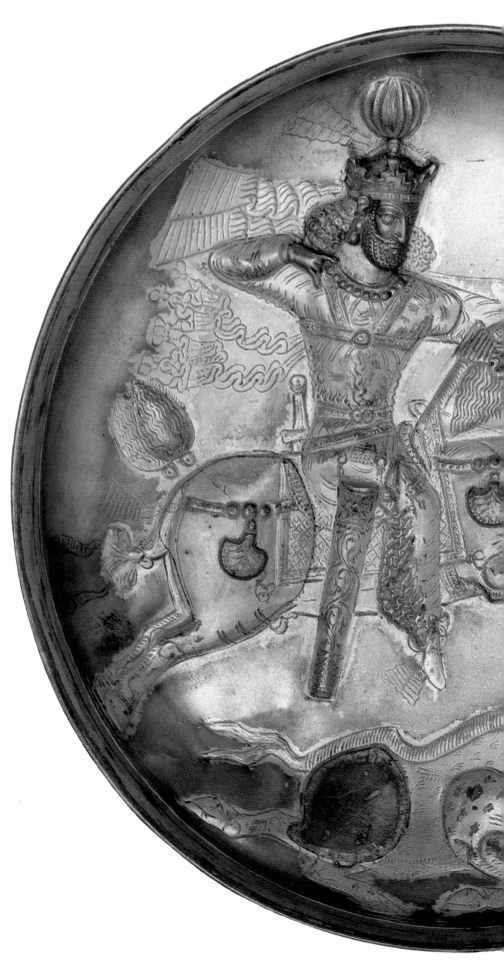

Iranian art delights the beholder with its grace and beauty, its exquisite detail. *Above:* An early 13th-century beaker, not quite five inches high, tells a love story from the Shahnama ("Book of Kings"), an epic history of Persia written by Firdausi around A.D. 1000. The beaker is roughly 100 years older than the earliest known illustrations of the book.

Right: The Sasanian dynasty (224–651) left behind a wealth of silver objects, among them many silver plates depicting the royal hunt. The king in the Freer's fourth-century plate is probably Shapur II (309–80).

Opposite top: *Shaykh Muhammad. Camel and Keeper. 1556–57. Color and gold on paper, 4⁵⁄₁₆ x 5³⁄₁₆" (11 x 13 cm). FGA.*

Opposite bottom: *Behzad. Old Man and Youth in Landscape. Early 16th century. Color, gold, and silver on paper, 3¼" (8 cm). FGA.*

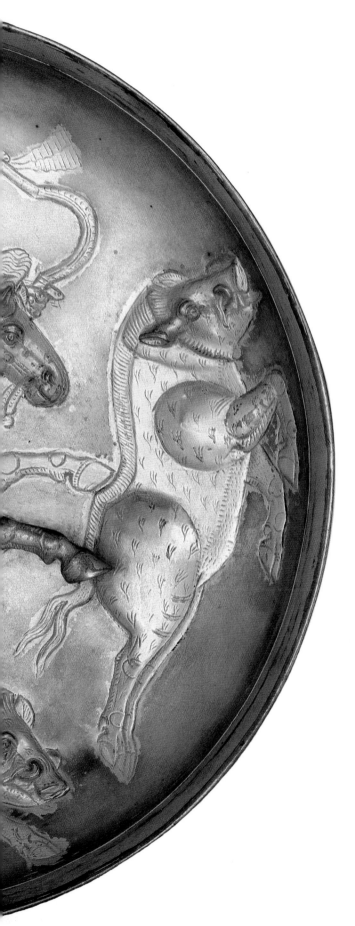

Bookmaking is probably the most exquisite of all Iranian art forms, calling on the talents of gifted bookbinders, calligraphers, illuminators, and painters. The top painting, surrounded by the poem it illustrates, is the only signed work of the painter and calligrapher Shaykh Muhammad, while the circular miniature, the frontispiece of an anthology, is one of few signed by the celebrated Behzad.

Opposite: The Freer owns four gray schist reliefs that once decorated the base of a *stupa* (funerary mound) in Gandhara, now northwestern Pakistan. They depict four cardinal events in the life of the Buddha: the Miraculous Birth (shown here), the Enlightenment, the First Sermon, and the Death. *Above:* This tenth-century statue of Parvati, divine consort of the Hindu deity Siva, is an outstanding example of Indian bronze casting during the Chola dynasty. Parvati is the Daughter of the Mountain (her father Himavat is a personification of the Himalayas), and her grace and beauty are derived from her mother, an ancient fertility deity.

Left: *Mushfiq*. Rama and Lakshman Fight the Demoness Taraka. *Mughal, late 16th century. Color and gold on paper, 10⅞ x 6″ (28 x 15 cm). FGA.*

This is one of 130 illustrations in the Freer's Persian translation of *Ramayana*, one of the venerated stories of India. It was set down soon after 500 B.C., but it derives from an older oral tradition. Its hero is Rama, an incarnation of the Hindu deity Vishnu and the restorer of moral order. In this painting, upon the request of the great sage Vishvamitra, the young Rama and his brother Lakshman confront the demonic Taraka. Once a beautiful young bride, Taraka went mad upon the death of her husband and began to attack any man who had the emotional control that she lacked. Here she grows gigantic and murderous with rage, but Rama calmly kills her with his bow and arrow. As a reward he receives weapons that endow him with divine powers.

Opposite: *Bichitr*. Jahangir Preferring a Sufi Shaykh to Kings. *Mughal, c. 1615–18. Color and gold on paper, 18⅞ x 13″ (48 x 33 cm). FGA.*

This painting celebrates the triumph of the divine over the worldly, of holy men over secular rulers. The Mughal Emperor Jahangir, sitting on an hourglass throne, presents a book to Shaykh Husain, a direct descendent of the great saint Mu'in al-Din Chisti, ignoring the three important men—a Turkish sultan, a Hindu, and James I of England and VI of Scotland—who crowd the lower left corner. The likeness of King James is copied from an English portrait almost certainly presented to Jahangir by Sir Thomas Roe, British Ambassador to India from 1615 to 1619. The borders of the painting, works of art in their own right, were executed by Muhammad Sadiq in 1727.

351

352

The Ottomans (1299–1923), the longest line of rulers in history, involved themselves in the development of the arts in Turkey by supporting royal academies that employed the best talents of the Empire. They greatly admired the ceramic traditions of China: more than 10,000 pieces of Chinese blue-and-white porcelain were kept in the imperial kitchens of the Topkapi Palace. Some of these were imitated at the imperial kilns at Iznik, which by the mid-16th century had created an indigenous type of ware using blue, green, turquoise, and red pigments, and depicting naturalistic flowers. This became the classical Ottoman style, which in turn was imitated widely in Europe. The Freer's mid-16th-century plate, *above left,* is typical of this style, with its jewel-like tones, the twisting leaves of the central cyprus tree, and the roses and rosebuds. The early 17th-century tile, *above right,* may well be one of a series designed to decorate the walls of a pavilion that looked out onto beautiful gardens filled with fountains and exotic birds. Flower motifs that were used in the ceramics of the 16th and 17th centuries are also to be found in textiles of the same period. Probably intended as a cushion cover, the Freer's textile, *opposite,* has an intricate pattern of tulips, carnations, and hyacinths.

In Japan, *cha-no-yu*—"boiling water for tea"—brings people together for a special kind of spiritual and social encounter. Although green powdered tea was introduced from China in the 13th century, it was only in the 16th century that it became the medium for a ceremony that is highly complex in procedure yet elegantly simple in mood and aesthetic. Toki Miyakawa of the Urasenke Tea Society of Washington, *above*, gazes at her ladle in preparation for her role as hostess of a tea ceremony demonstration at the Museum of Natural History. Usually, *cha-no-yu* takes place in a tea room whose simple lines and lack of ornamentation enhance the sense of harmony, serenity, and refinement that is so integral a part of the tea ceremony and that lends itself to the contemplation of beauty. There are two focal points in a tea room: an alcove where a hanging scroll or a floral arrangement is displayed and a hearth or a brazier where the water is boiled and the tea prepared. The soothing sound of the boiling water is often likened to the rustling of pines or the breaking of waves on the shore, hence the decoration of the Freer's Kamakura period (c. 1300) iron kettle, *right*.
Overleaf: A detail from one of a pair of six-fold screens painted by the Rimpa school master Ogata Korin shows gray cranes, popular symbols of longevity, moving across a brilliant gold background. *Ogata Korin.* Cranes. *Edo period, 17th–18th century. Ink, color, and gold on paper, 5'5⅜" x 12'2" (1.66 x 3.71 m). FGA.*

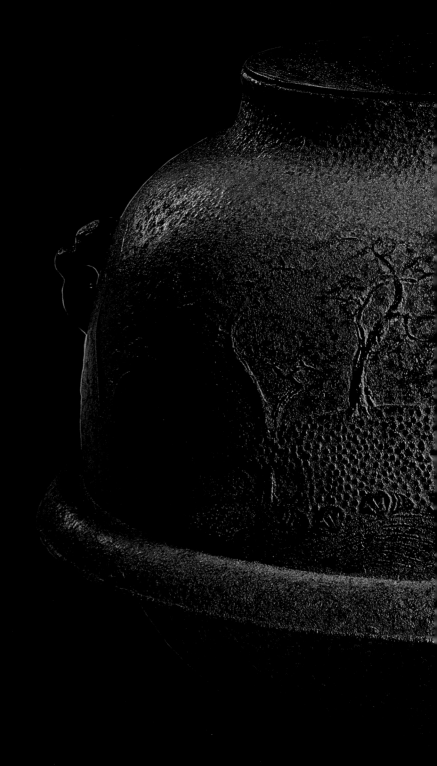

Part of the tea master's art lies in his choice of utensils, which he selects as both pieces of individual beauty and parts of a harmonious whole. *Opposite top:* This 17th-century drinking bowl would be chosen for its openness of form as a summertime vessel. In it rest a scoop and a whisk. *Top left:* This black Raku bowl, attributed to the great 16th-century potter Chojiro, is considered the ideal type of tea bowl. Thick and porous—a wintertime bowl—it represents the reverence for utmost simplicity established by the 16th-century tea master Rikyu. *Top right:* More elaborately carved and glazed, this Momoyama period (1568–1614) jar holds fresh water with which to replenish the kettle. *Above:* This early 17th-century caddy for the powdered tea also reflects the late Momoyama departure from severe simplicity.

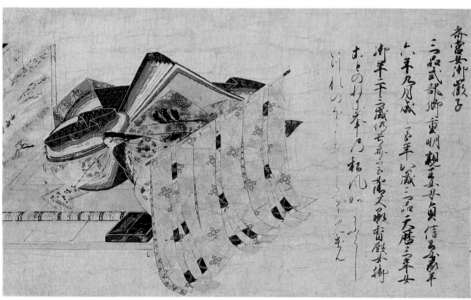

Above: This late 12th-century Buddhist sculpture depicts a Bodhisattva—one who has attained enlightenment (*bodhi*) but who has postponed his entrance into Nirvana in order to alleviate the suffering of others.

Top left: Some of the fans shown in this detail of a screen by the great painter Sotatsu depict animated warriors and may be related to the lost Kamakura (1185–1334) illustrations of the Heiji and Hogen wars of the 12th century.

Sotatsu. Decorated Fans. *Edo period, 17th century. Ink, color, gold, and silver on gold, 5'¹³/₁₆" x 11'10³/₄" (1.54 x 3.63 m). FGA.*

Center left: During the 11th century, the great poet and critic Fujiwara Kinto selected the 36 major poets of Japan for an anthology. This painting of the poetess Saigu-Nyogo Yoshiko, originally part of a handscroll showing all 36 poets, shows her reclining on her *tatami* mat, her head peeping out from the voluminous folds of her 12-layer robe.

Attributed to Fujiwara Nobuzane. Portrait of Saigu-Nyogo Yoshiko, Poetess. *Kamakura period, 13th century. Ink and color on paper, 11 x 20¹/₈" (28 x 51 cm). FGA.*

Bottom left: This early 17th-century lacquer *tebako* (a case for a lady's personal effects) is decorated in *maki-e,* a technique that is unique to Japan. One type of *maki-e* is the reddish pearskin ground embedded with powdered gold.

Opposite: This bronze Kamakura period pendant (*keman*) was once suspended from a beam near the altar in a Buddhist temple, the bells at the bottom jingling in the wind. The design of the *keman* originated in the garlands of flowers offered in India to royalty and deity, the cord tied in a bow as if binding a bouquet.

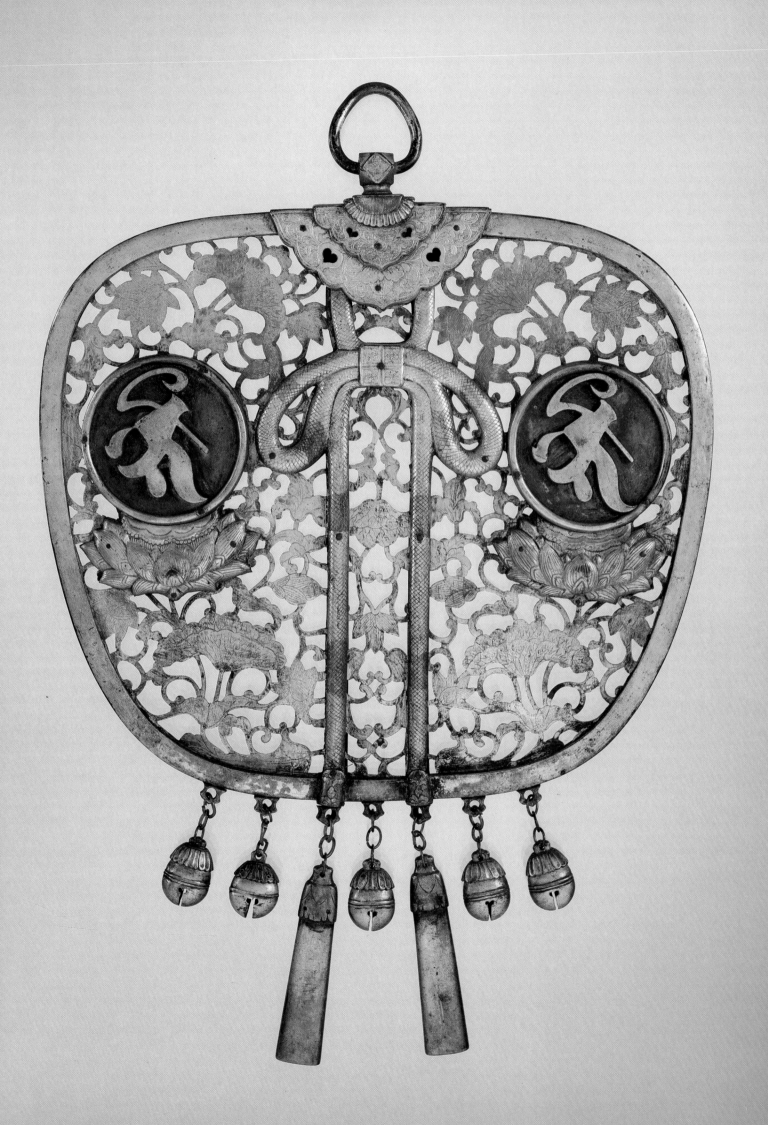

Above: In this Korean Buddhist painting, the artist has captured the shimmering translucence of the overgarments of the Bodhisattva Avalokitèsvara, whose foot is resting on a lotus, the Buddhist symbol of purity.
Unidentified artist. Avalokitèsvara with Willow Branch. *Koryo dynasty, late 14th century. Ink, color, and gold on silk, 38³⁄₄ x 18¹³⁄₁₆″ (98 x 48 cm). FGA.*
Right: This delightful 12th–13th-century celadon ewer from Korea is in the shape of a closed lotus flower. Two small boys are perched on the neck of the ewer picking small lotus flowers while a frog sits astride the handle. Originally a string was threaded through the frog's eye and attached to the lid, which is now lost.

Whistler at first signed his work with his full name, but after being chastized by a potential buyer for taking up so much canvas with eight letters, he developed a monogram of J, M, and W which, stylistically rendered, came out in the shape of a butterfly. This pleased his sense of showmanship. He used it a lot. You see it all over the Peacock Room, for example. He signed himself "Butterfly" at the end of his clever, expressive letters, and when he took a dig at some critic he called himself the butterfly with a sting.

The Smithsonian has sometimes used live animals in its exhibits to make a special point. I don't believe the Freer ever kept butterflies in its atrium courtyard—at least not intentionally—but for a while there were peacocks wandering about.

He got on tolerably well with some of the expatriate crowd, though, including John Singer Sargent. When I was being wrenched up in Boston, I heard his name, inevitably, when portraits were mentioned. He was as much a Boston institution as the Public Library, whose murals he painted. He was the inescapable choice to paint the portrait of Boston's Henry Cabot Lodge that graces our National Portrait Gallery.

John Singer Sargent was born in Italy (into a *very* old Boston family) and lived mostly in London. When he visited the States it was of-ten to do a portrait of a socially prominent American. His ladies—there are examples at the Museum of American Art—are wonderful. They are sufficiently rich and self-assured to wear simple—but expensive—clothes, and they look at you with candid appraisal: "Who are *you*? Were you at my coming-out? Or are you one of my brother's friends from the Hasty Pudding Club?" Personally, I always feel put down when I stare into those confident eyes. I suppose it's good for me.

Sargent worked fast and could knock off oils and watercolors in no time. He did seven portraits in one winter spent in Boston. Charles Freer picked up a sunny little Italian scene of Sargent's, *Breakfast in the Loggia*—bright and graceful with two animated figures in wonderfully feminine attitudes.

Freer also collected some fine paintings by Thomas Wilmer Dewing who, almost uniquely, caught the rather mystical Victorian opinion of women—gracefully posed in the background, beautiful, even sensuous, with soft bare shoulders and smooth, rounded arms, but never obtrusive. He would put these lovely, unattainable creatures in a room or a garden where they blended with other lovely things: objets d'art or vague blossoms and foliage. They are always misty and yet deliciously exciting. I would like to see into the soft eyes of a Dewing lady the way I am

362

Opposite top: *Thomas Wilmer Dewing.*
Early Portrait of the Artist's Daughter.
*1894. Oil on canvas, 3'4⅞" x 5'7¾" (1.04 x
1.72 cm).*
Opposite bottom: *Winslow Homer.* Early
Evening. *1881–1907. Oil on canvas, 33 x
38¾" (84 x 98 cm).*
Above: *John Singer Sargent.* Breakfast in
the Loggia. *1910. Oil on canvas, 21¼ x 28"
(51 x 71 cm).*
Right: *James McNeill Whistler.* The
Thames in Ice. *1860. Oil on canvas, 29⅜ x
21¾" (75 x 55 cm).* FGA.

Abbott H. Thayer. The Virgin. *Oil on canvas, 7'6⅜" x 5'10⅞" (2.30 x 1.80 m). FGA.*

forced to meet the haughty, almost amused stare of Sargent's women.

Dewing's paintings hang in the Museum of American Art as well as the Freer. So do those of Abbott H. Thayer, another of Freer's favorites. Thayer used very free, sweeping brush strokes so that his work raged with emotion. His faces are beautiful, but they strike me as idealized, perfect. Purity isn't all that interesting to me, I'm afraid. I am, of course, a minority. Thayer's *The Virgin*, with its exalted atmosphere of childhood innocence, is one of the Freer's most popular American paintings.

Freer collected the works of other contemporary Americans. Winslow Homer's *Early Evening* is here, completed in 1907. It's a "down east" scene, figures on a granite hillside where a blueberry bush has found a niche between sloping slabs of rock. They are facing the wind, and I think the sea, though that's out of sight. Behind them are scurrying clouds and the sliver of a new moon. Homer's beloved Maine coast.

The Freer's sixth-century gold cross, which reads ZOE (life) horizontally and PHOS (light) vertically, may refer to the Gospel of St. John, chapter 4, verse 1: "In Him [God] was life, and the light was the life of men."

I swear that if you stand alone in Whistler's special room at the Freer—perhaps I should call it his haunt—surrounded by gilded peacocks on turquoise walls, and let your mind dwell gently on the story of Whistler, you will hear faint echoes of voices, of carefully constructed witticisms met with bursts of laughter, of elegant repartee, of endless conceits. . . .

The Freer Gallery has that special aura of the theatrical about it. It is at least half illusion. I find it a bit spooky, actually. But I never hurry out of the Freer before allowing myself a final, thoughtful reflection before a piece of art that somehow sums up the place for me. It's a tiny Greek cross in gold with two inscriptions that meet, linked by the common letter at the intersection of the arms. The alphabetic trick doesn't work in English, but translated the two married words are Light and Life. The interplay between appearance and reality, I suspect, fascinated Freer, as it had Whistler, Sargent, and all the rest of that crowd. It has not lost its fascination. ✸

Out of Africa

Being concerned with museums, I have always been intrigued with how they get started. The buildings are no problem: I've seen them being built or adapted and refurbished. But you don't put up a museum building with empty halls and galleries—at least the Smithsonian doesn't—and the formation of a major collection of articles can be a baffling process, infrequently experienced and inadequately described.

In the 1960s, however, Washingtonians were presented with the birth pangs and infancy of a major museum, small but vastly important since it was the first of its kind in the United States: the Museum of African Art. It was conceived in the mind of a scholarly, enthusiastic, determined former Foreign Service officer, Warren Robbins, and supported by the mighty political clout of the late Vice President Hubert H. Humphrey. And it consisted of a few thousand African items—sculptures, textiles, artifacts, musical intruments, among other things—augmented by the bequest of some 68,000 photographs from Eliot Elisofon, the famous *LIFE* photographer and collector of African art.

Mr. Robbins had bought the old Frederick Douglass house near the Capitol (Douglass was the black abolitionist writer and lecturer who was a friend and adviser of Abraham Lincoln) and moved his African collection into

Overleaf: *Dramatic masks play an important role in the vital ceremonies that bind people together in Africa. The masks at far left and far right are worn by the Ligbe people of Ivory Coast and Ghana at popular Islamic festivals. Museum of African Art, bequest of Samuel Rubin. The center left mask appears in female initiation rites of the Mende people of Sierra Leone. Museum of African Art, gift of Lawrence Gussman. The Yoruba people of Nigeria use the center right mask in their Ede/Gelede festival honoring the special attributes of womanhood. Museum of African Art, bequest of Samuel Rubin.* Right: *Eliot Elisofon's photograph of Goundam, Mali, one of the cities on the trans-Saharan caravan route, is one of the most popular at the Museum of African Art.*

Africa throbs with the sounds of music and the rhythms of dance. Eliot Elisofon caught the fun and happiness of it all in his photograph of a musician from Timbuktu, Mali, accompanying dancers on her bowed guitar.

it. Some rare old maps and around 6,000 books and periodicals arrived, along with paintings by Afro-American artists who had never enjoyed much reputation in this country because until recently their color prevented them from it.

All of this produced the new Museum of African Art in 1964. Fifteen years later the Smithsonian acquired it and almost immediately Secretary Ripley began making plans for a new building on the Mall to house the collections adequately and allow room for expansion, as well as for seminars and lectures.

So the museum took shape right in front of me, and still I knew an ingredient was missing. It was, of course, myself. Half of a museum lies within the beholder. I'd looked at the place academically, and never really experienced it. So one summer afternoon I came in out of the heat and simply roamed around among the sculptured figures that serve various African cultures as symbols of authority or personality, as good luck charms and evocations of nature.

Still pretty remote stuff, I thought to myself. Then I heard a great commotion from the auditorium and, curious, I drifted over for a look. Here a teacher was showing visitors how to do an African dance. I found it impossible to watch without joining in.

He made everyone clap with a sort of driv-

ing rhythm, and we all began to forget silly things like dignity and rocked the room with our clapping. Then he got a couple of musicians going on African drums. They doubled the basic beat and feet started to tap unobtrusively—after all, this was a pretty uptight crowd of Washington people, far more accustomed to bureaucracy than to African dancing. But before we knew it, we were all singing out *"Hey! Hey!"* and clapping and bouncing around the room in a sort of samba line. And all those carefully defensive faces cracked open into broad, friendly grins—the well-dressed young man and his sleek, slender girlfriend, the three "mean teens," the two buttoned-down Ivy League types, and the Sarah Lawrence grad with an alligator on her shirt—and so the Museum of African Art was born in my head as a place to have fun.

It has never failed me since. I love wandering among those wooden sculptures with heavy-lidded eyes and outthrust breasts, the totemlike figures astride tiny beasts, the strange dolls and stylized human heads atop staffs. I love the carved utensils and the bright textiles and beaded ceremonial regalia. All reflect, it seems to me, action and zest. These objects don't just sit back and contemplate life—they express the acts of living.

With that gut feeling about African art, plus the fact that I have fun in the museum, I've

taken a sort of cram course in the subject. Like any new student, I'm most eager to sound off with my new and very uncertain knowledge. First, I think it's right to say that the works of art here are differently motivated from those westerners produce. Picasso and Matisse, who were introduced to African art by André Derain, were much affected by it. Picasso painted to express deep feelings within himself, and his fascination with the abstraction of African art led to the movement in art called cubism, which, of course, hadn't much to do with African art in its society but rather with the self-expression of Picasso. Since he was a complicated person, his self-expression isn't readily understood, but his paintings intrigue you, and you find that you can keep on looking at such paintings day after day, discovering new things about them, and that they give you delight.

African art doesn't just hang on the wall. It may be a mask used in a rite of passage, a post supporting a roof or the lintel of a door, a wooden figure guarding the burial site of a long-dead grandfather, a doll carried by a young wife hoping to bear a child, or a rice ladle honoring a particularly hospitable woman. In other words, this art, its designs and contours sometimes exaggerated, sometimes almost erased by abstraction, is directly involved with the whole business of living.

Opposite left: *In the gay courtyard of the Museum of African Art, decorated in the geometric designs of the Ndebele people of South Africa, Alex Akoto and Peter Pipim play their drums while fourth-graders from Washington's Webb Elementary School perform an impromptu dance.* Opposite right: *Only eight-and-a-half inches long, this thumb piano or* sanza *from the Chokwe people of Zaire is held in both hands, the tips of the keys plucked by the thumbs. Museum of African Art, gift of Donna and Lee Bronson.*

AFRICA

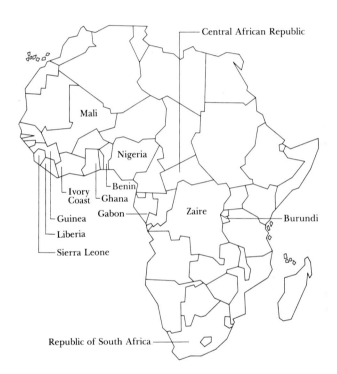

"Fertility" in Africa is almost synonymous with "increase"—increase of babies, food, rain, money; increase of whatever it takes to survive. Opposite: *The male and female figures from the Baga people of Guinea may represent spirits who live in or near the village and are believed to govern fertility and procreation. Museum of African Art, gifts of Samuel Rubin.* Left: *The headdress mask from the Bambara people of Mali, who depend upon farming for survival, symbolizes Chi-wara, the half-man, half-antelope who taught the Bambara how to farm. Bequest of Eliot Elisofon.* Above: *Elisofon's photograph shows young men reenacting Chi-wara's original lesson in rites that assure fertility to both people and the fields.*

The Museum of African Art is a bright window on the entire spectrum of African life. Since life differs somewhat from people to people, so does their art. But almost all of it shares one element, and it is expressed as the "life force"—the dynamism, energy that permeates all things, animate and inanimate. It is desirable in African life to attract to oneself and to the community as much of the life force as possible. So it is with this belief that a carver creates beautiful objects that will draw the life force into them.

Having achieved this level in my schooling, I began to get the uneasy feeling that I was delving into anthropology, which for me would be a fatal plunge from the frying pan into the fire. Anthropology should be left to that old and world famous department at the Museum of Natural History, not entrusted to a perpetually bemused voyeur of Smithsonian wonders. I cannot go on about African art, however, without mentioning obvious links that anyone can see for himself.

I trotted over to the Museum of Natural History and discovered a great deal of African art displayed there, all upholding the concepts I had learned. And there were, indeed, striking near-duplications of some African items in displays from the other side of the world—the lands of the Pacific, even the Pueblo villages of the American Southwest.

Take fertility—a vital part of the life force. Dozens of symbols refer to it in every African culture. The most important of those displayed in the Museum of African Art is the museum's own symbol, the antelope head-dress, bequeathed by Eliot Elisofon.

This intricately shaped wooden sculpture from the Bambara people of Mali represents Chi-wara, a part-human, part-animal deity who, according to one myth, sprang from the union between a snake and the original "Earth Mother" in the form of an antelope. He was born with claws, and used them and a pointed stick to dig the soil, and men followed his example and prospered. They prospered so well that they grew wasteful with the corn, and incurred Chi-wara's anger. He dug himself right into the ground and disappeared forever. So people built shrines to his memory and wore masks and these headdresses in the Chi-wara rite for the land's fertility. And since the sun and earth create and nurture humanity as well as crops, the Chi-wara also represents human fruitfulness.

Snakes are often connected with fertility, partly because they symbolize masculinity and partly because they give birth to so many young during their lifetime. And because they shed their skins, they're associated with continuity and renewal of life. Snakes also have spiritual associations because they can travel

above and beneath the ground, they can climb trees and swim, getting in touch with a lot of spirits who reside in these places. It's for that reason that Hopi people in the American Southwest perform their famous snake dance, during which (amid the gasps of tourists) men dance with live rattlesnakes held in their mouths. As I understand it, the snakes thus get the message that the people need to water their crops, and so when they are let loose, they pass the request along to the gods responsible for sending rain. You can learn all about that at the North American Indian displays at the Museum of Natural History. And in a little exhibit from New Hebrides in the Pacific, I found a lovely pearl-shell bracelet—in the form of a snake.

Other animals in Africa are important to the concept of fertility; also parts of animals. Big horns or tusks in a sculpture symbolize virility. In human figures, large breasts and bulging navels indicate, quite naturally, fertility. But there are some dolls with highly stylized features that serve a more specific purpose. One type is carried by Ashanti women who wish to become pregnant. The dolls evoke the Ashanti ideal of beauty—long necks, round, flat faces, high foreheads, small mouths—and the would-be mothers gaze at those features to be sure they will impress them upon their future embryos, and then they carry their dolls at the small of the back, where they would carry their live babies. When they do conceive, Ashanti wives try not to look at anything ugly.

Prenatal suggestion. Years ago, when my wife was pregnant with our first child, there was a joke going around which dealt with a speech impediment. I told it quite well (at least I thought so), but my wife forbade it for fear that our baby might grow up with such a serious problem.

"That's ridiculous," I said.

"I know," she said, "but still. . . ."

Surely many people have felt the same as the Ashanti women with their dolls.

In Nigeria, the Yorubas have the world's highest rate of twin births. It's over four times the twin rate in the United States. This is a mixed blessing. It suggests the remarkable fecundity of the mothers of twins, but it also puts a strain on family resources. So twins are sacred. Everyone tries to keep twins happy and spoil them outrageously because if they're not placated they can bring a heap of trouble to the community.

One of the bad things twins can do is die. Along with that high twin rate, the Yorubas have a high infant mortality rate, and since twins are often premature, one or both may die. The Yorubas then replace the lost twin with a carved wooden figure, an *ere ibeji*. It is

Above: *A woman's success is measured by her
ability to bear children. The Ashanti women of
Ghana carry an* akua'ba *doll, left, at the small
of their backs to encourage the conception of a
healthy, beautiful child. Among the Yoruba of
Nigeria, twins are thought to bring good
fortune and wealth. If one dies, an* ere ibeji *or
image, right, is carved as a resting place for
the soul. The mother nurtures, bathes, and
feeds it as she does the surviving twin.
Museum of African Art, gifts of Emil Arnold.*
Opposite: *The woman and child figure of the
Yombe people of Zaire symbolizes, among other
things, human fertility. The woman, wearing a
hat reserved for chiefs, represents maternity,
while the enlarged genitals of the child are said
to reflect his future role as an adult. Museum
of African Art.*

Eliot Elisofon's photograph shows Dakpa youths from the Central African Republic returning to the community after their coming-of-age rituals. They are painted with white clay to indicate that they are on the threshold of manhood.

The most common initiations in Africa, and those that involve the most art, are the coming-of-age rituals. In most cases, boys and girls are taken away from their villages to separate secluded places where they go through various puberty rites. Then they enter the betwixt-and-between stage: they have left their previous life but before they can enter their new life they must be given the sometimes sacred and secret knowledge that prepares them for adulthood. The initiates are often likened to the dead during this transition period, and their subsequent reincorporation into the community is celebrated as a rebirth. They are welcomed back, then, as new people, with new names and new responsibilities. Initiation doesn't stop with the advent of adult life, however. Later there will be initiation ceremonies celebrating a change in status or the entry into a special society. *Left:* Originally a raffia fringe was attached to this coming-of-age mask from the Biombo people of Zaire. Museum of African Art, gift of Josefa Carlebach. *Opposite:* The somewhat menacing dancers in Elisofon's photograph are the *minganji* of the Pende people of Zaire. The *minganji*, who are in communication with the spirits of the dead, serve as the policemen of initiation camps, ensuring that the young boys obey all the rules. When the initiates return to the village, the *minganji* don their raffia costumes for a celebratory dance. *Opposite bottom left:* Representing Mwaash A Mbooy, a mythical king of the Kuba people of Zaire, this mask is used mainly in the royal court but also at some initiation ceremonies in dramatic reenactments of the legendary founding of the Kuba kingdom. Museum of African Art, gift of Eliot Elisofon. *Opposite bottom right:* When newly initiated Chokwe boys of Zaire return to their villages they are greeted by cavorting dancers wearing hyena costumes like this one. The hyena—dirty, gluttonous, and cruel—cautions the boys against socially unacceptable behavior. Museum of African Art, gift of Robert C. Reif, Jr.

specially fashioned for the mother, having the same sex as the deceased and bearing the family scars on the face. The mother then bathes, clothes, and feeds it just as she does the surviving child.

If the mother loses both twins, then two figures are made. These are the center of weekly rituals in the hope that the infants will be born again, and this time reach maturity. That's why the *ere ibejis* have adult genitals.

All peoples have rites of passage into adulthood. You might say that in our western society, every time Dad hands the car keys over to a new driver he makes a symbolic act signifying this passage. In Africa, as in many other lands, dancing is a frequent part of this initiation process, and the masks of the dancers have important meanings.

At the Museum of African Art are several masks used in the initiation dances so important to Zaire's Yaka people. When adolescent Yaka boys have been circumcised they stay in a secluded camp to learn the skills of manhood—especially singing and dancing. Finally they return to their village, adults now, and dance in pairs wearing masks. The best dancer of the group, however, dances alone. He wears a special mask called a *mbala* which often depicts an event from adult life. A successful performance enhances the villagers' prestige within their region and qualifies the dancers to travel to other villages to perform and to bring back wives.

Animals are teachers for Africans. From them, they learn useful arts and necessary survival skills. Certain animals are models for conducting oneself as a member of a family and a community, and are depicted on the masks. Mali's Bambaras—the same ones that use the Chi-wara—have hyena masks which are worn by one of the highest grades of initiates. The hyena is considered a filthy scavenger, gluttonous, cruel, and dangerous to humans. So the initiate, who may one day be a priest, wears the mask to indicate that he knows he has a lot to learn before he's considered much better than a hyena. The museum has a hyena costume from the Chokwe people of Zaire. Dressed in this, a dancer crouches and sways clumsily in front of the initiates to warn them not to behave crudely.

Other animals have similar reputations for bad behavior, and masks of them are used to demonstrate these traits as something to avoid. A black monkey mask, for example, shows antisocial behavior. Wearing it, a dancer refuses to dance, but sits on the sidelines in a sulk, making lewd gestures at everybody else. In a chimpanzee mask, a Dan dancer of Liberia or the Ivory Coast dashes about throwing sticks at onlookers, scattering trash piles and trampling on clean clothes that have been left out to dry, exhibiting the destructiveness of noncooperative members of the community and of the uninitiated.

Of course leopards and lions are admired for their superior hunting skills, as is the fish eagle. The elephant dominates other animals not just by its size, but also its intelligence. And the chameleon is a favorite subject in art because of its extraordinary characteristics. It's strangely human in some ways: it carries its young on its back as African mothers do, and its little toes can grasp like human hands. It walks deliberately, as though thinking carefully about where it's going. One myth has it that the chameleon was one of the first creatures to walk on the still-fiery earth after creation, and it tests the ground before putting down its feet. Africans assign spiritual powers to the chameleon for all those reasons as well as for its ability to change its color to blend in with its surroundings. And, as if that weren't enough, its eyeballs rotate independently so that when it's after prey it can look backwards and forwards simultaneously.

And speaking of living creatures as symbols, there is a fish figure that appears on gold weights and personal jewelry of the rulers of Ghana's Akan people. This is the mudfish, which can cope with the dry season by leaving a shrinking pool of water and trundling along terrestrially on its fins to a better one. It has rudimentary lungs to keep it going. And its ability to transcend its environment, to shape its destiny in an extraordinary way, gives it characteristics of a king. Incidentally, the mudfish is easy to catch when it's en route on dry land—and it's delicious to eat.

In Chapter One I mentioned symbolic Chokwe chairs on display in the Museum of African Art. The Dan people use "grandfather" chairs in a special rite of passage for their village girls. As they reach maturity, Dan women dance to celebrate their coming of age and hold before them these chairs, which symbolize heritage and authority and ultimate wisdom. It's their way of saying that they're ready for marriage, for the increase of the people, the upbringing of new members who will honor and strengthen the community and help preserve it.

Other symbols of marriage or readiness for marriage are baskets used for weighing, measuring, and storing food, and beaded aprons whose decoration indicates a girl's progression through the stages of womanhood.

Carried in public ceremonies by young women who have gained the knowledge that makes them eligible for marriage, the grandfather chairs of the Dan people of Liberia symbolize heritage, order, authority, and ultimate tribal wisdom. Museum of African Art, gift of William Brill.

Women's and men's roles in Africa are clearly defined and rarely overlap. For example, both women and men work in the market, but women sell the baskets and pots they have made and the produce they have grown, while men sell the meat they have butchered. Women weave on horizontal looms, men on vertical looms. Similarly, their possessions are different from each other's. *Left, clockwise from top:* A cane and wood box once containing the personal possessions of a Kuba woman of Zaire; a set of nested baskets for weighing, measuring, and storing foodstuffs, traditionally given as a wedding present to Lobi women of Ivory Coast; a conical basket from Burundi; a raffia bottom cover, the woman's counterpart of the man's loincloth, from the Mangbetu people of Zaire. Museum of African Art, gifts of Mr. and Mrs. William N. Hart, Mr. and Mrs. William Brill, and John Kauffman. *Above left:* Eliot Elisofon's photograph shows dancing Mangbetu women wearing their bottom covers. Used by ordinary women all over Africa and for all types of activity, the bottom covers also serve as seats or cushions. *Above right:* This Ndebele woman from South Africa is wearing a *mapoto*, a beaded and fringed apron with brilliant geometric designs to indicate that she is married. The decoration of a beaded apron not only indicates the status of its owner but also her domestic aspirations.

Maturity, marriage, the transitions between the significant stages of a person's life—all confer status. Sometimes status is earned by a lot of hard work or by displays of courage in battle or hunting, sometimes it is divinely ordained. If you happen to be a member of a royal family or of the nobility, then you inherit it. In any case, the symbolic art inspired by status is rich indeed. Those figures that support a roof or a lintel indicate the wealth and importance of the people inside. A man astride a tiny beast is far more important than the animal that carries him. A huge head on the figure of a person indicates

that there's a lot of life force packed in there. There are combination figures—totemlike, with many elements, one atop the other—that serve as personal altars for successful leaders. There are silk robes and gold hair ornaments, and spoons and bowls, displayed in a home to show the hospitality of the owners.

Pipes, elaborately decorated, are smoked only by VIPs. Fly whisks with gold or ivory handles are the marks of the privilege and authority of a ruler. Decorated staffs, often topped with female figures, are held by attendants who follow a ruler. Ceremonial weapons—artistic evocations of a war ax or a sword

or knife—are more intricately carved than their functional counterparts.

Most African sculptures are wood, so they're not very old. Because of the climate—and termites—they rarely last more than a hundred years. This impermanence is accepted in Africa. One of our curators who worked in Nigeria explained that a new sculpture would be carved to replace a rotting old one. At a proper ceremony, the life force would leave the old piece and enter the new. After that the original would be worthless and could be laid to rest.

So the only old objects are of lasting materi-

In this brass miniature from the Museum of Natural History, a Fon chief from the Republic of Benin puffs luxuriously on his pipe while being carried in a hammock during a royal procession. The umbrellas, like the pipe, are symbols of his authority. Cast before 1930, this piece was probably intended as a gift for a distinguished guest of a chief.

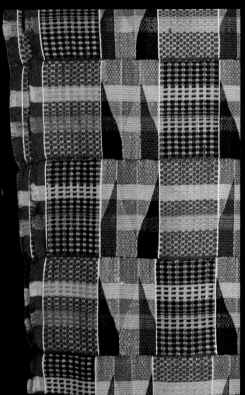

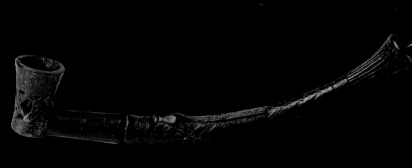

Top: The robes of high-ranking Hausa men of Nigeria are fuller than usual and require the work of various specialists—weavers, tailors, designers, embroiderers. Museum of African Art, gift of the Hon. Joseph Palmer II. Left: Worn as a toga-like robe, the Ashanti kente cloth of Ghana is extremely expensive because it's made of rare silk by especially skilled weavers. Museum of African Art, gift of Franklin Williams. Above: Kuba officials of Zaire smoke elaborately carved pipes such as this one which is 22 inches long. Museum of African Art, gift of Bob Bronson.

Above: A wealthy Ibo woman of Nigeria gladly suffered the encumbrance of wearing this pair of hammered brass anklets, which are more than 14 inches in diameter, for the greater the size, the more prestigious and valuable the ornament. Museum of African Art, gift of Arnold Newman. Left: Africans of great wealth can afford custom-made ornaments of gold and ivory. The bracelet at far left, from the Berber people of Northern Africa, is made of metal and inlaid with coral, while the other two, from the Guro people of Ivory Coast, are of ivory. Museum of African Art, gifts of Eliot Elisofon. Worn in the hair and shaped like a mudfish, the gold ornament at top right comes from the Baule people of Ivory Coast. Museum of African Art, gift of David Markin. At bottom right is a gold pendant in the form of a highly stylized human face, also from the Baule people. Museum of African Art, gift of Eliot Elisofon.

If they are elaborately carved or designed, household items become emblems of status. Dan women of Ivory Coast who have excelled as hostesses own specially carved wooden rice ladles, below, *which they dance with in public ceremonies. Museum of African Art, bequest of Samuel Rubin. Royalty among the Mangbetu of Zaire keep their jewelry in wood and bark boxes with a sculptured head on the lid,* right. *Museum of African Art.*

als: metal, earthenware, bone—gold trinkets for kings, cowrie-shell jewelry, buffalo-horn cups, ivory spoons, soapstone carvings. The very oldest objects are the terracotta sculptures from the ancient Nok culture of Nigeria. Some of these are over 2,000 years old. And they are remarkably similar to some of the wood sculptures of the last 100 years. Wood with metal added to it gains eminence. For example, a stool with brass studs hammered into its seat can only be used by the upper crust of Lega male society in Zaire.

The Benin bronzes are special treasures of African art, and the museum has two, a head

and a plaque, dating from the 15th, 16th, or 17th century. Benin, in Nigeria, maintained a fairly cordial trading relationship with the Portuguese from the 15th century (the first Portuguese to enter Benin arrived about 20 years before Columbus sailed the Atlantic). The Benin *oba* and the Portuguese king treated each other with respect. The Portuguese presence is often seen in the bronzework that Benin artists traditionally produced.

In the 19th century, however, relations with Europeans were strained. The British were having trouble establishing a trade treaty and their missionaries weren't getting anywhere

In many African societies important people drink their palm wine from elaborately carved and highly polished wood or horn cups; ordinary people use gourds. Kuba, Zaire. Museum of African Art, gift of Warren Robbins.

Most African pillows are made of wood and are designed to preserve the elaborate hairstyles of their users. The intricate decoration of this one from the Kuba people of Zaire tells us that it once belonged to someone of great wealth. Museum of African Art, gift of Bernard Simon.

Cowrie shells, gold measured by brass weights, iron blades, "kissi pennies," strips of cloth—all have been used in Africa as currency for internal trade.

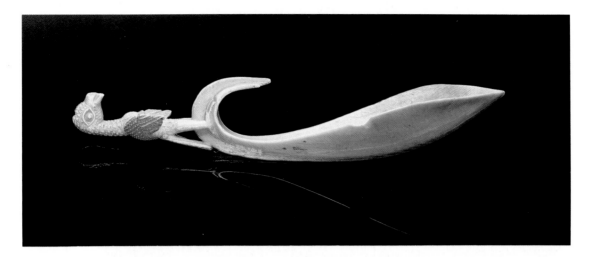

Our nickels and dimes and dollar bills appear rather ordinary next to traditional African money. *Opposite top:* The Akan people of Ghana and Ivory Coast used locally mined gold as their main medium of exchange before the 20th century and measured it with brass weights, which were often cast in a certain shape to represent a popular Akan proverb. Throughout sub-Saharan Africa delicately formed cowrie shells were the common currency. *Opposite:* Central Africans paid for their goods in iron ore, often shaped into blades, spearheads, and knives, while West Africans traded in bundles of "kissi pennies"—hammered and twisted pieces of iron. Homespun and handwoven cotton cloth strips were used as currency in areas like Liberia and Nigeria. The standard length of a strip was that of man's outstretched arms—so it paid to be long-limbed. Museum of African Art, gifts of Emil Arnold, Judith W. Ashelman, Robert Bevill, Alan Bresler, Gilbert Schulman, and the Commercial Museum. *Above:* The arrival of the Portuguese in Benin in the late 15th century prompted the beginnings of an overseas export industry. Benin's earliest export art consisted of beautifully carved ivory spoons, forks, vessels, saltcellars, and hunting horns that often reflected the prevailing tastes of the Europeans while retaining a peculiarly African style. This very fine ivory spoon, not quite seven inches long, was carved for export some time between the 15th and 17th centuries. Museum of African Art, bequest of Mrs. Robert Woods Bliss. *Right:* Bought in 1861 by a U.S. Navy paymaster, this tusk from Zaire appears to tell a long forgotten story. A foreign man sits stroking his beard atop a spiral of figures carved in relief. Museum of African Art, gift of Edward Elicofon (brother of Eliot Elisofon, who spelled his name differently).

Herbalist, pharmacist, psychologist, spiritualist, a diviner is endowed with special powers and can communicate with the supernatural world—the world of ancestors. Thus he is able to explain misfortune to those who go to him for help. A Lele diviner from Zaire uses the two-headed rubbing oracle, *above*, to determine the illness of a patient or the culprit of a crime or the cause of death. The heads represent dogs which, being hunters, help the diviner in his search for truth. He rubs the disc back and forth, calling out possible names until he hits upon the correct one, whereupon the disc suddenly fixes in place. Museum of African Art. Diviners often mix magic potions to make the impossible possible. A Holo diviner from Zaire mixes such a potion or medicine in the cylinder of the implement, *opposite*, and then stuffs it into the charms hanging from the figure's back. Museum of African Art. *Left:* This staff from the Yoruba people of Nigeria refers to the supernatural powers of a diviner: the gray heron is lord of the witches and sits astride the chameleon which is a messenger of the night and represents the power of transformation. Museum of African Art, gift of Herbert Baker.

394

with the Binis, the people of Benin. They were appalled at reports of human sacrifice, so in 1897 a nine-man mission set out to visit the *oba* at his palace to persuade him to stop the custom—an ancient rite to propitiate the gods and to ensure the continuity of the people. They were met on the way by messengers who told them that they couldn't meet the King just then. It was the time of the Ague festival—a time of human sacrifice—when the *oba* could neither see nor be seen by non-Binis. The British refused to turn back, the messengers then killed seven of them, and six weeks later a British punitive expedition entered the city.

They found two things. One was that Benin had practically become a bloodbath of human sacrifice. Ironically, the *oba* had intensified the rite in the dim hope that the gods would protect his people from the retribution that was sure to come. The second was this extraordinary bronzework. Most of it was seized and packed off to Britain to be auctioned. Experts

noted that the form of the figures lacked the exaggerated features that served the cause of symbolism in most African art. These were evenly proportioned, naturalistic. Surely they could not be African, said the experts, partly out of complacence and partly because (to give them credit) the bronzes were indeed very different from most African art.

In the years since their discovery, the Benin bronzes have at last become recognized as African and have added to western understanding of the long and sophisticated background of art from that continent. Heads similar to the one the museum acquired were kept at ancestral shrines, representing past *obas* in their coiled necklaces and coral crowns or headdresses. Plaques were affixed to the columns of an *oba's* palace and were engraved with scenes of his reign. They formed a visual history of the ruler and his court. Our plaque shows an African warrior in the foreground and, sure enough, Portuguese soldiers with distinctive helmets in the background.

Opposite: *This 16th or 17th-century plaque shows the* oba *flanked by attendants with two Portuguese soldiers in the background.* Right: *Some scholars think that this particular head from the 15th or 16th century may actually be a trophy head rather than a commemorative head—that is, that it may represent a stubborn conquered king whose head was cut off and then sent to the guild for casting.* Top: *Eliot Elisofon's photograph shows a king's shrine surrounded by commemorative heads supporting carved ivory tusks symbolic of royal wealth and power. Museum of African Art.*

Death in Africa is something of a journey from this world into the world of spirits, the world of ancestors. And ancestors are revered for they have influence in the world they left behind.
Opposite: *The Kota people of Gabon preserve the sacred relics of their important ancestors in basket containers. These are guarded by highly abstract wooden figures covered with metal, whose staring eyes keep constant vigil. Museum of African Art, bequest of Samuel Rubin.*
Below: *Agni women of Ivory Coast have traditionally made terracotta portrait figures (mma) of the deceased. These are kept in a special place (mmaso) in the forest where people can go to invoke the spirits of their ancestors. Museum of African Art, gift of Herbert Baker.*

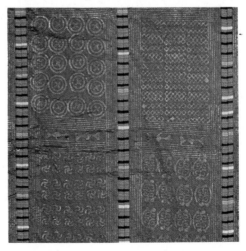

The Yombe people of Zaire apply white pigment to figures used as memorials to the dead. The female figure, top, would be placed on or near a grave to honor a woman. Museum of African Art, estate of Agnes E. Meyer, courtesy of Mrs. Katherine Graham. While they are in mourning, the Ashanti people of Ghana wear a red adinkra, *above, a special cloth whose decoration is stamped rather than woven. Museum of African Art.*

397

The final rite of passage in Africa is death. But death in Africa is really afterlife or a continuation of life—a world into which the deceased pass and join their ancestors. And funerals are celebrations of life, honoring the deceased's achievements during his lifetime and ensuring that he will live beyond death. Africans believe that the soul of the deceased remains active and so they provide a residence for it in the form of memorial images. These serve as an important connecting point between the world of the living and the world of the spirits—the afterlife.

For in Africa, ancestors are honored because of their wisdom and knowledge as well as their influence and power in the spirit world. They are often considered responsible for sending new children into the community. And so they must be appeased and guarded by carved likenesses, which house their souls and which are visited regularly to be venerated with sacrifices and prayers. I can't help thinking of all that statuary in our western cemeteries doing much the same thing.

Opposite: *The Dogon people of Mali have a belief in ancestors that is rich in symbolism. This wooden stool, only to be used by a* hogon *or ritual chief, is thought to depict the ultimate tribal ancestors and the primordial coupling of male and female. Stools of this kind have been interpreted by scholars as complete images of the creation of the world, with the two discs representing the earth and the sky joined by a tree. Museum of African Art, gift of Robert H. Simmons.*

In fact, the great impression I get of this almost matchless Smithsonian museum is that it seems to celebrate human similarities cloaked in widely divergent ways, sometimes telling exciting or amusing stories, always expressed in endlessly interesting art forms. The sculptures are as complex and sophisticated as a language. In fact, among those traditional groups that lack writing, sculpture takes its place. Carvings provide what writing expresses: ideas and hopes, reminiscences and theories, virtue and villainy, sorrow and humor, weakness and strength. And so African art becomes, routinely, a part of daily life.

Warren Robbins (it is impossible to write about the Museum of African Art without using his name at least twice) has noted that even the small squiggles on otherwise blank surfaces are often much more than the mere filling in of space with decoration. They may be, for example, a visual, tactile expression of the rhythms that I felt in my uneducated western bones when I pranced around the auditorium. That was a great afternoon. ✳

Collections By Design

Like most people addicted to the Smithsonian, I always took it for granted that the Institution's museums were in some way restricted to Washington. However far-flung the research establishments might be, the museum complex seemed to me purely a phenomenon of the capital.

I was wrong and I should have known better. The Smithsonian has a habit of defying such imagined restrictions. To prove it, in 1976 blares of celebratory trumpets echoed southward from New York as the Cooper-Hewitt Museum, the Smithsonian Institution's National Museum of Design, opened its doors in upper Manhattan.

As edified and delighted as they were with the museum's opening, many New Yorkers did not regard the gift as new. After all, the Carnegie Mansion, occupying the block between 90th and 91st streets along Fifth Avenue, had been a showplace since the turn of the century. And the remarkable collections that now filled it had been pleasing interested Manhattanites since 1897.

It was in that year that Sarah, Eleanor, and Amelia Hewitt (known as the Misses Sally, Nelly, and Amy), granddaughters of inventor Peter Cooper, opened their long-dreamed-of "Museum for the Arts of Decoration." Miss Sally and Miss Nelly particularly used their resources to set up, as a tribute to their grand-

father, the kind of useful museum that he had wanted at the Cooper Union, the foundation that he had established some 40 years earlier in what is now Astor Place in lower Manhattan. In essence, Peter Cooper wanted to offer free education to the city's working classes. His granddaughters kept that in mind when they built their museum on the top floor of the Cooper Union. And public education in design still remains a priority at the Cooper-Hewitt.

Bursting with enthusiasm and blessed with many munificent friends, the Hewitt sisters crammed their museum with decorative arts. J.P. Morgan bought up Spanish and French textiles and shipped them home to the Hewitts. Intricate metalwork, glass, furniture, sketches, paintings, and engravings flooded into the Cooper Union Museum. The Hewitt sisters spirited some of the *objets d'art* away from the old Cooper mansion to fatten up the collection. The Homer family came through with the world's largest single collection of Winslow Homer drawings and paintings. Miss Nelly and Miss Sally tracked down the rare and beautiful *Histoire Naturelle des Oiseaux* by Georges-Louis Buffon, the renowned French naturalist. Scores of watercolors and drawings by Thomas Moran, painter of sweeping western landscapes, came to the museum; so did more than 2,000 oils and sketches by Fred-

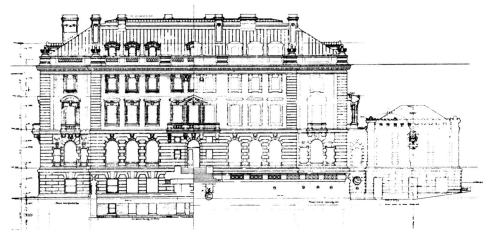

Overleaf: *A déjeuner service of Sèvres porcelain, c. 1813, gift of Mrs. Katrina Becker of Charleston, South Carolina, in memory of her parents, Mr. and Mrs. Charles V. Hickox.* Left: *This cutaway of the Carnegie Mansion on Fifth Avenue appears on the Cooper-Hewitt's letterhead.*

Wide-eyed Eleanor Hewitt, "Miss Nelly," and her sister Sarah, "Miss Sally," were the driving force behind the Cooper-Hewitt collection, begun in the 1890s. Never married, they spent their lives amassing examples of fine design from all over the world—prints, drawings, paintings, textiles, objets de vertu such as the Japanese box with flowers in mother-of-pearl, right.

Above left: *Antonia de Bañuelos.* Eleanor Hewitt. *1888. Oil on canvas, 34¼" x 23¾" (87 x 60 cm).* CHM, *bequest of Erskine Hewitt.*

Above right: *Carroll Beckwith.* Sarah Hewitt. *1899. Pastel, 24¼" x 19" (62 x 48 cm).* CHM, *bequest of Erskine Hewitt.*

erick E. Church, who was a leading member of the Hudson River School and painted wild and distant landscapes in such places as the Andes and Labrador.

This is just a sampling of the museum's works of art. European and Asiatic drawings and prints seem to go on forever. And then there are ceramics, fabrics, jewelry, wallpaper . . . the fact is that the words "design," used today to describe the museum, and "decoration," used by the sisters, are loose enough to encompass hundreds of widely varied subjects and about 300,000 objects spanning some 3,000 years and every continent.

The Cooper Union Museum, on the top floor of the old Cooper Union building, made its collections available for study, sketching, and copying by students. But costs mounted, and in the 1960s the museum was closed. New Yorkers (many of whom are fond of tradition) howled in anger. Officials buzzed; committees hummed; special groups whispered; in 1968 the museum was transferred to the Smithsonian, becoming the Cooper-Hewitt as a well-deserved nod to the two sisters. Four years later the old Carnegie Mansion was also given to the Smithsonian. Museum and mansion were thereupon wedded.

Andrew Carnegie, millionaire-steel tycoon-philanthropist of the late 19th and early 20th centuries, sought a simple home, nothing like the ostentatious imitations of French châteaux that were going up farther down Fifth Avenue. Carnegie wanted "the most modest, plainest, and roomiest house in New York." He chose a small height of land, rock-strewn and rather thinly settled, south of Harlem and beside Central Park. The slight rise of Fifth Avenue here is still called "Carnegie Hill."

The house Carnegie built is hardly modest and plain by today's standards, and its roominess is remarkable: 64 rooms; six floors; space enough for 19 servants, for a white-tiled boiler room with coal-fed furnaces and every piece of equipment doubled in case one set failed. Space enough for the proper entertainment of famous guests; for the kitchen and laundry facilities required to take care of lots of people; for the everyday comfort of Carnegie, his wife, and his daughter. The whole mansion was steel framed—the first private residence to be built thus.

Russell Lynes, in his vastly entertaining book about the Cooper-Hewitt, *More Than Meets the Eye*, tells how important guests would pull up under the copper and glass canopy on 91st Street and be ushered into the Great Hall, completely paneled in Scottish oak. It is still the entryway into the Cooper-Hewitt. In the music room with its ornate ceiling—Louis XVI style, except for one bagpipe, thrown in out of deference to the owner's native land— such guests as Eve Curie, daughter of Marie Curie, Jan Paderewski, or Mark Twain might have gathered for an after-dinner concert. It's the same room today, but is now transformed into a gallery hung with prints, or displays of laces and jewelry.

To reach the dining room, Carnegie's guests would have passed through a wide foyer that opens onto the garden. In the dining room, the famous visitors were asked to sign the tablecloth. The signatures were then traced with embroidery and so preserved. The dining room is now a gallery; so is the small breakfast room beyond it.

Beyond the breakfast room is the conservatory, glass-enclosed and heated by its own

Jungle scenes with butterflies adorn the pages of a rare book of 1730, Surinaamsche Insecten. *Its illustrator, Maria Sybilla Merian, braved South American rain forests to render specimens from life. The Cooper-Hewitt possesses many antique volumes, prized for their artwork depiction of flowers, greenery, and animal life.* Top: *Various turtle shapes and patterns from another rare book,* Locupletissimi Rerum Naturalium, *by Albertus Seba, 1734, reflect a Golden Age of art for naturalists in Europe and America.*

This lordly oak staircase, opposite, once led Andrew Carnegie, his wife, and daughter up to their bedrooms and dressing rooms. Today its chandelier lights the way for visitors to the Cooper-Hewitt Museum. The Carnegie Corporation deeded the turn-of-the-century neo-Georgian mansion to the Smithsonian in 1972. The south facade, right, bedecked with blossoms in the spring, looks out onto a splendid garden.

special furnace. Mrs. Carnegie loved flowers, and the conservatory was her domain. It has been restored much as she knew it, with many tropical plants among its greenery. The garden was also her territory. It takes up roughly half the city block that forms the property and was planted with azaleas and wisteria and other happy things, as well as flowering trees. It's the same now: a big, pleasant garden that is open to the public.

The galleries continue on the second floor where members of the family had their suites—a bedroom, dressing room, and bathroom for each—also a sitting room and a library. A large section of this floor has been converted into a long display room. The museum library is now on the third floor, where the Carnegies had guest rooms and a small gymnasium. Here and on the topmost floor are study rooms where examples from the collections can be examined.

The mansion is rich in memories of the Carnegies. When they retired after a dinner party at which they may well have entertained a president, they probably mounted the broad, beautiful oak staircase, and found their way to the floor above by the light of a splendid chandelier. Ascending the stairs today always makes me feel like a multimillionaire.

To one end of the Great Hall on the ground floor was Carnegie's private library and study. The doors are small—a signal of his territorial rights, for he stood only about five feet three inches. By the time he had moved into his house he had made his pile. And what a pile! His steel plants and related holdings amassed a huge fortune for him even before he sold out to J.P. Morgan (who then founded the U.S. Steel Corporation) for $480 million—an unheard of amount for an individual. Morgan reportedly shook hands with Carnegie to seal the deal and lauded him for being "the richest man in the world."

Carnegie had, however, a strict Scottish sense of morality. He believed that it was a moral duty for the rich to use their wealth responsibly. Huge fortunes, he wrote, should be disbursed for the maximum benefit of mankind.

So, sitting in his study on Fifth Avenue, the little titan of steel spent much time meeting with important people and working on countless philanthropic projects. His job—to which he devoted his enormous skill and energy—now was to give money away, not make it. It was during the years in this house that he got the Carnegie Institution of Washington under way; also the Carnegie Foundation for the Advancement of Teaching, the Carnegie Endowment for International Peace, and the Carnegie Corporation of New York City.

In 1919, Carnegie's daughter Margaret was married to Roswell Miller, and the couple

Medallions in miniature, 27 buttons sparkle on a page from a sales sample book from 18th-century France. Eleanor and Sarah Hewitt donated these metal-foil dazzlers.

moved into a 45-room town house, a gift from her parents. It was the house next door, facing 90th Street, its west front overlooking the Carnegie garden. The Miller House is now crammed with stored collections, with a few rooms available for administrative offices. As I write this, plans are underway to remodel the interior of the Miller House so temporary exhibitions can be held. The old Carnegie Mansion will then have permanent exhibition rooms with their own storage areas nearby.

This will mark a change for the Cooper-Hewitt, for since it opened its doors in 1976 it has offered one temporary exhibition after another, rotating its collections so that all the myriad interests, all the army of star attractions get their chance to appear on stage. There have been shows of buttons, laces, glassware, architectural drawings, textiles, costumes, stage sets, you name it. The field of design is so broad that its boundaries fade from sight. Every object fashioned by man has design. I think every good one is here.

What one recalls after many visits to the Cooper-Hewitt are the things that touch on one's personal interests. Items that spring to my mind reveal more about me than about the collections. So do the items I *don't* talk about. With that caveat, I'll name a few treasures that especially delight me and also mention things that may delight everybody else.

The figures amaze: more than 2,000 buttons, including some painted by great miniaturists; more than 4,000 match safes—the little metal boxes that held "strike anywhere" matches before the introduction of safety matches in cardboard "books." The match safes come in every shape from General Grant's head to a violin. They are carved and

In the days of touchy, strike-anywhere matches, myriad little match safes kept the gentleman smoker from igniting himself. The Cooper-Hewitt has more than 4,000, gifts of Carol B. Brener and Stephen W. Brener.

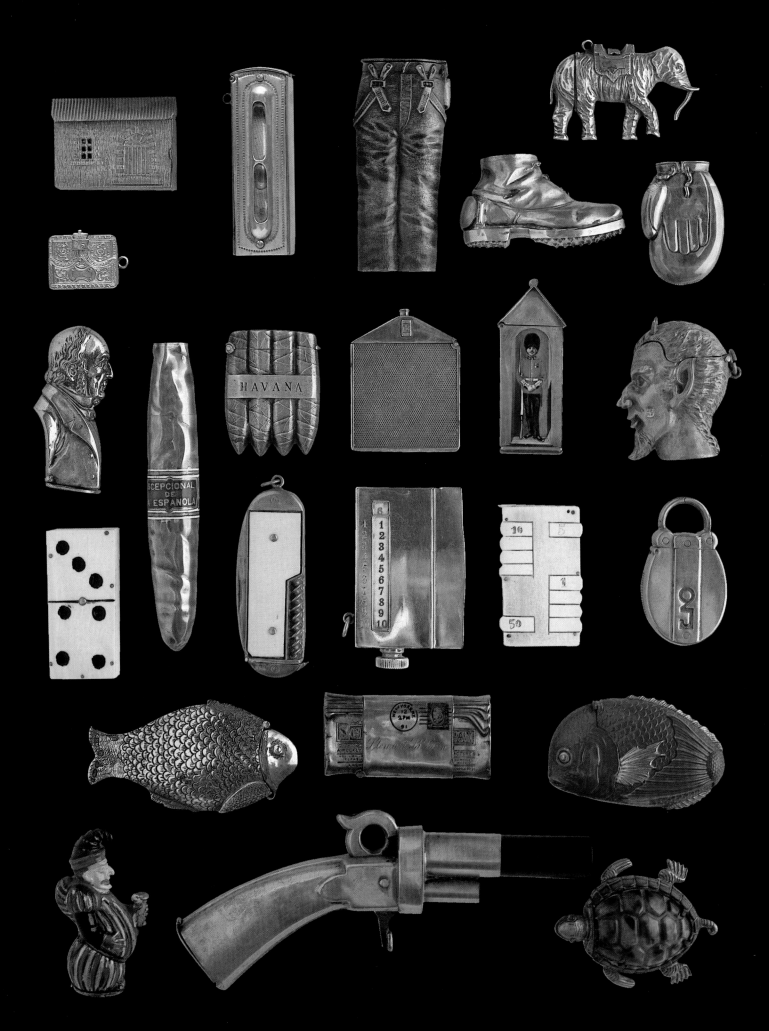

412

painted; they carry symbols and advertising slogans. Some have royal emblems. Some are silly. Some are beautiful.

The large textile collection encompasses a wide range of techniques, cultures, and periods. The oldest textiles are silks from the Han Dynasty of China, which dates from 206 B.C. to A.D. 220. They consist of a pair of mitts and a bonnet, and were found inside a box that was dug up in Hunan Province. The museum acquired these valuable examples of ancient Chinese fabric in 1951. This was more than 20 years after the death of the Hewitt sisters, but they undoubtedly would have loved this fine acquisition.

Since J.P. Morgan's generous gifts of Spanish, French, Eastern Mediterranean, and pre-Columbian textiles in 1902, the Cooper-Hewitt has picked up 17th-century velvet from Persia and dyed fabric of the same era from India, fourth-century embroidery from Egypt, and a screen print dated 1976 from Los Angeles. And lace.

I must say I'm partial to luxury items, and some of that Cooper-Hewitt lace is so intricately worked, so lavish, that when I stare at its endless patterns and tiny details, I find myself longing for the good old days of Louis XIV (assuming that I was at least a courtier and not some wretched peasant). My favorite piece of lace, however, is Flemish, not French. It's a lace collar from the 1600s. It was done with bobbin lace—wherein several threads are used at once—and it holds its shape so firmly that when I saw it at a museum show I was convinced it could still be worn. The idea of slipping it on, stiff and wondrously ornate, over your shirt and under your dark blue, all-wool, four-buttons-on-the-sleeve blazer fills me with pleasant thoughts.

There are some 6,500 examples of wallpaper and related accoutrements at the museum, the world's most comprehensive collection. The Hewitt sisters were not charmed with American design when they started putting this trove together, so they

Opposite: *Textile treasures abound at the Cooper-Hewitt, including "Tree of Life," a dyed hanging in silk by Lydia Bush-Brown Head. Gift of the artist.* Top: *Silk and metal threads add luster to a Persian panel in velvet from the 17th century.* Left: *Elephants and mythical beasts appear on this Eastern Mediterranean silk from the 11th or 12th century. Gift of J. P. Morgan.*

scoured around for early French and English wall coverings. The Cooper-Hewitt has since picked up an especially fine collection of American wallpaper. I wince a little when I see some of them, for I recall helping strip layers of old wallpaper off an early New England farmhouse so that the new owners could restore the broad paneling originally cut from the "King's pines" of colonial days. Certainly the paneling was beautiful and historic, but now I wonder how much beautiful and historic early American wallpaper was trashed in order to reach the wood.

When I investigated the wallpaper collection I had just been deeply involved with James McNeill Whistler and the Peacock Room at the Freer (Chapter 6), so I was interested in leather wall hangings such as those that Frederick Leyland bought and Whistler painted over. The Cooper-Hewitt doesn't have anything that might have belonged to Catherine of Aragon, as Leyland's was supposed to, but it does have a beautiful late 19th-century imitation of Spanish leather which adorned the walls of John D. Rockefeller's dining room at West 54th Street.

Some late 18th- and 19th-century wallpapers were painted rather than printed, even though their patterns sometimes repeated themselves. An example is in the Royal Pavilion at Brighton, the huge, ornate, beautiful summer palace built for the high-living George IV. The museum has some of these wallpapers, and also a watercolor of one of the walls, showing the wallpaper. This coverage of a museum object by museum art, and often by written description in the museum library, is typical of the Cooper-Hewitt. It remains true to its original concept as a museum for studying. You can learn about a kind of textile, for example, first by seeing it, then by poring over drawings or patterns of it, then by reading about it in the library. It sounds like overkill, but it is simply an opportunity for thorough scholarship—what the Hewitts wanted. This backup in research capability seems appropriate in the Carnegie Mansion with all its backup amenities.

Back to wallpaper. I found myself charmed by paper designed to carry a motif around a corner. I'm uncertain as to how this worked, but it's interesting to see. And a sample of paper from a children's room in England stirred memories of having seen something similar—only undoubtedly much less expensive—in a room that belonged to a small friend.

There are 112,000 prints and drawings at the Cooper-Hewitt. They are an endless resource for study, but they also include invaluable works by Mary Cassatt, Whistler, and Thomas Moran, in addition to Winslow Homer. The Homer drawings and paintings,

Flower and leaf patterns grace wallpapers from three countries: Englishman William Morris' "Pimpernel" paper, far left; *"Domino" paper,* left, *created with woodblocks by French artisans known as* dominotiers; *American wallpaper,* below, *based on the work of English artist Kate Greenaway.*

415

Below: *A Parisian named Paul Poiret designed the "Lampshade" dress and hobble skirt shown in this 1913 issue of* Gazette du Bon Ton. Bottom: *This day dress from a 1921 issue of the same gazette is a forerunner of the flapper's dress.* Opposite: *A fashion plate from 1809 shows the latest Parisian mode. Two printsellers of Paris, Jacques Esnauts and Michel Rapilly, hold credit for the original fashion plate. In 1778, they issued the earliest known colored illustration of the latest styles.*

donated by his brother, give me a special sensation when I see them, just as the Wright brothers' plane does at the National Air and Space Museum. Like that wonderful artifact, these canvases are real and authentic. They came off the easel of Winslow Homer just as surely as the old *Flyer* came out of that Dayton bike shop and that windblown shed at Kitty Hawk. To one whose knowledge of great events and great art is as plebeian as mine, authenticity adds a special dimension.

Among the Cooper-Hewitt prints are some 9,000 fashion plates which I personally find delightful. In color, they follow fashion trends from the late 18th and early 19th centuries (the latter showing simple Grecian gowns for women, Beau Brummell's tight little trousers for men), through the 1820s (women's waistlines right under the bust), and '30s (the women all fussed up and the men given big hips and narrow shoulders), and on through the multipetticoat years and the bustle era and the hobble skirts of World War I. Even fashions for children (poor little devils) are included in the plates. It's all very good fun.

This collection had once belonged to Vyvyan Holland, who was the son of our old friend Oscar Wilde. Holland? It turns out that when Wilde's cruel and regrettable trial for homosexuality came up and he was hustled off to Reading Gaol, the disgrace that was heaped on him by the Victorians spilled over onto his wife and, to a lesser extent, onto his two sons. She legally changed her name and that of the boys to Holland, an old family name on her side.

The Cooper-Hewitt's architectural and interior design drawings are also fascinating. They comprise one of the largest such collections in the country, and grew, in part, from the Hewitt sisters' purchase (for a pittance) of about 3,500 drawings from the private collection of an Italian art curator. Many of the drawings were from various sketchbooks and show adornments to Italian facades, doorways, details. New purchases supplemented the early one. Some sketches

LAQUELLE ?
Robe de soirée de Paul Poiret

2.

1.

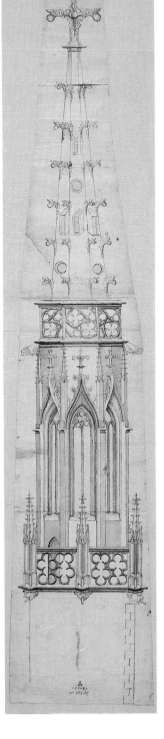

are of relatively plain architecture, unembellished with rearing steeds or the fluttering drapery of classical figures.

Recent sketches are of ideas for New York skyscrapers and of the villa built by Corbusier for Gertrude Stein's brother, in a Paris suburb. As she seems to have done with everybody, except Alice B. Toklas, the formidable Gertrude fought with her brother and he left the house of the salons at 27 rue de Fleurus.

The more you get to know the Cooper-Hewitt, the more you are intrigued with its role as an enormous repository of items once familiar, now often forgotten. But the acquisitions have not come without discrimination. The stuff that packs the rooms of the Miller House right now, and will eventually form permanent displays in the mansion, is most carefully chosen.

About 4,000 metalwork items, for example. It sounds like a wholesale warehouse, but it includes a 17th-century silver charger—a sort of platter—embossed with intricate reliefs which include symbols of four continents. No one knew much about the fifth continent, Australia, when this was done. The museum considers this bit of "metalwork" one of its most precious items—surely a Smithsonian treasure.

The Cooper-Hewitt's glass items stretch back to the Roman-Syrians of the first century, include Tiffany wares, and remind people such as me of how pleasing the design of a perfume bottle can be.

Household hardware fills shelves—locks and keys, knobs and knockers. The door knob and face plates from the old Woolworth Building (in my youth always the unbeatable world's tallest) have a special nostalgia.

The ceramics start with Etruscan earthenware and include tiles, pottery, Wedgwood, and porcelain. My favorite is the Meissen piece that holds a clock. I also like the clocks that are more important as clocks than as ceramic or metal. The biggest stands about nine feet tall, since a life-size bronze statue by Carrier-Belleuse rises upon the marble base wherein sits the clock.

The Cooper-Hewitt collection grew in an age of mansions, and it is most fitting that today the splendid Carnegie home on upper Fifth Avenue in New York should house the treasures of the art of architecture and building fixtures. Above: *Four architectural drawings, "Elevations of Mansions," by Whitney Warren from about 1894. Opposite, clockwise from top: Brighton's Royal Pavilion in watercolor and gouache by Frederick Crace, purchased in memory of Annie Schermerhorn Kane; a drawing from Germany for a Gothic steeple, c. 1500; a baluster in iron from a staircase in Chicago's Carson, Pirie, and Scott department store, designed by the Louis H. Sullivan firm; and an early 19th-century detailed scheme for an iron and glass gate.*

419

*Silver, responsive to both
human needs and artistic
whims, was chosen for this
1978 American traveling
flatware set by Anna Krohn
Graham. The pieces interlock,
the fork and spoon folding into
the knife. Gift of Aaron Faber
Gallery.*

A 20th-century four-piece tea service in silver and walnut by French designer Jean Puiforcat.

Above: *An American cocktail mixer in plated silver is fashioned into this playful penguin that dispenses drinks from its beak. The amusing denizen of Antarctica even frosts up when ingredients are shaken with ice.* Left: *This shallow platter, called a charger, gleams with silver and gold. Adolf Gaap of Augsburg, Germany, embossed it in 1689 with a figure of Alexander mourning Darius, fallen emperor of Persia, in the center and medallions representing the four continents on the rim. Gift of the Trustees of the Estate of James Hazen Hyde.*

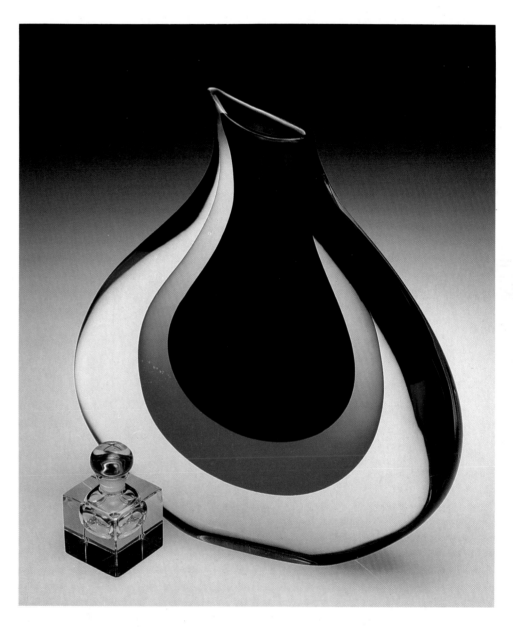

Opposite: *This vase of shimmering blown glass was designed by Louis Comfort Tiffany, who was intrigued by the peacock iridescence of ancient glass and developed a way to create this lustrous effect in the studio. From the collection of Stanley Siegel; gift of Stanley Siegel.* Above: *A tiny perfume bottle designed by Ben Kotyuk for Ralph Lauren (gift of Primary Designs Galleries) stands next to a vase of massive, multicolored glass from the Salviati Factory, Murano, Italy, gift of Michael Lewis Balamuth.*

Left: *This German porcelain from the Ludwigsburg factory was made around 1760–65 and depicts the popular four continents theme. Gift of the Trustees of the Estate of James Hazen Hyde.* Below: *A lovers' boat brooch in gold, from late 19th-century England, attributed to Carlo Giuliano. Purchased in memory of Annie Schermerhorn Kane and Susan Dwight Bliss.* Bottom: *An original design for a verrière (wine-glass cooler) from the famed porcelain factory at Sèvres, France. Purchase of the Friends of the Museum Fund. The Cooper-Hewitt owns such a vessel in porcelain.*

425

Other items at random have special appeal for me, and perhaps for you: a silver tea urn, again adorned with the four continents, whose spout is a woman's head that is swung into place before it pours. I also favor a set of 1814 coffee cups with cracks painted into them to give you that nice feeling that they're very antiquey (which now they are).

And as modern as tomorrow, sleek, slender flatware from Scandinavia—stainless that glows as richly as platinum. Another set, sterling, with the spoon and the fork stored within the handle of the knife.

Slabs of sculptured stone from the facades of New York buildings—the sort of thing that decorated a cornice or the lintel of a door and which I, for one, took entirely for granted un-

til I saw these. An 18th-century birdcage made of mahogany and wire and designed like a gothic turret. A cast-iron radiator in the shape of a shrine with a woman under the arch holding two goblets so you can pour water into it. It's six and a half feet tall, so it must have come from a pretty good-sized New York home.

Chairs! Far too many wonderful chairs to list. There's one designed by Frank Lloyd Wright, and one from the 19th century with papier-mâché embellishments. There's a roll-back office chair, deep purple, with a soft, round cylinder of upholstery held by a chromed bar which runs through it like an axle. But the bar is adjustable and the roller at the chair's back can be turned, and since it's

eccentric it takes a new position with every turn and. . . . Don't ever try to describe a roll-back office chair. It's enough to feel its infinite adjustments for tiny shades of comfort.

There's a liquid-looking plastic chair and an extravagant beanbag chair (remember beanbag chairs?). And there's the Chiquita Chair, so-called because it's adorned with carved banana leaves. It's mahogany, but you'd never know it because it's been lacquered richly and has come out a bright red-orange. The curator told me it weighs a ton. It's unforgettable.

That's a key word for this museum. Design is transitory, changing with our whims, seeming almost to orbit our lives so that a style sometimes recurs like Halley's Comet. And when a style, a mode, a little twist or method of design has passed beyond our ken, off on its apogee in far space, it's easily forgotten. We can recall beanbags, but who remembers much about Prohibition? The answer is: the Cooper-Hewitt, that's who. I found on one of the crowded shelves in an upstairs room (once a maid's room, I suppose) in the Miller House a cocktail shaker of the 1930s and '40s in the shape of a penguin. The museum had snared it before it disappeared on its orbit, and now keeps it especially for my delight—and per-

haps that of a few others.

There is no end to design as long as man's work continues. It stretches back through the centuries and it includes the vast and the tiny. Lisa Taylor, the director of the museum since 1968, once told me that the Cooper-Hewitt is concerned with everything from buttons to cities. Buttons I knew, but cities? She referred me to a museum publication, *Cities, the Forces that Shape Them*, a stimulating view of urban living from about 60 highly qualified contributors. Their thoughts add vastly to the museum's resources for they display the essence of a mighty subject, just as two thousand buttons give a taste of all the world's billions of them.

The museum can't quite put a city inside the Carnegie Mansion, but it can and does show elements in drawings, models, publications, displays of design. And why be restricted to the building? The Cooper-Hewitt show dealing with subways went on display first at a 42nd Street subway station, then went on the road to 18 cities.

In the truest spirit of the entire Smithsonian, this proud old New York establishment collects moments from the passage of time and charms us into standing still with it and looking upon ourselves with understanding and candor, revelation and enjoyment. ✹

Opposite: *A diminutive "Starfish Dancer" emerges in bronze, gold, and ivory. Demetre Chiparus created her about 1925. From the collection of Stanley Siegel; gift of Stanley Siegel.* Right: *This 19th-century Japanese guard for a ceremonial sword, made of iron and gold by Bairiuken Kiyonaga, resembles a pair of folding screens.*

Filigrees, Furbelows, and Flowers on Flywheels

A soft glow penetrated the frosted panes of the massive double door and bathed us as we approached. I reached for the brass plate, but before I touched it the door swung open magically, and we stepped through, gladly escaping the cold, drear street.

Warm light sparkled around us. A wave of gentle sound washed over us as guests greeted each other, the ladies in exquisite gowns, glittering with jewelry, the gentlemen, in full evening dress. Strains of "Tales from the Vienna Woods" floated down from the second floor.

A liveried footman bowed. I produced a card from my white waistcoat and handed it to him. In stentorian tones he announced us, and the trumpeters atop the broad stairway sounded their fanfare. With little ado, we mounted the crimson-carpeted steps, sniffing the tantalizing aroma of hot savories, the fleeting scent of expensive perfume.

The stairs led us straight into a vast and lofty room echoing with the lilt of Strauss. On the gleaming floor a score of couples whirled through the waltz, ladies clutching their fans, rich silks and satins rustling, gentlemen with coattails flying, bright black pumps flashing, hands carefully white gloved lest they defile those soft, bare shoulders so daringly submitted to the tender grasp of a mere man.

I turned to my partner in unspoken invitation. She paused for a moment with becoming modesty, then graciously inclined her head. And I glimpsed a sparkle in her eye as we joined in. . . .

No, this didn't happen in 1880 at an imperial palace of old Europe. It took place about a century later at a treasure of a building that belongs to the old Smithsonian. It was a Viennese waltz party at the one gallery in the Institution with enough Victorian elegance to carry it off: the Renwick.

The splendid old building next to Blair House on Pennsylvania Avenue had been carefully prepared for the event. The music came from an orchestra in Viennese costume. My wife's gown came from a dark corner of the closet where it had hung for years awaiting just such an occasion. My white tie and tails came from a rental agency.

In the Grand Salon, focal point of the Renwick Gallery, the musicians clustered in the center of the long north wall. The huge carpet had been removed and the floor waxed. Marble-top tables were set up around the dance area and in the center of the two circular couches or "poufs" were plinths bearing statues which in turn carried gasoliers.

The music was magically evocative. Everyone waltzed divinely. The food came from service areas on the second floor and was marvelous. The champagne . . . oh, my! I have loved the Renwick ever since.

No one loved it very much for the first sixty-odd years of this century. It was then the United States Court of Claims, a grim old government building where legal bureaucracy reigned, where many a heart was broken, where the original purpose of the building was forgotten and its future was always in doubt. Even its looks were regarded with indifference, for its architectural style was passé, and the modern trend was to get rid of the old wherever possible. Fortunately, the old Renwick was never quite gotten rid of.

Overleaf: *Nostalgic trappings of a Victorian ball that serve as elegant reminders of another age include gloves, top hat, dance card, and nosegay holder (the latter on loan from the collection of Frances Jones Poetker). So, too, does the many-splendored Renwick Gallery, below, originally designed by James Renwick in 1859 as the Corcoran Gallery of Art. The Renwick became part of the Smithsonian in 1965. A bronze bust of Renwick,* right, *resides in the gallery's Grand Salon, gift of Mr. and Mrs. Paul Garber.*

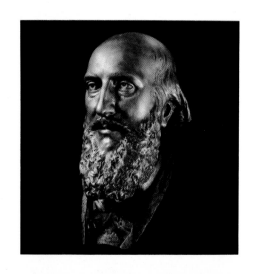

Its beginnings go back to about 1859 when James Renwick, fresh from his architectural triumph of the Smithsonian Castle, designed a building across the street from the White House to become the original Corcoran Gallery of Art, the first public art museum in Washington. Renwick pulled out all the stops, going for what is called French Renaissance or Second Empire style. The mansard roof, the mixture of arches and gables, the pilasters and cornices and embellishments are as French as Le Petit Palais in Paris; the red brick and brown sandstone snap you back to young America. All Washington awaited this fine expression of culture which would house the private art collection of the popular William Wilson Corcoran, merchant and banker, friend of Presidents Fillmore and Buchanan, of such luminaries as Daniel Webster, Stephen Decatur, Robert E. Lee, and Jefferson Davis.

Then the Civil War broke out and work on the new building stopped. Soldiers jammed into the capital. Like many other Washingtonians, Corcoran's sympathies lay with the South. He moved to Europe while the war raged. And his unfinished gallery became a warehouse for Union army uniforms, then headquarters for the Quartermaster General of the Union Army.

The army used the unfinished building for the duration of the war and for four years thereafter. Not until 1869 did the builders get back to work on Mr. Corcoran's gallery, and it wasn't really finished until 1874. But Washington society got a preview of it in 1871 when Corcoran invited President and Mrs. Grant to a gala ball there to raise money for yet another unfinished structure—the Washington Monument. The building held the Corcoran collection until 1897. By then the collection had grown too large and the building itself too small. A new, larger Corcoran Gallery arose nearby (it's still there as a private museum), and the old one slipped into its dismal period as a minor governmental edifice. In 1965 it was turned over to the Smithsonian and soon its restoration began.

I can remember the amazement with which my friends and I watched the results of the work in progress. Stone embellishments and scrollwork, turned lumpy and shapeless with the accumulated dirt and deterioration of decades, had to be taken down and new ones painstakingly made from molds. One by one, pilasters returned to the freshness of youth, their capitals again rich with the carvings that had been there all along. The interiors of the Grand Salon and Octagon Room were brought back to Renwick's original plum color. And the other rooms were also repainted. Paintings were hung in the Grand Salon in the Victorian manner from eye level to ceiling, lit by the long skylight overhead. Electricity, of course, had taken over from gaslight. Not counting those gasoliers near the poufs, the room had about 285 gas jets.

The second upstairs display room, the Octagon Room, had been designed by Renwick to show off Hiram Powers' controversial nude statue, *The Greek Slave*. This, of course, was moved to the new Corcoran, but the Smithsonian restored the elegant room. Downstairs rooms became additional display areas as well as administrative quarters. Renamed for its architect, the Renwick Gallery opened in January 1972, as a new Smithsonian star, the crafts, design, and decorative arts division of the Museum of American Art.

No building in the Institution can quite match the Renwick's ardent espousal of the Victorian look. The Castle is more important, and looks it. Its ghosts are those of scientists and philosophers. The Arts and Industries Building celebrates a particular time, the nation's Centennial, and looks it. Inventors and engineers haunt it. But the Renwick, despite its focus on contemporary crafts, runs wild with Victorian details, from its architectural adornments to the concave poufs upholstered in plush plum-colored velveteen that back up against the four sides of those gasolier-bearing statues. The chairs around its marble-top tables are in the bentwood style. Others are gilded Louis XIV-style ballroom chairs.

In 1972, when the Renwick re-opened as an art gallery, the Grand Salon, opposite, *had just been refurbished and repainted, making it an impressive showplace in its own right, as well as a fine backdrop for the paintings adorning its walls.*
Below: *Emile Renouf.* The Helping Hand. *1881. Oil on canvas, 5' x 7'5" (1.52 x 2.26 m). In the Collection of the Corcoran Gallery of Art, a private museum, Washington, D.C., museum purchase, 1885.*
Bottom: *Elizabeth Nourse.* Fisher Girl of Picardy. *1889. Oil on canvas, 46¾ x 32⅜" (119 x 82 cm).* NMAA, *gift of Elizabeth Pilling.*

The Renwick's ghosts are surely of the bon ton, accustomed to ballrooms and suppers with crystal punch bowls, appreciative of the works of Abbey and de Chavannes, Howe and van Lerius, Nourse and Renouf. These painters of the late 19th to early 20th century are all represented (along with many others) on the walls of the Grand Salon. Renouf comes through very strongly as you enter the room. Remember *The Helping Hand*? That appealing picture of the little girl with tentative hands on the oar that the crusty old pipe-smoking fisherman is pulling? You used to see it in every shop that sells prints. And here it is, the actual canvas by Emile Renouf, a big one, too. And I shouldn't even mention it because it doesn't belong to the Renwick. It's on loan from the Corcoran, which, of course, is not affiliated with the Smithsonian. But it's so evocative of that time (1881) that I can't help staring at it with delight, and feeling that I know the Renwick all the better for it.

A couple of other paintings—one is a portrait of Mr. Corcoran—are on loan from the Corcoran Gallery. The rest are from the Museum of American Art. Though the emphasis of the paintings is the Victorian years, the earliest on display here are two by Richard Wilson and one attributed to him. Wilson was a great British landscapist of the 18th century, reflecting the classicism of his time. He was very prolific, and it is quite in character for a Victorian gallery to display a few of his works.

Among the sculptures is a marble bust of Proserpine—the one I mentioned in chapter one—by Hiram Powers. At least the design was by Hiram Powers, but the carving may well have been done by the artisans he employed in his studio in Italy. After all, there are more than 150 of his Proserpines around. Certainly whoever completed her added that same old classical face—straight nose, small mouth, lofty brow, wide-set eyes with aristocratic haughtiness strongly implied. Go look again at the first ladies. Same face. Different sculptor, but identical.

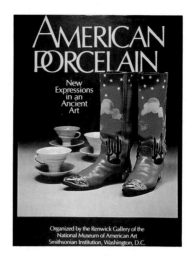

The strength of the Renwick is not in its own permanent display of paintings and sculpture but in its unending series of special shows, each wonderfully surprising and imaginative, as though trying to outdo the one before. An exhibit of the designs of Raymond Loewy included an actual automobile—a Studebaker Avanti, that beautiful vehicle that told the world what American designers and car builders could do if the economy allowed it. Of course the economy didn't allow it, Studebaker folded, and the Avanti is now considered a classic.

I think it's great to have things like the Avanti in an art gallery. It's not really "far out" for the Smithsonian. Some New Yorkers will remember when the Cooper-Hewitt got the Beatles' Rolls Royce as a gift from John Lennon and displayed it. It was bright yellow with brilliant orange and blue psychedelic designs and had a horn that played, I think, the opening bars of *Lili Marlene*. The Rolls made a stop on the Mall before being shipped to New York. Secretary Ripley drove it around. He said it handled like a truck, but that the horn was fun.

The Rolls went into a Cooper-Hewitt show called Ornament in the Twentieth Century— much the kind of show that the Renwick puts on. I don't know how they got the Rolls into the Carnegie Mansion. I know that they had to turn the Avanti on its side to get it through the front door of the Renwick.

There have been other wonderful shows at the Renwick—it's a regular theater for craft and design exhibitions. I remember a Frank Lloyd Wright show which opened my eyes to all the designs he did that weren't buildings: wallpaper, stained-glass windows, tables, flat-ware, chairs, other items that I never dreamed of associating with this eminent American architect, whose talent and taste were, at least to my eyes, enormous.

Then—as though to forestall complaints that all the Renwick displayed were outrageously extravagant items—Lloyd Herman, the gallery's director, put on a show called Good as Gold. It exhibited jewelry made of glass and ceramics and plastic and other everyday things. The results were incredibly imaginative, especially the designs fashioned from "found objects." There were ivory trinkets made from piano keys and a belt made of electric wiring that clipped together with terminal jaws.

In 1982, the Renwick marked its tenth birthday with the offbeat flair that was by then expected of it. First it displayed a collection of birthday cakes, carefully selected from scores that had been submitted. They had one thing in common: they were inedible. They were made by artists and craftsmen out of things like fabric, plastic, metal, glass tubing. One was crocheted. Then there were souvenirs of the Renwick, similarly fashioned. Pigeons, for example. The Renwick has lots of pigeons, so these were souvenirs. But they were soft sculpture.

I suppose it's obvious that the Renwick is one of my favorite Smithsonian places. The fact that this wonderful Victorian building, so rich in history and redolent of Victorian tastes and sensibilities—which still hung on a bit when I was a boy—is the home of an endless, ever-surprising parade of smashing modern design amuses me. And add those special shows when the artists are encouraged simply to have fun . . . well, I'm totally won over.

Opposite: *In 1977–78, the Renwick featured a show of Frank Lloyd Wright's decorative designs, including this dining room furniture set, complete with lamp stands-cum-flower holders. Wright designed it in 1908 as part of his overall plan for the Frederick C. Robie house in Chicago.*

Top: *From the whimsical to the scholarly, three posters reflect the diversity of the Renwick's exhibits. From left to right: A 1982–83 anthropological exhibit on celebrations around the world, a 1982 show commemorating the Renwick's tenth birthday, and a 1980–81 retrospective on American porcelain.*

There are a few buildings "of a certain age" in Washington—the Renwick is one—that call to mind those elegant gatherings that sparkled with brilliant repartee, the salons. Salons formed so naturally around James McNeill Whistler that the very word was often associated with him. One of the American artists who visited Europe, met Whistler, and was delighted by the salon idea was a wealthy woman named Alice Pike Barney, who in the 1890s settled in Washington with her equally wealthy husband. Both before and after their arrival in the nation's capital, Alice spent some time abroad, soaking up the cultural delights of Paris. And once back in Washington, she began to feel the need for a salon there. Even at the turn of the century, it was hardly more than a sleepy little town, blazing hot in the summer, drenched in humidity, choking in dust when it was dry, gluey with mud when it was not, and culturally rather barren.

Members of Congress were still of the tobacco-chewing, gallus-snapping school, and no one else in town had much influence over the fate of the city. But there were some bright, interesting people nonetheless, and Mrs. Barney decided to set up a permanent salon and drag culture, willy-nilly, into Washington.

The result was Barney Studio House, now a special small treasure of the Institution. It

stands on Sheridan Circle among a number of embassies, all facing the statue of General Philip Sheridan on his faithful steed, our friend Rienzi/Winchester (see pages 16–17). The house is tall and narrow, richly paneled and furnished and designed for the entertainment of the interested elite. A sort of stage is set up in the ground floor reception room and a gallery for musicians overlooks the upstairs studio room. Guests were encouraged to take part in small theatricals, wearing costumes and reading meaningful lines. Mrs. Barney seems to have been particularly interested in drama.

At any rate, Sarah Bernhardt used to appear here, also Ruth St. Denis. Music floated through the rooms of the house and guests gazed at works of art—many of them Alice Barney's—on the walls. Among the paintings are portraits of the Barney daughters, Natalie and Laura. Upon growing up, the girls spent most of their time in Europe. Natalie became a poet and writer.

The Barney Studio House can be visited on appointment and sometimes offers dramatic or musical presentations for the public. It's worth seeing—a real, honest-to-goodness salon transplanted to the cultural desert of Theodore Roosevelt's Washington.

It's haunted of course. Pianos play in the evening in darkened rooms that are quite empty of mortals. Bursts of laughter can be heard behind closed doors, shadows flit along faintly lit hallways. A friend and colleague of mine once made his digs in the upstairs accommodations of Barney Studio House—the servants' quarters, I suppose—while awaiting permanent assignment to Washington. Visiting him in the evening was always a scalp-tingling adventure because of the sounds and movements in the darkened lower rooms.

He told me that he was returning to his rooms late one evening when, mounting the gloomy stairway toward the second floor, he heard muted laughter and the tinkle of glasses, saw a glow of discreet light. Gathering his courage, he peeked around the corner and saw an elegant dinner table, candle-lit, set with places—13 he suspects—and around it were sitting ladies in the fashions of 1900 and gentlemen in old-fashioned dinner attire, all engrossed in quiet and genteel conversation.

It took him a moment to realize that they were, actually, real. It was a costume party, appropriately staged at the Barney Studio House. My friend still nourishes a soft spot for the place, but he moved out of there as soon as he could.

Top, left to right: *Alice Pike Barney.* Laura Attentive. *1912. Pastel on pulpboard, 19⅝ x 18⅜" (50 x 47 cm);* Natalie With Flowing Hair. *c. 1895. Pastel and pencil on paperboard, 23⁹⁄₁₀ x 17¼" (61 x 44 cm);* Self-Portrait With Hat And Veil. *c. 1906. Pastel, 25⅛ x 18¾" (64 x 48 cm). NMAA, gifts of Laura and Natalie Barney.*
Opposite: *In this studio room, Alice Pike Barney staged musicals and other cultural events. She also exhibited works of art here, her own as well as those of other artists. One of her self-portraits is displayed on the easel.*

In another part of late 19th-century Washington, another extraordinary woman was making her mark in what was really a man's world. Her name was Anna J. Cooper—teacher, lecturer, scholar, author, feminist, human rights advocate, above all education reformer—and she was teaching Latin at the Washington Colored High School, familiarly known as the M Street School because of its location. Her lifelong credo was *education for service*—service to her race.

For Anna Cooper was born a slave in North Carolina in 1858, on the eve of the Civil War. At a time when the necessity of education for both blacks and women was being questioned, she earned a masters degree from Oberlin College, taught languages and science at Wilberforce College in Ohio, then Latin at the only high school for blacks in Washington, D.C. Eventually she became principal of the M Street School (now Dunbar High School), and secured scholarships to Harvard, Yale, Brown, Amherst, and Dartmouth for her most promising students. She also taught Latin and Greek at Lincoln University in Missouri, shared the rostrum at Hampton Institute with the great black educator Booker T. Washington in 1892, and was chosen as the American delegate to the Pan African Conference in London in 1900.

The life of this indefatigable woman—in her fifties she took in the five orphaned children of her nephew, in her sixties she earned a PhD in French from the Sorbonne in Paris, in her seventies she became President of Frelingheusen University, a Washington, D.C., institution of higher education for employed blacks—was the subject of a major exhibition at the Smithsonian's Anacostia Neighborhood Museum in 1980. The museum, devoted to black American history and culture, was started in 1967 in a former movie theater in Anacostia, a Washington neighborhood rich in black history. More than any other Smithsonian museum, it involves the community in which it is based, encouraging Anacostia residents to participate in its myriad programs and adventures.

In the words of director John Kinard, the museum's aim was "to put people in touch with their history," and what better place to start than the local neighborhood? So the first major exhibition examined the history of Anacostia from 1608 to 1930. The next step was to look back to Africa, to the beginning, as it were, before coming back to the United States and taking an overall view of Afro-American history, which is, after all, American history.

The Anacostia Neighborhood Museum is in a unique position to mount the type of exhibitions that it does, for it has a wealth of oral information to draw upon. Some of Anacostia's older residents were Anna Cooper's pupils and remember her Latin classes well—and fondly. And a few of the real old-timers even remember watching Frederick Douglass' funeral cortege as it proceeded through the streets of Anacostia in 1895. They were very young then, of course, but the impression left behind by the event was powerful indeed. For Frederick Douglass, the great abolitionist, civil rights leader, lecturer, and orator, who like Anna Cooper was born into slavery, was the "Sage of Anacostia." He had moved there in 1877, and he was easily the most prominent citizen. Far from allowing his many achievements to remove him from his neighbors, he involved himself in all kinds of community affairs, attending church meetings and picnics, checking in on Sunday schools. All of Anacostia grieved his death.

And of course the Anacostia Neighborhood Museum has organized a couple of exhibitions on this great figure of American history. Today the museum is building up its collection, expanding its areas of research, gaining national prominence with its publications and traveling exhibits. But it hasn't forgotten its Anacostia roots. And the age that produced Frederick Douglass, Booker T. Washington, and Anna J. Cooper—that incredible Victorian age—will forever remain an era of vital interest to this innovative museum.

Left: *Addison N. Scurlock.* Anna J. Cooper *(1858-1964). c. 1923. Photograph, 5 x 7" (13 x 18 cm). Mrs. Regina Bronson. Anna Cooper was 65 at the time this photograph was taken. When she died in 1964 she was 105 years old.*
Below: *Anna Cooper sits at her teacher's desk in the Anacostia Neighborhood Museum's reconstruction of her M Street School classroom.*
Bottom: *In the Anacostia Neighborhood Museum's collection is this broadside of a poem by Langston Hughes, who was considered the poet laureate of the Harlem Renaissance movement of the 1920s.*
Bottom left: *Frederick Douglass, who remained active during his last years in Cedar Hill, Anacostia, is shown here hard at work in his parlor.*

The other great memory of Victoriana at the Smithsonian is the Arts and Industries Building. I've saved it until last because it's my own, my home for 13 years. That's more than three times the number of years I spent in my university, and I get good and emotional about that—so forgive me if I get personal about the A & I, as we call it.

It was the ghosts that I first knew, for my first visit was in the evening after the doors were secured and the only access was through the ancient tunnel that connects A & I to the Castle. I was met and led through this brick-walled burrow with arched roof where pipes and conduits run—clad in sponge rubber to protect the scalps of anyone over five feet nine. Trudging along that vaulted tunnel, I instantly transported myself into the fantasies where I am often so comfortable. This time it was Mr. Toad of *The Wind in the Willows*, being led away under arrest: "on and on, past the rack chamber and the thumbscrew room, past the turning that led to the private scaf-fold, till they reached the door of the grimmest dungeon that lay in the heart of the innermost keep." Surely I heard an eldritch scream echoing beyond those bleak stones? But no, it was only a door creaking at the end of the tunnel.

Through it we passed, and on into the gloomy innards of the A & I Building. Then along a shadowy, deserted corridor and through another great oaken door into the vast exhibit area. And as I hurried after my guide, the eyes of mannequins followed me, costumes rustled as I passed, a bust gravely winked and the wings of the *Spirit of St. Louis* rocked gently in greeting.

This was in the days when aircraft were displayed here. Lindbergh used to come and look at the *Spirit* to recall his experiences in it for a book he was writing. He'd usually arrange to come by after hours to avoid unwanted publicity. There he'd stand—a tall, quiet figure, absorbed in the small silver plane hanging beside him.

A flag-bedecked sign beckons visitors into the Arts and Industries Building and the world of Victorian wonders that awaits them. Originally called the United States National Museum, the A & I, as it's commonly known today, was built to house objects from the Centennial Exhibition of 1876. Right: One of the Smithsonian's flower gardens lies along the east side of A & I.

Smithsonian magazine, as yet only an embryo, grew gradually in one office area after another, practically all over the Arts and Industries Building. As new kids on the block, we had to make do with cast-off sites—great heights and cramped closets under the eaves. I found it all immensely romantic and exciting, especially the tower where I spent many happy months—until its air conditioning system collapsed of a fatal aneurysm, spilling its life-giving fluid to such a depth on my floor that I felt my aerie was turning into a rather large aquarium.

By the time the magazine was born in 1970 we had come to understand and love our building. And it is extraordinary, this second-of-all Smithsonian structures. Work started in 1879 and was finished in time for President Garfield's inaugural ball in 1881. Because the building was completely symmetrical, it was erected at a cost of only $3.00 per square foot, making it the cheapest building ever completed by the government in Washington.

The building was a triumph of modern mechanics and materials. Its huge iron roof was stabilized by long iron tie rods, threaded at their ends to take the giant nuts that held everything together. While our office was perched in an attic, some of us, in the throes of editorial frustration, would climb up to the nearby tie rods, vowing that we would unscrew the entire building if things didn't improve.

The architectural style is listed as "modernized Romanesque," but that doesn't really do it justice. I used to tell prospective visitors to look around the Mall until they spotted the transplanted capitol of some remote and obscure Soviet state. That never failed to set them straight. Inside, the exhibition bays are cruciform, coming together at the great rotunda where the fountain splashes. Yet the building is square, so the areas between bays are available for administrative purposes and for such projects as our magazine.

The original purpose of the National Museum, as it was called, was to display some of

Originally engine No. 3 for the Santa Cruz Railroad, the Jupiter, left, *was built in 1876 by the Baldwin Locomotive Works. Its long service career finally came to an end in the 1950s in Guatemala. Opposite: Massive Rodman guns, a model of the 312-foot cruiser* Antietam, *and other military objects in A & I collections recall War Department displays at the Centennial in Philadelphia.*

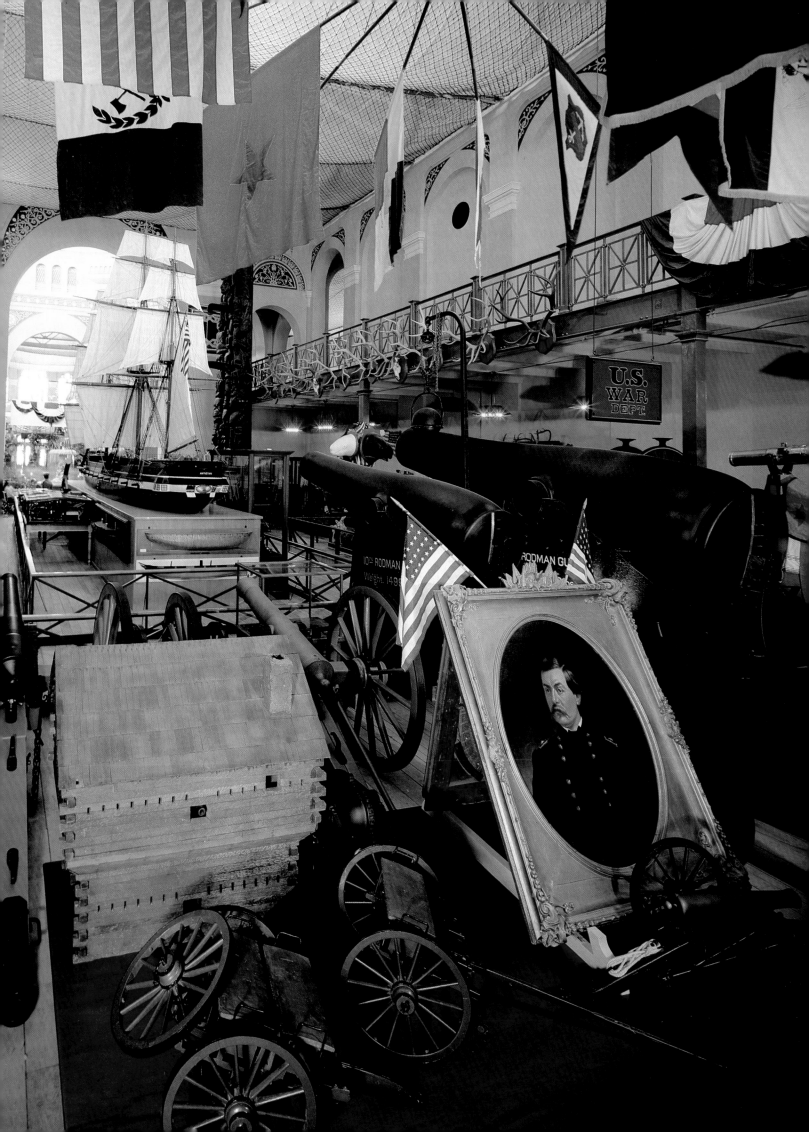

the wonderful items that had appeared at the Philadelphia Centennial Exhibition in 1876 to demonstrate the strides the youthful republic had made. So when the Bicentennial rolled around, a decision was made by the Smithsonian to restore A & I to its original looks, and to fill it with those same Centennial objects wherever possible and with others of the same vintage wherever necessary.

A new generation of architects explored the old building and realized that over the years it had lost its color. The Victorians, with all their neo-Gothic leanings, loved bright colors, but these had faded or been replaced. So new polychrome tiles were set into the floors and new stenciling enlivened the walls. The airplanes went to their new and magnificent museum, and old machinery and ordnance and household furniture and carriages began to take their place. The fountain under the rotunda dome had been covered over and forgotten long ago. Now it was rebuilt, to be surrounded by ever-changing plants from the horticultural department, and soon was burbling away and collecting small change tossed in for luck.

I was fascinated by the great steam engines that were inched into place for this 1876 exhibition. They had been idle for years, but the curators and their assistants polished the old piston rods, refitted the bearings, cleaned, oiled, greased, repainted the mighty flywheels, adjusted the whirling governors, filled the little glass oil cups that nourished the bearings and finally fed a little compressed air (steam would have been too dangerous) into the cylinders. I remember the groans with which the great pistons first moved and the clacking of the moving parts as they grudg-

ingly turned on their bearings. More oil, more tightening, more adjusting, then more air. And at the end of one day the engines were clicking over gently, the cylinders panting, the wheels whispering. Even now, I can never get enough of watching those engines turn.

Just looking at them immobile is a pleasure. When these were first built and first moved with the thrust of steam they were a new enough concept to merit special care, pride, affection, even reverence. Kipling caught the feeling in *McAndrew's Hymn*:

> From coupler-flange to spindle-guide
>   I see
> Thy Hand, O God—
> Predestination in the stride o' yon
>   connectin'-rod.

No wonder, then, that they carry adornments—bands and stripes along the great spokes, a posey, perhaps, on the casing of the cylinder.

One of the old engines drives a belt which then powers a series of shafts, each with its countershaft, each countershaft carrying its own belt drive to turn a lathe or a bandsaw or a drill press or a planer—whatever can be driven by a turning wheel. This was the essence of the 1870s machine shop, and the concept was so simple and effective that it lasted for decades in both the huge factories and the workshops of country towns. I remember the shop in New Hampshire where our old Buick was repaired—the steady hum of the shafts, the mechanic's hand reaching up to clutch that dark wood lever, shiny-smooth where his calluses had ground against it for so many years, then the slap and whine

of the belt and the inexorable spinning of a drill, the wisp of smoke as metal shavings peeled away, the smell of burning oil as the heat was soothed. To see that same setup at A & I stirs more memories, almost, than I can handle. And I've seen others of my age stop and stare and listen and sniff, their eyes looking back to a distant past.

The greatest engine of all, the star of the Philadelphia Exhibition, is no more. This was the giant Corliss steam engine, some 700 tons in all, with a flywheel 30 feet in diameter. It powered the entire machinery display at Philadelphia, and was later bought by George Pullman to power his railroad passenger car works at Pullman, Illinois, until 1909 when it was demolished. Arts and Industries displays a model of a Corliss that looks a lot like the one from the Centennial.

George H. Corliss of Rhode Island, developer of the huge engine, was an inventor of a specialized sewing machine. We think of these machines as being entirely the province of Elias Howe and Isaac Singer, but there were dozens of other sewing machine patent models, and a lot of them are gathered in the 1876 exhibit. I stumbled across them one time when I was exploring a dark corner, and I started to list the inventors and the years in which their brainchildren were born. It was hopeless. I jotted down 17 names with dates ranging from 1857 to 1876 and then gave up. I remember reading that William Dean Howells, visiting the original Exhibition, was overwhelmed by the sight of what amounted to a half a mile of sewing machine displays.

Howe got his patent in 1846, and Singer made his patented improvement in 1851. And one cannot talk about Isaac Merrit Singer

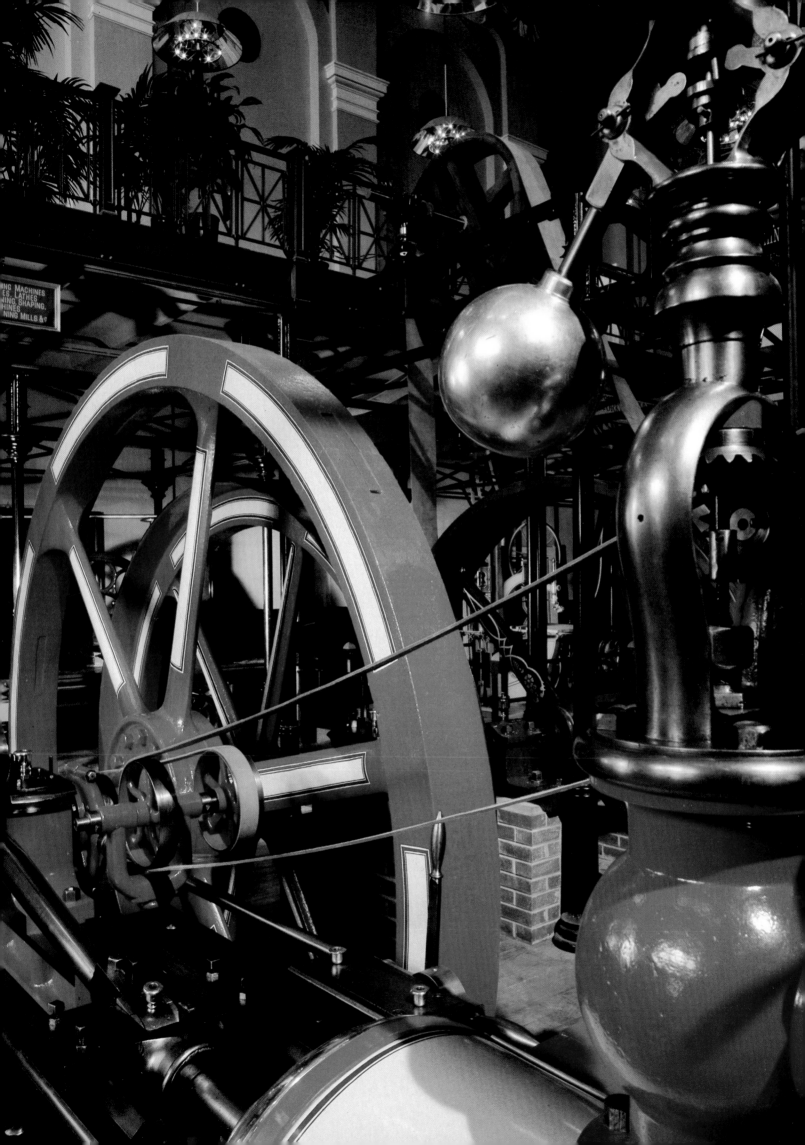

An overhead lineshaft drives lathes, a planer, and a milling machine in a composite of a mid-19th-century machine shop, left, at the Museum of American History. Power would have been provided by steam or water, depending on the geographical setting. Below: A couple is dwarfed by a giant Corliss steam engine similar to the one that drove all the machinery in Machinery Hall at the Centennial Exhibition.

without dashing straight over to the National Portrait Gallery for a look at the bright and revealing painting that Edward Harrison May did of him in 1869 (see page 44). Singer was a self-made millionaire, the 19th-century American dream come true. By 1863, the Singer Company was reportedly selling a thousand sewing machines a week. The money poured in after various lawsuits were settled (he had a huge patent war with Howe), and Singer was able to do just what he pleased—juggle a number of mistresses and sire about a score of illegitimate children, among more prosaic pursuits.

He got into trouble when his common-law wife encountered him on a New York street with one of his mistresses and caused a scene. Singer, furious, followed her home and apparently beat and choked her. She survived and had him arrested. Eventually, he settled down to a monogamous existence in Paris

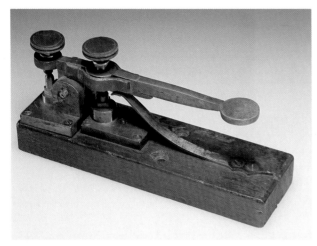

Flowering of Yankee ingenuity before and during the 19th century produced such inventions as Eli Whitney's cotton gin of 1794, top right, *and Samuel F. B. Morse's telegraph key,* top, *which sent first U.S. telegraph message in 1844. Above: Ornate jar of the late 1890s dispensed Coca-Cola syrup, which had been invented in 1886 and was a popular nerve tonic of the time.*

Above: *Mr. Barnes of New York enjoys a ride on Goodrich tires in this poster, c. 1898, from the Smithsonian's Warshaw Collection of Business Americana.*

Left: *Christian Schussele painted an imaginary gathering of 19th-century inventors. Joseph Henry, physicist and first Smithsonian Secretary, leans on the column at center.* Christian Schussele. Men of Progress. *1862. Oil on canvas, 4'3⅜" x 6'4¾" (1.30 x 1.95 m).* NPG, *transfer from the National Gallery of Art, gift of Andrew W. Mellon, 1942.*

with a French wife. And it was here that he had his portrait done. Personally, I love it—so arrogant, so dissolute, so rich.

Transportation is caught at the exhibit with carriages and a red and green pung—that tiny sleigh for two. But there are among these vehicles two marvels. One is a Baldwin locomotive (see page 446), built right in 1876 and used in California. Brasswork abounds on its engine parts, and the paint is fresh and new. The engineer's cab was originally done in cherry, but the more readily available walnut has been used for its restoration.

Another stalwart reminder of yesteryear is a delivery wagon, a plain, flatbed wagon with a canvas top. Nothing complicated about it. In fact, the design was so effective that this kind of wagon was used as long as horses were—it was to wagons what a DC-3 was to air transport. I even remember one being used in my boyhood Boston by an Italian fruit vendor.

One other wagon needs mentioning. It's a simple farm wagon, plain wood, and very old. It's been trundled off into a corner across from the carriage display, and I suspect that the reason is old age. Its isolation also saves those genteel carriages from being reminded that the farm wagon has one of the oldest, most aristocratic names in all wagondom: Studebaker. The name is written right on its side where every neighboring vehicle can read it. And I suppose it would be terribly humiliating for a coach with a coat of arms on its door to be reminded constantly that a miserable old farm wagon is the ancestor of the Avanti that had pride of place over at the Renwick that time.

Wagons were beautifully built in the 1870s, and so was furniture. Complicated inlaid desks with all sorts of pigeonholes make the mouth water. And right near these are a couple of Steinway pianos. One is often played at lunchtime by a costumed docent, a talented lady who, sitting at the Steinway in her 1870s fashions, really makes the clock turn back. She plays the old songs and sometimes is surprised by the response she gets. I walked past the Steinway one noontime when she was playing Stephen Foster—"Jeanie with the Light Brown Hair"—quietly, as though to herself.

Singing was a great family entertainment in the 1870s, and so was reading aloud. So it's fitting that not too far away are some of the books that would have been newly published at the time of the Centennial. Louisa May Alcott's *Little Women* is here, open for you to read, and also *Little Men* which came out two years later, in 1871. I always liked *Little Men* better when it was read aloud to me. It wasn't concerned with who was going to marry Laurie, and it wasn't so damn *sad*.

One forgets that tragedy was still fairly close at hand in 1876. The horror of the Civil War had been over for barely a decade. Part of a bay is filled with military displays, dominated by two huge Rodman guns, one of about seven tons, one of about 25—a 15-inch cannon whose enormous round shells were raised to its muzzle by a hoist. I watched the monstrous gun being inched into place, the mighty barrel last, and tried to work out just where it was being aimed. As near as I can tell, had one of those massive shells been fired, it would have passed through the front wall of A & I, soared across the Mall and probably struck the new FBI building on Pennsylvania Avenue, a rather ponderous structure known in Washington as Fort Hoover.

To my mind, the treasure of the war displays is the mock camel with the Gatling gun mounted on its hump. It was in June of 1876 that Custer's command was wiped out at the Little Bighorn, but I often wonder if that battle might have swung the other way if Custer had brought along a couple of armed camels. The gun is a ten-barrel Gatling, the barrels mounted in a gleaming brass jacket. It fired the big .45–70 bullets of the day as fast as a man could turn the crank at the breech. It sits up on the single hump of a dromedary (made of plaster, here), and I suppose it was dismounted and staked into the ground before anyone fired it. If an army gunner had tried to shoot it from the camel he would have

A & I's exhibit bays brim with relics and reminders of the Centennial Exhibition. Never before seen in the East, totem poles, above, dominated the Centennial's Indian exhibit. These were carved by the Haida Indians of the Pacific Northwest, and were included in a trainload of objects that came to the Smithsonian after the Centennial closed in Philadelphia.

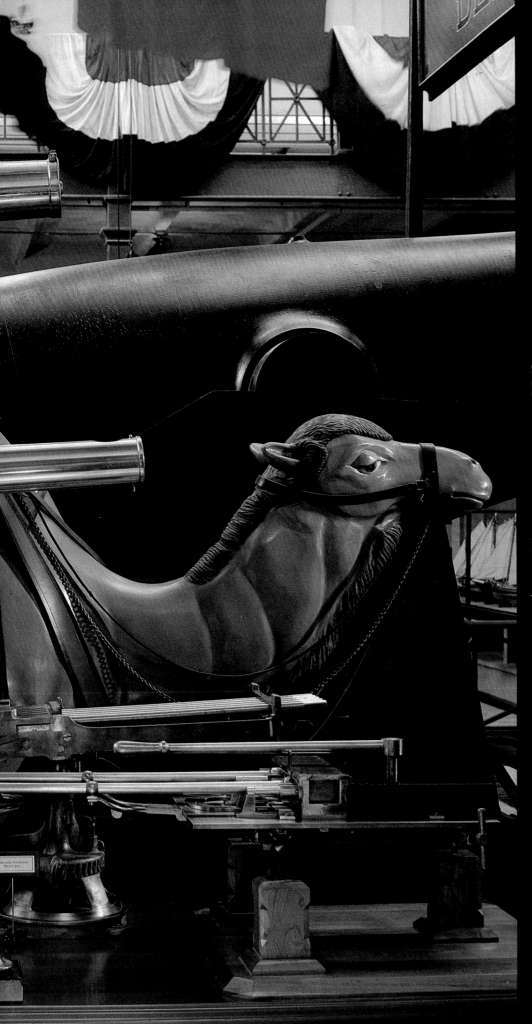

A ten-barrel Gatling gun sits atop the hump of a plaster dromedary camel, left. Some military minds of the mid-19th century were considering the camel as a possible mode of transportation for the big gun. Luckily, however—for both camel and gunner—such a plan was never realized. Manufactured by the Colt Patent Repeating Arms Co., this gun is the same model as the one exhibited at the Centennial, which was attended by Richard J. Gatling himself. Above: Military uniforms and other material portrayed the Army's heritage in the Quartermaster section of the Centennial's War Department display.

1) shot the animal's ears off; 2) given its hump a fantastic massage with all that recoil; and 3) slid inexorably off the rump of the camel and received a well-deserved kick from a hind leg. But the Sioux warriors undoubtedly would have been incapacitated by laughter.

The best part of this wonderful display is the painted eye of the camel—drooping eyelids and an expression of utter boredom.

In all the time that I have lived in this strange old building amid these memories of the last century, I have never yet seen all there is to offer. I think I have, and then I find a bentwood chair from Vienna, a Liberty Bell made out of tobacco leaves, a portrait of Cyrus Field, the man who in 1858 stretched the transatlantic cable between New and Old England. And even the items I think I know by now always, suddenly reveal new facets—carvings on the silver servers, the American flags on the great Limoges vases (Centennial gifts from Haviland & Co. of France, which were finished off on the inside by having a man lowered into them). Only the other day I saw green-tinted spectacles near the vicious surgical-instrument display. I never knew dark glasses went back so far. I thought General MacArthur invented them.

It is a strange place to work. When I had to stay late to meet a deadline I would walk through those empty, darkened bays with an unmistakable sense of being watched—by the pretty fashion model in her bustle; by the great statue of Gambrinus, supposed inventor and patron saint of beer; by the staring eyes of the Haida totems; from under the sleepy eyelids of the gun-toting camel.

And the only route out of the building at night is through that dank tunnel and then the Castle, with all *its* ghosts. I hurry through those corridors, hoping not to hear the tower elevator climb to the eighth level and then down again with no one in it on either trip, praying I won't see a heavy electric typewriter jump on a vacant desk, determined not to notice if a light in a deserted room goes on then off again.

I say all this, but I don't really worry. The Smithsonian celebrates people—the human race. Every museum, every research establishment is the work of people, for people. Displays of rocks mean nothing but for the human minds that tell us how to see the tracings of the past upon them. Teddy Roosevelt's mounted lions would be only a silent zoo except that they add to human knowledge of a distant environment—and therefore of all the world's environment.

Knowing this, I feel all right in the old Castle, even walking through it alone, when the high-tower clock shows midnight. Surrounded by ghosts as I may well be, I recognize them as the shades of the same dedicated humans who have, in all the past decades and today, made the place what it is and will continue to be—a forum of human ideas and theories and memories, of knowledge among all mankind. *People* always have been and always will be the greatest Smithsonian treasure of them all. And if, like Abou Ben Adhem, in the poem of the same name by Leigh Hunt, you can be written "as one that loves his fellow men," you'll feel that the old Institution, even on a dark, gloomy night that is filled with rustles and creaks and half-seen flutterings, is your welcoming home. ✳

Morning sun highlights the rich colors and the picturesque towers, turrets, and spires of the A & I Building, and of the Castle beyond. This lofty view faces west.

Index

(Numbers in italics indicate pages on which illustrations appear.)

The following are abbreviations used to identify Smithsonian Institution museums and other collections in captions, index, and credits:

Picture Credits

The type in this book is eleven point Baskerville with Caslon Old Style heads, typeset by Byrd PrePress, Springfield, Virginia. Color separation and film preparation were provided by the Lanman Companies, Washington, D.C. The book was printed in New Berlin, Wisconsin, by the W. A. Krueger Company on Warrenflo Web Gloss with Strathmore Grandee endsheets, bound in Centennial Buckram supplied by Joanna Western Mills, and jacketed in Westvaco Sterling Litho Gloss. For the deluxe edition slipcases were furnished by Alexander Ungar and leather was supplied by Essex Tanning. The design is by Komai, Watermark Design, Alexandria, Virginia.